THE

PUBLICATIONS

OF THE

THORESBY SOCIETY

ESTABLISHED IN THE YEAR
MDCCCLXXXIX

SECOND SERIES
VOLUME 12
FOR 2001

Anglican Resurgence under W. F. Hook in Early Victorian Leeds

Church Life in a Nonconformist Town, 1836–1851

by

Harry W. Dalton, BA (Hons), MA, PhD

THE THORESBY SOCIETY
23 CLARENDON ROAD
LEEDS
2002

© The Thoresby Society and H. W. Dalton

ISSN 0082–4232

ISBN 0 900 741 60 0

The Thoresby Society is a registered charity no. 227526

Published by The Thoresby Society
(The Leeds Historical Society)
and produced by Maney Publishing, Leeds
2002

For my three children, Margaret, Helen, Ian

and

in memory of their mother,

Mary Dalton (1929–1993)

Contents

CONTENTS   ix

List of Tables

Author's Acknowledgements

For their valuable contribution to the form and content of the present rewritten and condensed version of my PhD thesis, I acknowledge a debt of special gratitude to the present Honorary Editors of the Thoresby Society, Mrs Ann Alexander and Dr David Thornton, and to their predecessors, Mrs Joan Kirby and Mrs Rosemary Stephens. For the original research I owe much to my supervisors, Mr G. C. F. Forster and Dr D. E. Steele, and also to Dr Simon Green, Fellow of All Souls, who was appointed as my specialist adviser on Victorian religious affairs shortly after his arrival at the University of Leeds.

Heartfelt thanks go to my wife's cousin, Jean Booth, who voluntarily offered to type the manuscript draft, and similarly to her husband, John Booth, for word processing and printing. I would also like to thank Mrs Ann Hudson for indexing the book. Without the skill and knowledge of Mr Andrew J. Morrell, Consultant Ophthalmic Surgeon and Dr Colin T. Pease, Consultant Physician and Rheumatologist, it would not have been possible to complete this work.

Finally, it is a pleasure to record my deep appreciation of the encouragement and practical help of Peter and Jean Beeley over the years.

Honorary Editors' Acknowledgements

The Thoresby Society is most grateful for the assistance given by the following in enabling this work to be published.

The Marc Fitch Fund
The Scouloudi Foundation in association with the Institute of Historical Research.
Mrs E. Bishop
Various anonymous donors

Front cover illustration showing The Parish Church, Leeds 1841.
W. Richardson/G. Hawkins. Courtesy of The Thoresby Society.

Abbreviations

Additional Curates Society (ACS)
Bodleian Library, Oxford University (BLO)
British and Foreign Bible Society (BFBS)
British Library (BL)
Church Building Commission (CBC)
Church Missionary Society (CMS)
Church Pastoral Aid Society (CPAS)
Ecclesiastical Commission (EC)
Hook Archives (HA)
Incorporated Church Building Society (ICBS)
Index of Attendance (IA)
Journal of the Statistical Society, (JSS)
London Society for Promoting Christianity among the Jews (LSPCJ)
Old Style (OS)
Percentage Share (PS)
Pusey House, Oxford (PH)
Rhodes House Library, Oxford University (RHL)
Ripon Diocesan Church Building Society (RDCBS)
Ripon Diocesan Church Building Society, Leeds District (RDCBSLD)
Society for Promoting Christian Knowledge (SPCK)
Society for the Propagation of the Gospel (SPG)
West Yorkshire Archive Service, Leeds (WYASL)

Mary Forster, Librarian 1960–2002: An Appreciation

Commenting on the appointment of Mrs Forster as Librarian to succeed G. E. Kirk, whose sudden death in March 1960 had shocked the Society, our *Annual Report* for that year remarked that her experience would be of considerable value. Nobody then imagined that the new Librarian would give more than twice the twenty years' service of her predecessor.

Since Mary has kindly agreed to talk to the Society at its Members' Evening in December 2002 about those forty-two years in the history of our Library, it would be both inappropriate and unkind to upstage her at this juncture by focusing on the Library rather than its Librarian. Mary brought with her to this post a degree in English taken at St Anne's College, Oxford, and some years of professional employment in the Brotherton Library. In contrast, her part-time voluntary work in our Library must have seemed small beer, yet despite the many vicissitudes which the Society and its Library were to face through the four decades of her service, she remained devoted, resourceful and reliable. She keenly encouraged all members to use the Library. Moreover, in a very real sense she became the public face of the Society because almost invariably queries from non-members about aspects of the history of Leeds were referred to her, and to answer them she developed an enviable knowledge of the stock of the Library. Furthermore she has become a valuable source of oral history about the principles and customs of the Society: it is always a salutary experience for new officers to be reminded why things are done as they have been. Her contributions to the work of our Council, whether as Librarian or as a Vice-president, have always been welcome. She has trained and directed a small band of helpers, and it was in no small part due to her and to them that the recent exhibition, 'Impressions of Leeds', developed from an idea into reality. The Society is hugely indebted to her for such lengthy and unselfish voluntary service: we wish her a happy and well-earned retirement.

P. S. Morrish
President

Introduction

Subject and Perspectives

Christianity, according to F. K. Prochaska, is not simply a theory about past and future events but something that actually happens to people. Prochaska's standpoint is the basic premise of this study, dealing with what occurred in the Church life of Leeds Anglicans from 1836 to 1851. Following the death of Richard Fawcett in 1837, the parish obtained in Walter Farquhar Hook (1798–1875) an energetic and gifted successor as Vicar of Leeds. Hook so channelled and directed the already reviving Church spirit in the parish, that with the willing co-operation of his clergy and parishioners, it gained a reputation as the model parish of England.[1] In his biography of Hook, his son-in law, W. R. W. Stephens, seldom allowed his account of events in Leeds to focus on the work of others. This eventually led to an incomplete picture of a time when the parish of Leeds was alive with new initiatives and activities, in which many participated.[2] For the present purpose Church life was taken to cover both the ways in which Leeds Anglicans organized their affairs, and also their involvement, from time to time, with the wider community. We need to bear in mind that, for those involved, Church life in Leeds was essentially a continuous and indivisible experience in place and time. Here, however, these various aspects are considered in separate chapters by topic in order to depict the progression of events more clearly. Studies of nineteenth-century Anglicanism in the parishes, C. S. Ford has observed, are relatively few. The present work, dealing with one of the most difficult parishes for Anglicanism in England, represents an addition to their number.[3]

The first sign of Anglican renewal in Leeds occurred early in 1836, with the successful launch of a Church extension scheme, in a conscious effort to recover ground lost to Dissenters.[4] Although the scheme required his formal

---

[1.] W. F. Hook, *The Duty of English Churchmen, and the Progress of the Church in Leeds* (1851), pp. 18–20, 22–23, 25–26; *L(eeds) I(ntelligencer)*, 2 Aug. 1845; F. K. Prochaska, 'Philanthropy', in *Cambridge Social History of Britain*, III, ed. by F. M. L. Thompson (Cambridge, 1990), 357–93.

[2.] W. R. W. Stephens, *The Life and Letters of Walter Farquhar Hook, DD, FRS*, 2 vols (1878), II, 90, 323–26.

[3.] C. S. Ford. 'Pastors and Polemicists: the Character of Popular Anglicanism in South-East Lancashire, 1847–1914' (unpublished PhD thesis, University of Leeds, 1991), pp. 4–5.

[4.] *LI*, 13, 20, 27 Feb., 12 Mar. 1836; *L(eeds) M(ercury)*, 27 Feb. 1836; E. J. Connell and M. Ward, 'Industrial Development, 1780–1914' pp. 142–76; C. J. Morgan, 'Demographic Change, 1771–1911' pp. 46–71; N. Yates, 'The Religious Life of Victorian Leeds', pp. 250–69; all in *(A History of) Modern Leeds*, ed. by D. Fraser (Manchester, 1980); *New York Review*, April 1838, cited in J. Stoughton, *Religion in England from 1800 to 1850*, 2 vols (1884) II, 59; R. J. Wood, *Church Extension in Leeds* (Leeds, c. 1964), pp. 9, 29.

approval, the Vicar of Leeds, Richard Fawcett (1760–1837) otherwise took little active part. His powers were failing, and he died in January 1837.[5] Announcing that merit would be the sole criterion in searching for a successor, the patronage trustees provided further evidence of renewal. Walter Farquhar Hook, of Coventry, their choice in March 1837, proved to be the sought-for parish priest whose vision was 'large enough to grasp the future'.[6]

Hook's Parish and Hook's Vision

Hook's new parish was extensive and populous, approaching 150,000 inhabitants with over half living in the crowded central township, where the Parish Church and several district churches were situated. The out-townships contained a number of chapelries at some distance. Apart from two small independent parishes, Hook as Vicar of Leeds possessed full parochial jurisdiction and sole cure for souls. The responsibilities and status — and expectations — were of a different order of ecclesiastical magnitude from those of Holy Trinity, Coventry. However, Hook arrived to one priceless advantage. Church spirit was very much alive and giving convincing proofs of Church renewal.[7] From Hook's arrival Church life acquired pace and excitement, becoming more satisfying than in living memory. Active Evangelicals, however, found problems with his High Churchmanship.[8] Events in time brought better mutual understanding, as parish renewal progressed.[9]

Hook's vision informed his personal endeavours. After training assistant clergy to his own high standard, he was able to 'exhibit the Church . . . in her beauty' in the conduct of divine service, baptisms, marriages and funerals.[10] Hook himself kept highly visible. People of all classes crowded St Peter's.

[5.] *LI*, 27 Feb. 1836, 28 Jan. 1837; *LM*, 17 Dec. 1836; R. V. Taylor, *The Biographia Leodiensis . . . from the Norman Conquest to the Present Time* (1865), pp. 368–70.

[6.] *LI*, 18, 25 Mar. 1837; *LM*, 4 Feb., 18, 25 Mar. 1837; Morgan, p. 48; J. Rusby, *St Peter's at Leeds, being an Account Historical and Descriptive of the Parish Church*, ed. by J. G. Simpson, (Leeds, 1896), pp. 54–65; Stephens, *Hook*, I, 295–97, 314–16, 332; Taylor, pp. 123–28, 158–60, 183–85, 259–60, 368–70; R. G. Wilson, 'Georgian Leeds', in *Modern Leeds,* pp. 24–43; Wood, pp. 4–6; Yates, pp. 250–53.

[7.] Anon, *The Parochial System of the Church of England Opposed to the Present Condition of the Parish of Leeds* (Leeds, 1842), pp. 15–16; A. D. Gilbert, *Religion and Society in Industrial England: Church, Chapel and Social Change, 1740–1914* (1984), pp. 100–01; Morgan, pp. 48, 52.

[8.] *LI*, 28 Jan., 7, 21 Oct., 11 Nov. 1837, 21 Apr. 1838; *LM*, 4 Feb., 25 Mar. 1837, 11 Aug. 1838; Rusby, p. 61; Taylor, pp. 368–70.

[9.] Stephens, *Hook*, II, 67–69, 73–74, 76–77, 255.

[10.] Morgan, p. 48; Rusby, p. 66; Stephens, *Hook*, I, 372, 401–02, 405; Taylor, pp. 368–70.

Very soon a parishioners' meeting suggested church enlargement.[11] Hook's aim was parochial unity of doctrine—'Church principles'— based on the Catholicity and Apostolicity of the English Church. He found like-minded clergy at St Peter's, and by 1838 through the Additional Curates Society (ACS), had five curates working in poor districts.[12] Hook invariably selected High Church clergy for such vacancies until beyond 1851. Similarly in 1837, he influenced St George's trustees to appoint William Sinclair as first incumbent. Unexpectedly for Hook, Sinclair proved decidedly Evangelical, and gave fresh heart to local Evangelicals. Eventually Hook realized that unity of doctrine was 'impracticable'.[13]

The increased numbers of Leeds churches during Hook's incumbency (1837–1859), mentioned regularly since Stephens's biography (1878), represented part of his vision for Leeds.[14] Of the twenty churches involved (two being replacements) sixteen were from public subscriptions, four privately donated. Hook was directly responsible for the rebuilt St Peter's (1841) and also for St Luke's (1841), in a poor district.[15] Hook's vision for his parish comprised more than buildings. The principles he instilled encouraged 'a certain kind of spirit', a confidence among Anglicans about their religious standing in a Dissenting town. This resulted in Church people's increased sensitivity to the spiritual needs of the poor, mainly for whose spiritual care thirteen churches were consecrated between 1847 and 1855, thus fulfilling Hook's parochial vision for the poor to have complete pastoral care near their homes. For this purpose Hook also obtained a private Act (1844) to supplement national legislation for parish division.[16]

Hook as 'Champion of the Church'

From 1837 Hook greatly enhanced Anglican morale and standing locally. His exclusive High Church attitude, however, caused offence to Dissenters, and

---

11. W(est) Y(orkshire) A(rchive) S(ervice) L(eeds), L(eeds)P(arish)C(hurch) 41/5, 1st, 2nd, 3rd. Subscription Lists; *LI*, 21, 28 Oct., 4, 11, 18, 25 Nov., 9, 16 Dec. 1837; *LM*, 14 Oct., 11 Nov. 1837; Stephens, *Hook*, I, 378–79, 407.
12. *LI*, 13 May, 15 July 1837, 7 Apr., 1 Dec. 1838, 25 May 1839, 4 Jan. 1840; Stephens, *Hook*, I, 401–02, II, 324.
13. B(ritish)L(ibrary), Gladstone Papers, Add. MS 44, 213, fols 5–8, Hook to Gladstone, 26 Mar. 1838; P(usey)H(ouse), Transcripts, fols 103–16, Hook to Pusey, 9 June 1840; *LI*, 10 Feb. 1838, 18 Mar. 1848, 6 Dec. 1851; E. D. Steele, 'The Leeds Patriciate and the Cultivation of Learning, 1819–1905: A study of the Leeds Philosophical and Literary Society', *P(roceeding of the) L(eeds) P(hilosophical and) L(iterary) S(ociety)* (1978), pp. 187–88; Stephens, *Hook*, II, 255.
14. *Church and Town for Fifty Years (1841–91)*, ed. by C. G. Lang (Leeds, 1891), p. 14; Rusby, p. 69; Stephens, *Hook*, II, 392; W. R. Ward, *Religion and Society in England, 1790–1850* (1972), p. 224; Wood, p. 15.
15. See Chapter 7.
16. Stephens, *Hook*, I, 184, 404, 408, II, 159–77; Wood, pp. 9–15, 29–30; see also Chapter 7.

presented a marked contrast to Dr Longley, the new diocesan, who on his first official visit to Leeds in 1836 had referred to Dissenters' efforts in appreciative terms.[17] That said, Hook experienced few problems from 'religious' Dissenters. His difficulties came from 'political' Dissenters over their still remaining 'grievances'. For both, however, Hook's High Church doctrines were novel and therefore suspect. The independent editors of the *Leeds Mercury*, Edward Baines, Senr., and Jr., derided Hook constantly,[18] whilst the biting invective of the Baptist minister, J. E. Giles, also featured prominently.[19] Giles had a personal and denominational axe to grind. Dissenters generally found Hook's practice of referring to their ministers as 'teachers' both condescending and hostile.[20] Popular votes enabled political Dissenters to control Leeds churchwardens until 1842 and the Town Council from 1835 onwards. Their relations with Hook were uneasy.[21] In 1841, however, the Council became co-operative. They wished Hook to surrender vicarial rights to further graveyards in favour of a municipal cemetery. Hook agreed. Parliament insisted on partial compensation. Once the cemetery opened, in 1845, the Council attempted to 'claw back' statutory payments by imposing higher charges for Anglican burials, and later by paying token stipends to Anglican cemetery chaplains. Hook resisted this municipal injustice consistently. In 1850 he even accepted frugal commutation to ensure equal treatment permanently thereafter.[22]

Doctrinally, Hook was the champion of Church principles — the *via media* between Dissent and Rome. In 1837–38 he experienced an upsetting polemic from Miles Jackson, unreconciled Evangelical curate of St Paul's,[23] and in 1840 contention from Evangelicals in his own Sunday Schools.[24] As Vicar, Hook worked hard for the 'orthodox' sister-organizations, the Society for Promoting Christian Knowledge (SPCK) and the Society for Propagating the Gospel (SPG), but disparaged the Evangelical Church Missionary Society (CMS), and the Church Pastoral Aid Society (CPAS). In criticizing and

---

[17.] *LM*, 17 Dec. 1836; A. M. G. Stephenson, 'The Formation of the See of Ripon and the Episcopate of its First Bishop, Charles Thomas Longley' (unpublished BLitt thesis, University of Oxford, 1960), p. 197.

[18.] *LM*, 23 Dec. 1837, 13 Jan., 10 Mar. 21 Apr. 11 Aug. 1838, 23 Feb. 1839; B. I. Coleman, *The Church of England in the Mid-Nineteenth Century: A Social Geography* (1980), p. 41; E. P. Hennock, *Fit and Proper Persons: Ideal and Reality in Nineteenth-Century Urban Government* (1973), App. III, p. 357; Stephens, *Hook*, I, 378; Yates, pp. 251–52, 258, 260–61.

[19.] *LM*, 2, 9 Mar. 844, 13 Sept. 1845.

[20.] *LI*, 6 Jan. 1838; Stephens, *Hook*, I, 185–87, 396.

[21.] D. Fraser, 'The Leeds Churchwardens 1828–1850', *P(ublications of the) Th(oresby) S(ociety)*, LIII (1973), pp. 3–14, 18, 21.

[22.] *LI*, 20 Nov., 18 Dec. 1841, 5 Jan. 1850; *LM*, 27 Nov., 4, 11, 18 Dec. 1841, 5 Jan. 1850.

[23.] PH, Transcripts, fols 48–51, Hook to Pusey, '2 in Advent 1837', fols 60–61, Hook to Pusey, 3 Mar. 1838, fols 62–69, Hook to Pusey, 24 Apr. 1838; *LI*, 28 July 1838; *LM*, 13 Jan., 28 July 1838, 2 Nov. 1839.

[24.] *LI*, 25 Jan. 1840; *LM*, 25 Jan., 1, 15 Feb. 1840.

allowing criticism of the latter at a meeting he arranged in 1841 to support the High Church Additional Curates Society (ACS), Hook set in train events leading to a public check from the diocesan. He learned his lesson and troubled Evangelical societies no more.[25] Hook's great fear of damage to Church principles came from advanced Tractarian clergy staffing St Saviour's, Pusey's church in Leeds which opened in 1845. Secessions to Rome of its clergy and laity from 1847 brought Hook much closer to his Evangelical colleagues.[26] Hook did not confine his activities to Church affairs. He was also prominent in projects for the social and economic betterment of the working classes. Here, however, the purpose has been to show how Hook fulfilled the central directing, co-ordinating and representative role for Leeds Churchpeople. Subsequent chapters depict his activities within the wider context of Anglican resurgence in Leeds.

Leeds Church Life under Hook during the Anglican Resurgence: the Need for Reassessment

From 1878 Stephens's version of events in Leeds Church life has been accepted almost without question. He placed Hook centre stage without drawing much attention to others who contributed to the parish's remarkable transformation. Indeed, the resurgence began in 1836, before Hook's arrival, with an imaginative Evangelical-led Church extension scheme, about which Stephens was silent. Similarly he gave no space to Evangelical achievements under Hook, which included nearly half the subscription churches consecrated during Hook's incumbency.[27] For Hook's life prior to Leeds, Stephens's biography is still indispensable. That said, for Church life in early Victorian Leeds, the available primary sources furnish a better guide, showing Hook alongside his people, where he always wished to be.[28]

25. *LI*, 6, 13 Feb., 27 Mar., 3, 10 Apr., 1841; *LM*, 6, 13 Feb., 27 Mar., 3 Apr. 1841; Stephens, *Hook*, II, 67–78.
26. H(ook) A(rchive), S4, Pusey to Hook, 29 Apr. 1839; PH, Transcripts, fols 70–78, Hook to Pusey, 3 Apr. 1839, fols 81–91, Hook to Pusey, 16 Aug. 1839; S. Savage and C. Tyne, *The Labours of the Years: The Story of Saviour's and St Hilda's, Leeds* (Oxford, 1976) p. 2; N. Yates, *Leeds and the Oxford Movement: A Study of High Church Activity in the Rural Deaneries of Allerton, Armley, Headingley and Whitkirk in the Diocese of Ripon, 1836–1934*, P.Th.S., LV (1975), 28–31; *St Saviour's, Leeds, 1839–1929*, Borthwick Papers, 48 (York, 1975), pp. 2–3.
27. PH, fols 479–90, Hook to Pusey, 3 Aug. 1847; *LI*, 24 Dec. 1836; *LM*, 22 Feb. 1859; Stephens, *Hook*, I, 371–73.
28. *LI*, 6 Feb. 1841; *LM*, 6 Feb. 1841; Stephens, *Hook*, II, 67–69, 194, 290–91, 392; see also Chapter 9.

Primary Sources

It was the primary sources in Leeds, London, Oxford, and the Hook Archive elsewhere which made this study possible. All sources are duly referenced. For manuscripts and certain printed items the precise location is shown in abbreviated form (see key provided) and are followed by the individual archive's reference marking. Published works are shown on first citation by author, title, publication date and then by shortened title or more usually by author only. An important series of letters (1812–75), collated between Hook and his lifelong friend, W. P. Wood, later Lord Hatherley, which Stephens used in his biographies of both, is not listed among the surviving papers of either.[29] Fortunately, E. B. Pusey preserved Hook's letters to him (1822–1847). These were collated by H. P. Liddon and transcribed for his biography of Pusey. The transcripts available provide the most direct and sustained primary evidence of Hook's feeling about aspects of his ministry at Leeds from 1837 to 1847. Apparently unavailable to Stephens, they might well have modified his lukewarm summary of Hook's actions in relation to St Saviour's.[30]

The following printed primary sources have been of special value: Hook's pamphlets, government volumes entitled *Orders in Council Ratifying Schemes of the Ecclesiastical Commissioners for England* along with a separate *General Index to end 1854,* both covering parish formation; *Annual Reports* of Ripon Diocesan Church Building Society, SPCK, SPG, CMS and the London Society for Promoting Christianity among the Jews. The 1750 issues of the Anglican *Leeds Intelligencer* and the Nonconformist *Leeds Mercury* jointly provided chronology, structure and eyewitness detail unavailable elsewhere.[31]

Primary sources of the dispute between Hook and Pusey, covered specifically in Chapter Nine, are numerous. The *Statement of St Saviour's Clergy* (1851) provides their view of events, as does the more advanced Tractarian J. H. Pollen's more personal *Narrative of Five years at St Saviour's, Leeds* (1851). The Bishop of Ripon's *Visitation Charges* (1844, 1847, 1850) and his *Letter to Parishioners of St Saviour's* (1851), illuminates his actions.

29. W. R. W. Stephens, *A Memoir of the Right Hon. William Page Wood, Baron Hatherley*, 2 vols (1883), I, 15.

30. PH, fols 491–93, Hook to Pusey, 24 Dec. 1847; Stephens, *Hook*, II, 194; Yates, *St Saviour's*, p. 27.

31. *LI*, 19 Feb., 5, 12 Mar., 9, 16 Apr., 7 May 1842; *LM,* 16 Apr. 1842; C. Binfield, *So Down to Prayers: Studies in English Nonconformity 1780–1920* (1977), pp. 54, 62–75, 77–80; D. Fraser, 'Poor Law Politics in Leeds, 1833–1855', *P.Th.S.*, LIII (1973), 23–49; D. Read, 'North of England Newspapers (c. 1700–c. 1900) and their Value to Historians', *PL L S* (1957), pp. 200–03, 213; D. Read, *Press and People 1790–1850: Opinion in Three English Cities* (1961), pp. 74–79, 201, 203–08; *The Victorian Periodical Press: Samplings and Soundings,* ed. by J. Shattock and M. Wolff (Leicester, 1982) pp. xiii–xix; Taylor, pp. 435–42.

Secondary Sources

The earliest book dealing with aspects of Hook's work at Leeds is perhaps that by Huntington (*c.* 1864). However, W. R. W. Stephens, *The Life and Letters of Walter Farquhar Hook, DD, FRS,* 2 vols (1878) is still essential. Other works have largely rearranged his material: Gladstone (1879); Lang (1891); Simpson (1896); Wood (1910); Stranks (1954); and Sprittles (1969). Based mainly on newspapers and pamphlets, the present writer's Thoresby Society article (1990) discussed Hook's foundation years at Leeds (1837–48). For church life in wider aspects, especially the Evangelical contribution, newspapers proved necessary.[32]

The following works centre on St Peter's: Moore (1877); Rusby (1896); Kitson Clark (*c.* 1931); Bunnett (*c.* 1950); and Sprittles (1954). C. Webster's book on Chantrell (1992) provides insights about the rebuilding, as does D. Webster's (1988) about music's place in worship.[33] Derek Fraser's Thoresby Society's article on 'Leeds Churchwardens' (1970) discusses the Burial Grounds dispute. The following contain extended discussion and interpretation of the history of the early years of St Saviour's: Grantham (1872); Yate's Thoresby Society contributions on the Oxford Movement and St Saviour's (1975) and Savage and Tyne (1976).[34]

---

32. H. W. Dalton, 'Walter Farquar Hook, Vicar of Leeds: His Work for the Church and the Town, 1837–1848', *P.Th.S.,* LXIII (1990 for 1988) 27–79; W. E. Gladstone, *Dean Hook: An Address Delivered at Hawarden* (1879); G. Huntington, *The Church's Work in our Large Towns* (*c.* 1864), pp. 111–20; Lang; Rusby, Chapters 4 and 5—contributed by the editor, J. G. Simpson, pp. vi, 51–78; J. Sprittles, *Links with Bygone Leeds,* *P.Th.S.,* LII (1969) pp. 104–12; see also Stephens, *Hook;* C. J. Stranks, *Dean Hook* (1954); F. J. Wood, *Four Notable Vicars* (Leeds, 1910), passim.

33. See R. J. A. Bunnett, *Leeds Parish Church of St Peter* (Gloucester, *c.* 1954); E. Kitson Clark, *Leeds Parish Church* (*c.* 1931); R. W. Moore, *History of the Parish Church of Leeds* (Leeds, 1877); Rusby; J. Sprittles, *Leeds Parish Church: History and Guide* (Gloucester, *c.* 1954) C. Webster, *R. D. Chantrell, Architect: His Life and Work in Leeds 1818–1847,* (*P.Th.S.,* Second Series 2 (1992); D. Webster, *'Parish' Past and Present: 275 Years of Leeds Parish Church Music* (Leeds, 1988), passim.

34. See Fraser, 'Churchwardens'; G. P. Grantham, *A History of St Saviour's, Leeds* (Leeds, 1872); J. H. Pollen, *Narrative of Five Years at St Saviour's* (Oxford, 1851) Savage and Tyne; Yates, *Oxford Movement;* Yates, *St Saviour's,* passim.

CHAPTER I

Anglican Parish; Dissenting Town — Leeds 1836

The year 1836 proved a benchmark for religious and municipal affairs in Leeds. In February, when Protestant Dissenters were already visibly predominant, local Churchpeople began the process of parish renewal by successfully launching a church building subscription scheme, the first since 1727 (Table 1.1).[1] A significant change also occurred in municipal affairs. On 1 January a popularly elected Town Council, mostly Liberal Dissenters resentful of existing Anglican civil privileges, replaced the old Anglican Tory close Corporation. The mutuality of interest between Leeds Parish Church and the municipality abruptly disappeared.[2]

TABLE 1.1
Religious Provision for Leeds Township, 1837–39 (Population, 1839: 82,120)

Places of Worship, 1837: Places of Worship and Seating, 1839
(NC = No change)

NEW DISSENT

Wesleyan Methodist		New Connexion Methodist		Primitive Methodist	
1837 6		1837 3		1837 2	
1839 6 (NC)		1839 4 (+1)		1839 4 (+2)	
St Peter's	2600	Ebenezer	800	Ann Carr's	180
Rehoboth	400	Old Chapel	1200	Quarry Hill	500
Wesley	1410	Zion	400	Rehoboth	800
Oxford Place	2550	Bethesda	600	Woodhouse	200
Brunswick	2500		3000		1680
Woodhouse	500				
	9960				

[1.] See Table 1.1; see also Chapter 2.
[2.] D. Fraser, 'Politics and Society in the Nineteenth Century', pp. 270–300; T. Woodhouse, 'The Working Class', pp. 353–88; both in *Modern Leeds*.

Protestant Methodist

1837 4	
1837 2 (−2)	
Stone Chapel	700
Park Street	800
	1500

Inghamite

1837 1	
1839 1 (NC)	
Duke Street	200
	200

Independent

1837 6	
1839 6 (NC)	
George's St	530
Byron St	450
Salem	1200
Albion	800
Queen St	1400
Belgrave	1650
	6030

Baptist

1837 2	
1839 1 (−1)	
South Parade	1380
	1380

Southcottite

1837 −	
1839 1 (+1)	
Zoar	186
	186

Old Dissent

Friends

1837 1	
1839 1 (NC)	
Water Lane	1000
	1000

Unitarian

1837 1	
1839 1 (NC)	
Mill Hill	780
	780

Arian

1837 1	
1839 1 (NC)	
Call Lane	530
	530

Episcopal: Anglican and Roman Catholic

Church of England

1837 8	
1839 9 (+1)	
St Peter's	2800
St George's	1654
Christ Church	1500
St Mary's	1434
St Paul's	1400
St Mark's	1327
St James's	1200
St John's	1200
Holy Trinity	720
	13,235

Roman Catholic

1837 2	
1839 3 (+1)	
St Mary's	730
St Patrick's	340
St Ann's	900
	1970

SUMMARY

Denominations	Places of Worship	Seats	Seats/Population
Protestant Dissent	28	26,246	32.0%
Anglican	9	13,235	16.1%
Roman Catholic	3	1970	2.4%
Totals	40	41,451	50.5%

Sources: Statistical Report, Town council, October 1839, *Journal of the Statistical Society*, II, 1839–40; *Leeds Mercury*, 4 Mar. 1837.

The Parish

The external boundaries of the parish of Leeds, thirty-two miles in circumference, were fixed in medieval times, and enclosed an area of 21,766 acres. Within these boundaries two small 'district' parishes had recently been created, Woodhouse in 1826 and Kirkstall in 1829. Over the remainder of this vast area the Revd Richard Fawcett, Vicar of Leeds since 1815, possessed entire cure of souls and superintendence of its clergy.[3] In November 1836, to provide better episcopal oversight of Leeds and much of the West Riding, diocesan responsibility passed from the aged Archbishop of York to C. T. Longley (1794–1868), Bishop of the new diocese of Ripon, instantly effective and beloved.[4]

Of ancient foundation, the impressive Parish Church of St Peter-at-Leeds reflected the in-township's early and continuing importance. The eight out-township chapelries, at Armley, Beeston, Bramley, Chapel Allerton, Farnley, Headingley, Holbeck, and Hunslet exhibited the pattern of medieval settlement.[5] Later churches came in various ways: John Harrison founded St John's, Briggate (1634); subscribers built Holy Trinity (1727); St Paul's (1793), St James's (1801), and St John's, Wortley (1813) were privately provided.[6] Parliamentary Grants built Christ Church (1826), St Mark's, Woodhouse

---

3. *Parochial System*, pp. 15–19; G. C. F. Forster, 'The Foundations: from the Earliest Times to c. 1700', pp. 2–21; Wilson, p. 24; both in *Modern Leeds*; Taylor, pp. 368–70;

4. O. Chadwick, *The Victorian Church: Part One, 1829–1859* (1987), pp. 122–23; F. W. Cornish, *The English Church in the Nineteenth Century*, 2 vols (1910), I, 111–12; Stephenson, pp. 20–21, 31, 162–63.

5. *Parochial System*, pp. 15–18; Forster, pp. 2–4; Wood, *Church Extension*, pp. 3, 15 (note), 29.

6. *Parochial System*, pp. 16–18; M. Beresford, *East End, West End: The Face of Leeds during Urbanisation, 1684–1842*, P.Th.S., LX and LXI (1988 for 1985 and 1986), pp. 4, 6–7, 31, 133, 147, 155–57; Forster, p. 16; K. Grady, *The Georgian Public Buildings of Leeds and the West Riding*, P.Th.S., LXII (1989 for 1987), pp. 27, 39, 130, 161–63; Taylor, pp. 92–93; Wood, *Church Extension*, pp. 3–5.

(1826), St Mary's, Quarry Hill (1827), St Stephen's, Kirkstall (1829); and rebuilt Holbeck Chapel as St Matthew's (1832).[7]

Leeds Parish Church possessed four clergy: Richard Fawcett (1760–1837) vicar; Edward Brown, clerk-in-orders; Robert Taylor, curate; George Wray, lecturer.[8] Between them they conducted divine worship on Sundays, and marriages, burials and baptisms on weekdays. In 1836 there were 3087 baptisms, 1372 weddings, and 1558 funerals.[9] Fawcett's yearly stipend was £1257 supplemented by small tithes, chapelry surplice fees, and notional rent of £130 for his freehold house. From a total of approximately £1500 Fawcett paid £40 each to Brown and Taylor quarterly.[10] Wray's lectureships at St Peter's and St John's (stipends unknown) both conveyed tenure.[11] The two district incumbents both possessed full cure of souls. In 1831 James Fawcett's stipend at St Mark's increased from £70 to £140 but he felt obliged to supplement this by fees from private tuition.[12] By receiving £147 yearly from the outset, Robert Hodgson, St Stephen's, Kirkstall, had clearly fared better.[13]

In the parish of Leeds, incumbents of out-township chapelries and in-township district churches were technically 'perpetual curates without cure of souls'. Their status did not infringe the parish priest's prerogatives, but did guarantee tenure and income. They conducted Sunday services and funerals but not baptisms or normally marriages. Though not authorized to give spiritual counsel, some in the main township certainly visited the poor.[14] Central township remuneration varied. F. T. Cookson, St John's, received £375 by Chancery decision of 1768.[15] The stipend of the absentee pluralist of Holy Trinity, John Sheepshanks, Archdeacon of Cornwall, was £179. Since 1830 he had paid an undisclosed amount to Joseph Holmes (1790–1854), Headmaster of Leeds Grammar School, to officiate as his curate.[16] In

7. *Parochial System*, pp. 16–18; M. H. Port, *Six Hundred New Churches: A Study of the Church Building Commission, 1818–1856, and its Church Building Activities* (1961), pp. 21–26, 138–39; Wood, *Church Extension*, p. 5.

8. WYASL, LPC112/1, 'Parish Church Record', List of Clergy, entry for 1836.

9. *LI*, 7 Jan. 1837.

10. WYASL, LPC26, Election Papers 1837, MS note, 'Value of the Parish Livings. Parliamentary Return'; LPC49/1, Sequestration Papers, small red cash book; *LI*, 28 Jan. 1837.

11. *LI*, 4 Feb., 13 May, 2 Sept. 1837.

12. WASL, LPC26, Election Papers 1837, MS note, 'Value of the Parish Livings'; *LI*, 21 Nov. 1840.

13. WYASL, LPC26 Election Papers 1837, MS note, 'Value of the Parish Livings'. *LI*, 29 Dec. 1838; *LM*, 24 Mar. 1838; Port, pp. 168–69, Plate VIIb.

14. *Parochial System*, p. 19; Wood, *Church Extension*, pp. 6–8.

15. WYASL, LPC26 Election Papers 1837, MS note, 'Value of the Parish Livings'. *LI*, 28 Jan. 1837; J. Mayhall, *The Annals and History of Leeds and Other Places in the County of York, from the Earliest Period to the Present Time*, (Leeds, 1860), p. 90; Taylor, pp. 368–69, 480–81.

16. WYASL, LPC26, Election Papers 1837, MS note, 'Value of the Parish Livings'. *LI*, 28 Jan. 1837; Grady, pp. 39, 130 Plate 24b, 162; Taylor, pp. 280 (n.), 454–55, 459; Wood, *Church Extension*, p. 3; R. J. Wood, *Holy Trinity, Leeds: A Short History of the Church and its Ministers* (Leeds, 1966), pp. 1–3, 8–11.

1836 the stipend at St Paul's totalled £135, out of which the non-resident proprietor Christopher Atkinson, Vicar of Elland, maintained the belligerent Evangelical Miles Jackson, his curate since 1814.[17] St James's was also a proprietary church, owned by its incumbent, John King since 1801. He was old, unwell and anxious to retire. His remuneration is unknown.[18] Incumbents of the remaining two churches, both in desperately poor districts, almost certainly possessed private incomes. John Holroyd of Christ Church received £115 yearly whist Edward Cookson's annual income from St Mary's was a mere £47.

The out-township incumbents, similar in status to their in-township colleagues, nevertheless, probably enjoyed a degree of pastoral autonomy. Except for St John's at Wortley, consecrated in 1813, all were attached to ancient chapelries. Their stipends made them valuable preferments. Charles Clapham at Armley received £204; J. Wardle at Beeston £189; T. Furbank at Bramley £289; J. Urquhart at Chapel Allerton £361; T. Wilson at Farnley £204; and W. Williamson at Headingley £250. At Holbeck J. C. Brown received £170 while at nearby Hunslet, the incumbent, R. Foster was in receipt of £182. George Rickards who took up the incumbency at Wortley in 1814, received £147.[19]

Growth of Leeds Township and Consequences for the Church by 1836

Leeds as a manufacturing centre was fortunate in that nearby coalfields provided cheap fuel for industry, and associated layers of clay for building. The town exemplified the way a dominant and expanding industry in this case wool textiles could attract associated and auxiliary industries,[20] as, for example flax spinning and machine and toolmaking.[21] Men, women and children, over 37 per cent of the workforce, were employed in textiles. But there was also a demand for building tradesmen and labourers as well as transport and delivery men, garment workers, domestics and various specialist workers.[22] A parallel development occurred in the township's growth as a commercial, financial and retailing centre.[23] As part of wider demographic

17. WYASL, LCP26 Election Papers 1837, MS note, 'Value of the Parish Livings'. *LI*, 30 June 1838; 13 May 1843; *LM*, 30 June 1838; Beresford, pp 155–58; Grady, pp. 39, 163; Mayhall, pp. 172–73; Taylor, pp. 242–47.
18. *LI*, 28 Jan. 1837; Grady, p. 163; Mayhall, p. 181; Wood, *Church Extension*, p. 4.
19. WYASL, LCP26 Election Papers 1837, MS note, 'Value of the Parish Livings'; *LI*, 28 Jan. 1837; Beresford, p. 359; Grady, pp. 132, Plate 26, 165; Port, pp. 138–39 Plate Vd.
20. T. Fenteman, *An Historical Guide to Leeds and its Environs* (Leeds, 1858), pp. 25–31; Connell and Ward, pp. 150–51; Forster, pp. 2–3.
21. Fenteman, pp. 31–35; Connell and Ward, pp. 151–53.
22. Fenteman, pp. 39–41; Connell and Ward, pp. 156–57 (Table 14).
23. K. Grady, 'Commercial, Marketing and Retailing Amenities, 1700–1914': *Modern Leeds*, pp. 177–99.

changes nationally, the borough population increased from 30,609 in 1775 to 123,548 in 1831. C. J. Morgan's decennial table distinguishing migration and natural increase indicates that, for the ten years from 1821 to 1831, migration accounted for 66.5 per cent of the decade's increase.[24] The actual population increase in the borough was 47.2 per cent (83,943 to 123,548); 47.3 per cent in Leeds township (48,603 to 71,602); and the out-townships in aggregate 47.0 per cent (35,340 to 51,946). The near correspondence of actual percentage increases, in relation to the borough, suggests that the out-townships were as attractive to economic migrants as the main township.[25] However, in Leeds township especially, the poor paid a high price in loss of amenities for daily living. By the 1830s soot-grimed, filthy and squalid streets and courts encompassed the Parish Church, and extended eastwards.[26] Comparable conditions existed west of the central business and shopping district.[27] This situation had not arisen overnight. Of early Victorian Leeds M. W. Beresford writes, 'the accumulation of house alongside house, of factories, dye-houses, gasworks, had been measured in years and even decades'.[28] One visitor from York decided that Leeds was 'the filthiest and dirtiest town in England', where men seemed inured '. . . to live and die — like pigs in a stye'.[29] The Church in Leeds, as often elsewhere, had not kept pace with population growth. In 1836, eight churches, including three for pewholders only, and eleven clergy served Leeds's rapidly growing population, which by the 1841 census had reached 88,741.[30] Although three churches came to Leeds township through the Parliamentary Grant, it was not until 1836 that reviving Anglican confidence finally launched a Church extension scheme.[31]

Church and Dissent in Leeds Township, 1836

From 1740 onwards the Evangelical Revival's message of salvation through conscious acceptance of Christ as Saviour gradually changed the religious map of England.[32] Anglican Evangelicals mostly remained Calvinistic doctrinally, disagreeing with Wesley's extra-parochial Arminian preaching of

[24] Morgan, pp. 46–47, 48 (Table 2, Borough), p. 69, 2 (note).
[25] Morgan, pp. 48 (Table 2, Borough), p. 52 (Table 3, Townships).
[26] Beresford, pp. 381–97.
[27] LI, 16 Oct. 1847; R. J. Morris, Class, Sect and Party: The Making of the British Middle Class, Leeds 1820–1850, (Manchester, 1990), p. 48.
[28] Beresford, p. 383.
[29] LI, 9. Nov. 1844.
[30] LI, 27 Feb. 1836; see Chapter 1; SS Peter, John, Paul, James, Mark, Mary, Holy Trinity, Christ Church; and R. Fawcett, Wray, Brown, Taylor, J. Fawcett, F. T. Cookson, Holmes, Jackson, King, Holroyd, E. Cookson.
[31] LI, 27 Feb. 1836; Wood, Church Extension, p. 5.
[32] J. R. H. Moorman, A History of the Church in England (1963), p. 298.

salvation available to all.[33] Less popular in appeal, and more narrowly proclaimed, Evangelicalism neither enthused the whole Church, nor suffered total rejection.[34] By contrast, Wesley's Methodist Societies grew spectacularly. Similarly, many Independent and Baptist congregations of Old Dissent 'caught' Methodist beliefs and expanded markedly.[35] Unenthused by evangelicalism, Quakers declined, whilst Unitarian increases came mainly from heterodox Presbyterian and General Baptist congregations.[36]

Methodist preachers brought the Evangelical Revival to Leeds around 1743. By 1778 Methodist, Independent and Baptist congregations were fully settled.[37] Zealous and diligent, they opened new chapels as the population increased. Between 1770 and 1840, for example, Wesleyans in the out-townships opened twenty-two places of worship. In the same period Anglicans added just two churches to their out-township stock.[38] By 1836 the Anglican total of eight churches in the main township, the religious centre of Leeds, was completely overshadowed by the Protestant Dissenters' twenty-seven chapels.[39] Within Dissent itself twenty-four chapels testified to the proselytising vigour of evangelical congregations, in contrast to the non-evangelical Arians, Quakers, and Unitarians, each with one congregation, the same as in 1740. For Churchpeople evangelical tenets were proclaimed forcefully to private pewholders at St Paul's.[40] At the Parish Church, however, Richard Fawcett's standing as an Evangelical came more from his co-operative attitude to Dissenters than from his preaching.[41] Council statistics of Leeds township's sittings in 1839 (Dissenters 26,246: Anglicans 13,235) demonstrate the predominance of Dissent in 1836,[42] and are striking

33. K. Hylson-Smith, *Evangelicals in the Church of England, 1734–1984* (Edinburgh, 1988), pp. 10–11; Moorman, pp. 302–08.
34. Gilbert, pp. 70–74; Hylson-Smith, pp. 11–13.
35. Gilbert, pp. 31–32, 34, 37.
36. Gilbert, pp. 40–41.
37. F. M. Beckwith, 'The First Leeds Baptist Church: the Old Stone Chapel 1779–1826', *Baptist Quarterly*, New Series VI, pp. 8 (note), 74, 78; N. Curnock ed., *The Journal of John Wesley AM*, 8 vols (1909–16), III, 74 n. 1, IV 67, note 2; R. G. Lawn, 'The City of Leeds and its Methodism', *Methodist Magazine*, July 1930, p. 414 (extract); *Extracts from the Leeds Intelligencer and the Leeds Mercury 1777–1782*, G. D. Lumb and J. B. Place, *P.Th.S.*, XL (1955), 47, 91; H. McLachlan, 'Diary of a Leeds Layman, Joseph Ryder', *Essays and Addresses* (Manchester, 1950), p. 33, J. Nelson, *The Journal of Mr John Nelson, Preacher of the Gospel, written by himself* (1826), pp. 74–75; *The Jubilee of Queen Street Chapel, Leeds, with Memorials of the Church and its Pastors from the Beginning* ed. by W. Thomas (Leeds, 1875), pp. 5–6; W. L. Wade, *West Park Congregational Church (Queen Street Memorial), Leeds, 1672–1972: Three Hundred Years of Witness* (Leeds, 1972), pp. 1–2.
38. Yates, 'Religious Life', pp. 251–52, 257–58.
39. *LM*, 4 Mar. 1837.
40. M. Atkinson, *Practical Sermons (with a Memoir)* (1812), pp. vi, ix; T. Dikes, *A Sermon Preached on 17 February 1811 (on the death of the Rev. M. Atkinson)* (1811), pp. iii, 14; Mayhall, pp. 172–73; Taylor, pp. 242–47; Wood, *Church Extension*, pp. 4, 29.
41. *LI*, 28 Jan. 1837; *LM*, 4 Feb. 1837; Taylor, pp. 268–70.
42. Table 1.1 (Summary).

confirmation of the *Leeds Mercury*'s claim in 1837 that Dissenters were twice as numerous as Churchpeople there.[43] In 1836, however, three Anglican churches restricted their sittings to pewholders. The five churches open to the poor possessed 3,831 free places. It is likely, therefore, that in total the twenty-seven Dissenters' chapels existing in 1836 contained greater provision for the poor.[44]

From 1836 electoral strength in the municipality accompanied Dissenting religious predominance in Leeds. Liberal majorities, mainly Dissenters, were consistently returned at the annual Council elections. The Church, therefore, was disadvantageously placed whenever its role in the town's affairs was called into question.[45] Nationwide the steady increase of Dissenters had been observable for decades. Officially certified permanent Dissenting places of worship increased decennially from 1771–80 (158) to 1831–40 (2784).[46] By 1851 the Census of Religion indicated that mainstream Protestant Dissenters in total had reached 85.7 per cent of the total Anglican figure[47]. Dissenting strength was unevenly distributed, but manifested itself visibly wherever populous parishes refused Church rates, especially in Yorkshire and Lancashire. Elsewhere, anticipated opposition deterred requests for rates.[48] Despite Dissenting encroachment the Established Church was nevertheless still deeply embedded in the English social fabric, through its schools and recurring contacts with parishioners at baptisms, weddings, and funerals. Hence in 1836 the Church in Leeds proved well placed when reviving Anglican spirit there launched its own distinctive Church extension scheme.[49]

[43.] *LM*, 4 Mar. 1837.
[44.] Anglican free sittings, Leeds township 1836:

a	St Peter's (est. on 1450 total)	950
b	St John's (est. on 700 total.)	400
c	Christ Church (880), St Mary's (801), St Mark's (800)	2481
d	Holy Trinity, St Paul's, St James's	*Nil*
		3831

Sources: *Parochial System*, p. 16 (a, b), p. 22 (d); Port, pp. 138–39 (c).
[45.] Chadwick, I, 11; J. A. (Tony) Jowitt, 'The Pattern of Religion in Victorian Bradford', in *Victorian Bradford: Essays in Honour of Jack Reynolds*, ed. by D. D. Wright and J. A. Jowitt (Bradford, 1982), pp. 37–61 (Table 4, p. 45).
[46.] Gilbert, pp. 33–34, 218–19, note 23.
[47.] Chadwick, I, 365.
[48.] Gilbert, pp. 118–19.
[49.] Chadwick, I, 54–62, 100–06.

CHAPTER 2

Anglican Renewal begins in Leeds: Church Extension by Subscription, 1836–38

In the 1830s the Church of England became increasingly aware that if more churches were to be built for the ever growing population, it would be through Anglican self-help, since further Parliamentary grants looked unlikely. This recognition, along with the receding fear of disestablishment, stimulated the endeavours of subscription committees and private founders. Between 1836 and 1855 they built 1461 new churches in the counties of England and Wales.[1] The extent of this voluntary effort nationwide may be gauged in relation to the 515 new churches which received aid from the Church Building Commission (CBC), out of the second Parliamentary Grant, from 1825 to 1856. Of this number around 110 churches, mainly built between 1825 and 1835, received half or more of the cost from the CBC, whilst the remainder about four hundred, mostly churches built after 1835, were awarded a contribution representing about one-tenth. Hence in twenty years, from 1836 to 1855, subscription schemes and private founders were wholly responsible financially for erecting more than one thousand and fifty new churches in England and Wales, and almost entirely so for over four hundred.[2] M. H. Port prepared detailed summaries by county of all churches assisted by the CBC, including those receiving a modicum of assistance from the second Parliamentary Grant. With nine of these churches Leeds initiated more schemes than elsewhere. Similar schemes in industrial districts included: Sheffield (5); Bradford (2); Halifax (2); Huddersfield (1); Birmingham (4); Coventry (2); Wednesbury (2); Wolverhampton (2); Burnley (2); Liverpool (2); Manchester (1); Salford (1). Only in London did schemes approach the Leeds total: Bethnal Green (8); Westminster (7); Lambeth (6); Paddington (6); Islington (5).[3] The impressive total in Leeds owed much from 1837 to W. F. Hook's inspiration and active support, though his wider responsibilities usually precluded much direct personal involvement.

---

[1] Gilbert, p. 130.
[2] Port. pp. 125, 140–73.
[3] Port, pp. 146–57, 160–63, 166–71.

The Need for Church Accommodation in Leeds, 1836

Between 1826 and 1832 five new churches (including one rebuilt) arose in Leeds through the CBC, at virtually no local cost.[4] From 1836 to 1855 subscription schemes and private founders added another twenty which included two rebuilt ones. The CBC in nine instances defrayed a fraction of the cost.[5] The earliest nineteenth-century subscription scheme (1836), though possessing an eighteenth-century subscription precedent in Holy Trinity, Leeds (1727), was the most remarkable. Unaided by the CBC, it planned to build a new church, increase seating in others, and provide funds for extra clergy.[6] These extra aims made the scheme unique among those which followed, and, apart from the rebuilding of the Parish Church (1838–41), the most expensive. In 1836, however, its very novelty attracted interest and ready support, and its methods became a pattern for later schemes.

By 1836 Leeds Anglicans were uncomfortably aware of the glaring disparity in the main township of eight churches catering for some eighty thousand inhabitants, as against twenty-seven Protestant Dissenting Chapels.[7] Seating for the adult poor centrally was the problem: pew rents restricted Holy Trinity, St Paul's and St James's to the middle classes. Some free seats existed in St John's, however, and far more in the great Parish Church. Parliamentary churches served the north, south and east: St Mark's, Christ Church and St Mary's respectively. Two-thirds of their sittings were indeed free, 2481 in total, and largely occupied by Sunday School children.[8] The siting of these Parliamentary churches reflected the relative population needs around 1820. By 1836 the west ward was an obvious contender for a new church. Since 1822 industry and workers' jerry-built houses had obliterated the fields stretching beyond the high-class housing of the West End. In-migration and natural increase doubled the west ward's population between 1821 and 1831, when it reached 9797 and still increasing.[9]

Leeds Church Extension Scheme; Inauguration, 1836

The organizers of the scheme appreciated the value of publicity. Brief details appeared in the *Leeds Intelligencer* of 13 February 1836. The intention was to consider ways and means of erecting new churches under the provisions of

4. Wood, *Church Extension*, pp. 5–6.
5. Port, pp. 168–69; Wood, *Church Extension*, pp. 29–30.
6. P. Clarke, *Jubilee 150: Worship, Work and Witness at St George's Church, Leeds, 1838–1988* (Leeds, 1989), pp. 1–3: H. W. Thompson, *A Short Account of Holy Trinity Church, Leeds* (Leeds, 1927), pp. 7–11; Wood, *Church Extension*, pp. 3, 6, 9; Wood, *Holy Trinity*, pp. 1–4.
7. Table 1.1.
8. *LI*, 27 Feb. 1836; *Parochial System*, p. 22; Port, pp. 138–39; Wood, *Church Extension*, p. 9.
9. Beresford, pp. 286–95; Morris, p. 48; Webster, *Chantrell*, p. 85; Wood, *Church Extension*, p. 5.

the Church Building Act, 1831 (1 and 2 William IV *c.* 38), which required one-third of total seating to be free.[10] Shortly afterwards, at a private meeting, a preliminary committee was appointed to prepare a feasible scheme for erecting one or more new churches in Leeds township.[11] Though sparsely attended, the public meeting at the Court House on 22 February attracted many of the Anglican Tory elite. The occupations of all but one of those described as Esquires can be identified: merchants (6); cloth manufacturers (4); flax manufacturers (2); barristers (2); solicitors (4); physician (1); surgeons (4); banker (1); wholesalers (2); corn factor (1); and independent (4). According to the contemporary status ranking within the middle class of Leeds, as described by R. J. Morris, most and possibly all of these could be assigned to an upper middle class of merchants and manufacturers and their professional aides. Possibly some reason prevented Richard Fawcett, Vicar of Leeds, of similar status, from attending, but ten of his curates were among the thirteen clergymen present, along with named laymen who were less substantial figures, as the banker William Beckett noted.[12] Individuals and families in the higher ranking group were much wealthier, though far fewer, than the remainder. If the interest of both groups was fired, it augured well for subscriptions.

At the meeting different speakers voiced the religious and social concerns prompting the scheme. Evangelization of the poor was much in mind. Because of the shortage of free sittings in the township, Anglican churches were largely left with a limited number of the better-off, having lost most of the working classes. Active clergy were needed — those who would visit the poor in their homes and pray with them. Only thus could the Church attract them to regular worship. It was the duty of the rich and prosperous, declared William Beckett, to provide churches and clergy, so that factory labourers and their families could enjoy 'the comforts and consolations of religion'. The Liberal activist Joseph Bateson joined fellow Anglicans, mostly Tories, in this shared religious undertaking. He ascribed the Church's present difficulties to the laity failing to do their duty in the past.[13] He made a telling point. Within the past ten years the CBC had provided Leeds township with three churches at no local cost. Voluntary contributions for specific local purposes were welcomed by the CBC, but for these churches nothing came from the parish of Leeds. In contrast, places as diverse as Brixham, Gateshead, Ramsgate, Blackburn, Lambeth, Stepney and other parishes in London, all made substantial contributions towards their 'million' churches.[14] As chairman, J. R. Atkinson highlighted the vital role of churches in the formation of

---

[10.] *LI*, 13 Feb. 1836.

[11.] *LI*, 27 Feb. 1836.

[12.] *LI*, 27 Feb. 1836; *LM*, 27 Feb. 1836; *Leeds Directories, 1834, 1839; L(eeds) P(oll) B(ooks), 1834, 1835, 1837*; Morris pp. 165–66.

[13.] *LI*, 27 Feb. 1836; Fraser, 'Politics and Society', p. 291.

[14.] Port, pp. 132–39.

Christian character. Along with schools, they existed to provide young people with the religious and moral training which would enable them to take their place as good members of society. The first Mayor of the reformed corporation, George Goodman, a prominent Baptist, expressed his good wishes by paying a visit. It was his fervent hope that more religious provision would diminish crime. Such sentiments enabled the Tories present, still smarting from their displacement from municipal office, to give the Mayor a cordial welcome.[15] Perhaps the most pertinent observation about the incipient Anglican renewal locally came from J. R. Atkinson, when he stressed the need for perseverance in church building until every child could read the Bible and every individual received instruction 'in the genuine principles of the Protestant Established Church'.[16]

Those initiating the project had all agreed that a new church at the West End, in the vicinity of Bean Ing, near Gott's Park Mills, was an absolute and immediate necessity. The Court House meeting concurred. It regarded an additional church there as imperative for the district's rapidly increasing population. Because the needs of the poor for free seating were so continually iterated when the scheme was launched, it seems at first sight surprising that the new church was to be built under a statute which permitted two-thirds of the seating to be reserved for payment. Though not stated explicitly, the reason was economic. No endowments were available for a ministerial stipend, and the scheme organizers had obviously recognized that this would have to come from pew rents and fees. Important also to the organizers was the fact that the statute provided for the patronage of such churches to be vested in five trustees of the founders' appointment, rather than in the parochial incumbent.[17] In the 1830s, when differing doctrinal stances were sharpening, this opened the possibility of incumbents being appointed who were at odds doctrinally with the parish priest, their ecclesiastical superior. The remaining details of the scheme were unexceptionable. Three-fourths of the eventual total subscription were allocated for the erection of the new church. The residue would serve two purposes: construction of new galleries to provide additional free seating for the poor, at St John's in the north, Christ Church in the south, and St Mary's in the east of Leeds township; and for payment for additional clergy at these churches. A subscription in three equal instalments was then agreed, the first being payable immediately, the others on 1 June 1837 and 1 June 1838.[18]

[15.] *LI*, 27 Feb. 1836; *LM*, 27 Feb. 1836; Fraser, 'Politics and Society', pp. 279, 284.
[16.] *LI*, 27 Feb. 1836; *LM*, 27 Feb. 1836.
[17.] *LI*, 27 Feb. 1836; *Parochial System*, pp. 17–18; Port, pp. 107, 111, 191.
[18.] *LI*, 27 Feb. 1836.

The Progress of the Subscription, 1836

To achieve their purposes the organizers had estimated that £10,000 would be required. The alacrity and generosity of the response was heartening. Immediately the meeting ended, the sum of £3036 was subscribed. Five days later the total reached £5102. This impressive amount was crucial to the scheme's success, for fifty-five subscriptions of £20 upwards accounted for all but £200.[19] By 28 May 1836 nearly six hundred subscribers individually or collectively had promised £10,506.[20] This achievement owed much to the canvass of potential subscribers undertaken by thirty-seven committee members elected by the public meeting, but probably informally at work even earlier. All were Tories, except for Peter Fairbairn and Joseph Bateson. All were middle class, some indeed in the upper echelons, and in the same broad occupational categories as the Esquires present, but the social mix was probably deliberately wider, to gain access to a greater range of possible supporters. The 'retired' or 'independent' element was significantly absent, apparently to ensure that committee members were still actively engaged in regular contacts in business and socially.[21] Some Anglican Tory committee members were major subscribers and partners of well-known firms such as John Gott, J. R. Atkinson and Richard Bramley. Workers at Benjamin Gott and Sons gave £27 9s. 0d.; at Hives and Atkinson £15 16s. 1d.; and at Hirst, Bramley and Co. £13 1s. 4d.[22] Whether all these contributions were entirely spontaneous, or came from a sense of obligation to employers prominent in the scheme, will never be known, but that feeling could have existed at Hirst, Bramley and Co., who were notable for their efforts to keep their factory workers fully employed.[23] Some contributions arrived from unexpected quarters, especially £10 from the Revd R. W. Hamilton, the distinguished minister for the Independents at Belgrave Chapel.[24] In addition to the Mayor's attendance at the Court House, this handsome donation — not the only one — was evidence of the good will of prominent evangelical Dissenters towards the Anglican scheme in 1836.[25]

From Subscription to Foundation Stone, St George's, 1836

After the public meeting the subscription reached almost £10,200 in six weeks.[26] During this time the committee looked at four or five possible sites

---

[19] *LI*, 27 Feb. 1836; *LM*, 27 Feb. 1836.
[20] *LI*, 27 Feb., 5, 12, 19, 26 Mar., 2, 9, 16, 30 Apr., 28 May 1836; *LM*, 27 Feb. 1836.
[21] *LI*, 27 Feb. 1836; *LPB, 1834, 1835, 1837*; Morris, pp. 165–66.
[22] *LI*, 5, 12 Mar. 1836.
[23] Morris, p. 103.
[24] *LI*, 19 Mar. 1836.
[25] *LI*, 27 Feb., 19 Mar. 1836.
[26] *LI*, 9 Apr. 1836.

near Bean Ing. On 8 April 1836, with the first instalment of one-third presumably received, the committee unanimously resolved to site the church at Mount Pleasant, in part of a field belonging to the banker Christopher Beckett, one of three subscribers who each donated £300. The site, on rising ground, was a good one, and purchased on very favourable terms. When completed the new church would stand well.[27] Mount Pleasant was in a desirable still developing middle-class district. Three quarters of a mile distant, Bean Ing was a social world away. Its huddled houses in poorly cleansed streets had seen their share of cholera in the 1832 epidemic.[28] Because the final site was towards the north of Leeds township, rather than the west among the poor, an anonymous pamphlet in 1842 accused the committee of diverting the subscriptions to an unadvertised purpose.[29] It was indeed undeniable that the original resolution for a church in the West End had been circumvented. The reasons were probably social. Mount Pleasant was more likely to attract the middle-class congregations with funds sufficient for a stipend dependent on pew-rents. Also, perhaps, the religious poor might be deemed readier to journey on foot to Mount Pleasant than the still essentially carriageless middle class to thread their way through increasingly squalid streets to Bean Ing.[30] Nevertheless some uneasiness about the committee's decision apparently existed. In December 1836 the *Leeds Intelligencer* reported that, irrespective of the favourable purchase terms, the balance of eligibility 'preponderated' for Mount Pleasant over other sites available. Such a cryptic explanation posed more questions than it answered.[31]

Shortly after deciding on Mount Pleasant, the committee invited architects to submit plans and specifications. The brief was for a church in the plain, bold style of thirteenth-century Gothic, free from ornament. The design by the Leeds architect John Clark was selected, as best fitting the requirements.[32] On 16 December 1836 Dr Longley laid the foundation stone on his first official visit to Leeds as Bishop of Ripon. A grand civic procession accompanied him to the site of the new church — now known as St George's. In a lengthy prayer, the Revd Joseph Holmes referred to the district's current spiritual destitution. This was not the case. The west ward, where St George's was situated, was indeed populous, but not lacking in spiritual provision. Evangelical Dissenters had by 1836 already provided 5350 sittings in four nearby chapels, all but one within four hundred yards of St George's site. By 1839 there would be 15,483 inhabitants in the ward, one-third being children under thirteen. Dissenters' spiritual provision therefore in 1836 already bettered Peel's estimate (1824) that Anglican church-room for a quarter of

[27] *LI*, 9 Apr., 17 Dec. 1836; Beresford, p. 337.
[28] Beresford, pp. 279 n., 288–89, 292, 308–16, 323–24, 331–32, 337, 507–10; Morris, p. 48.
[29] *Parochial System*, pp. 17–18; Wood, *Church Extension*, p. 9.
[30] Morris, p. 51.
[31] *LI*, 17 Dec. 1836.
[32] *LI*, 16 Apr., 17 Dec. 1836, 10 Nov. 1838; *LPB, 1834*; Beresford, p. 340.

the population would be sufficient. Holmes's remarks typified the Established Church's affected ignorance of the efforts of other denominations, which Dissenters found so irritating.[33] Ironically, Bishop Longley in the presence of the civic party and prominent Dissenters at Christ Church had earlier that day in his sermon commended the exertions of Dissenters to propagate religion as something for his own flock to emulate.[34] On this bleak December afternoon the Bishop kept his own part intentionally brief: a short prayer in laying the foundation stone, and a few words of encouragement for local people to make full use of the new church after completion.[35]

The Gallery Extensions

In April 1836 the committee advertised for contractors for the gallery extensions. They selected designs for Christ Church by Robert Dennis Chantrell, its original architect who was also responsible for St Matthew's, the Parliamentary church which replaced Holbeck's ancient chapel.[36] Christ Church with its new galleries was reopened on 16 December 1836 as the first event of Bishop Longley's visit. The Mayor, Town Council, and the Borough Member of Parliament, Edward Baines, along with other prominent Dissenters, were among the crowded congregation. The Bishop's sermon addressed current issues. He commended the now tangible evidence of local zeal for Church extension, and reminded Anglicans of the need for moderation in expression when articulating doctrinal differences. In discussing this topic the Bishop delighted Dissenters by explaining that his remarks were aimed at preventing further Anglican disunion and were in no way condemnation of those departed in the past.[37] For Christ Church's reopening 'the new curate', the Revd Joseph Ware, was another proof of the local scheme's achievement.[38]

At St Mary's the new galleries for the north and south were designed by another Leeds architect, William Perkin. Other improvements, outside the scheme, were also made; installation of gaslighting, to institute evening services; and structural alterations to the nave.[39] As with Christ Church the scheme provided a new curate. St Mary's reopened on 31 March 1837,

---

33. 'Report upon the Condition of the Town of Leeds, by a Statistical Committee of the Town Council, October 1839', *J(ournal of the) S(tatistical) S(ociety)*, II (1839–40), 410, 415; Port, p. 93; see also Chapter 1. Table 1.1 (Oxford Place, 2550; Park St, 800; Queen Street, 1400).
34. *LI*, 17 Dec. 1836.
35. *LM*, 17 Dec. 1836.
36. *LI*, 16 Apr., 17 Dec. 1836; Port, pp. 138–39, 168–69, 179; Webster, *Chantrell*, pp. 43, 46, 54–55, 62, 85–87; Wood, *Church Extension*, pp. 5–6.
37. *LM*, 17 Dec. 1836.
38. *LI*, 10 Dec. 1836.
39. *LI*, 25 Mar., 8 Apr. 1837; *LPB, 1834*; Beresford, p. 359; Grady, *Georgian Buildings*, p. 165; Port, p. 185.

without episcopal or civic presence; the Bishop preached later, to assist in clearing the debt for the extras.[40] Situated in Quarry Hill, an impoverished district, the church was unlikely to attract more funds than those received from Parliament and the local scheme. Further external aid was essential, its source less obvious.[41] Financial salvation came from a bazaar, an innovation for Leeds Churchpeople which attracted great praise. Among the patrons were three titled ladies: the Countess of Harewood, the Countess of Mexborough and the Lady Elizabeth Lowther.[42] Held for three days in April 1838, the bazaar drew unprecedented crowds to the Music Hall. Many useful and ornamental articles were available, including newly made clothes for purchase to give to poor people.[43] The bazaar raised £2184, reflecting much hard work by the Ladies' Committee, especially Mrs Edward Cookson, the incumbent's wife. It cleared the debt on the church and Sunday school and financed the construction of better church approaches. The surplus of £840 was transferred to the church's endowment, the income being donated by the incumbent for church expenses.[44] Unlike Christ Church and St Mary's, no gallery reopening ceremonies were recorded for St John's, though the church was described as in a state of dilapidation in 1836, and closed for a spell in 1837.[45]

Appointment of Trustees and Minister for St George's, 1836–37

In May 1836 the committee advertised an election on 3 June for five trustees. As decided at the inaugural meeting, subscribers of £5 and above were eligible to vote. This provision was intended to secure a wide but responsible electoral constituency and to pre-empt a few principal subscribers from appropriating the power of appointment. To animate the dilatory it was announced that subscribers who had not paid their first instalment would be ineligible to vote.[46] J. R. Atkinson, committee chairman, presided at the subsequent count; J. H. Hill and T. T. Dibb, honorary secretaries, acted as scrutineers. The five elected were men of substance, but the result demonstrated that size of subscription was not the sole criterion for voters. William Hey, surgeon, subscribing £200, received 143 votes; J. R. Atkinson, flax manufacturer, £300, 123 votes; John Heaton, stuff merchant, £105, 112

40. *LI*, 1, 8 Apr., 7, 21 Oct. 1837.
41. Beresford, *East End, West End*, pp. 237, 262–64; M. W. Beresford, 'The Face of Leeds, 1780–1914': *Modern Leeds*, pp. 72–112. See illustrations 24, 25, 27.
42. *LM*, 13 Jan. 1838.
43. *LI*, 7, 21 Apr. 1838.
44. *LI*, 26 May, 2 June, 1838.
45. *LI*, 27 Feb. 1836, 22 Apr. 1837.
46. *LI*, 28 May 1836.

votes; William Beckett, banker £200, 90 votes; Thomas Shann, cloth manufacturer, £100, 85 votes.[47]

The trustees' search for a minister was not widely known until November 1837, when W. F. Hook was already some six months into a well appreciated High Church ministry as Vicar of Leeds, and at the request of many parishioners exploring the possibility of enlarging the Parish Church.[48] At this time four of the five St George's trustees (Hey, Atkinson, Heaton, and Shann) were pillars of St Paul's; two of them (Hey and Atkinson) were also Leeds Vicarage trustees who had opposed Hook's candidacy at the election for the new Vicar in March 1837.[49] Since its foundation in 1793 St Paul's had been an Evangelical beacon for the well-to-do in Leeds. After Hook's arrival its minister, the curate Miles Jackson, virulently opposed Hook for teaching High Church principles. Some of Jackson's congregation left, but not the four trustees of St George's.[50] Although William Beckett's doctrinal position never publicly emerged, it is clear that the power of appointing a minister for St George's rested with prominent Evangelical laymen.

On 15 December 1837 a majority of the trustees elected the Revd William Sinclair, son of the late Sir John Sinclair, Bt., as the first minister of St George's.[51] Sinclair was the only candidate publicly named. He had visited Leeds in November 1837, as his candidacy was announced, and preached in Evangelical Christ Church.[52] Sinclair was known as a friend of Hook, who had first suggested his coming forward for the position.[53] For St George's Evangelical trustees the High Church Vicar's support for Sinclair was possibly unappealing, but ultimately prevailed, though Hook admitted 'some difficulty in procuring' his appointment. In Sinclair Hook was expecting 'an advocate of sound [Church] principles'. Instead, after St George's consecration (1838) Sinclair's Evangelicalism was proclaimed 'with unusual resolution in his bearing and language'. Disillusioned, Hook used strong terms privately to Pusey about Sinclair's conduct.[54] Yet Sinclair's choice of Evangelical Christ Church for his sole pre-election preaching engagement was surely significant.

47. *LI*, 27 Feb., 4 June 1836; *LPB 1834*.
48. WYASL, LCP41/6, Leeds Parish Church Improvement Committee Minute Book, pp. 3–5; *LI*, 21, 28 Oct., 4, 11 Nov. 1837; *LM*, 14 Oct., 11 Nov. 1837.
49. WYASL, LPC25, Vicarage Book, Trustee Griffith Wright's list of votes cast; *LI*, 4 June 1836, 30 June 1838.
50. PH, fols 48–51, Hook to Pusey, '2 in Advent 1837', fols 60–61, Hook to Pusey, 3 Mar. 1838, fols 62–69, Hook to Pusey, 24 Apr. 1838; WYASL, LCP25, Vicarage Book, MS note on press report of meeting of 15 Mar. 1837, opposing Hook's candidacy; *LI*, 30 June 1838.
51. *LI*, 2, 16, 23 Dec. 1837; *LM*, 9 Dec. 1837.
52. *LI*, 4 Nov. 1837.
53. BL, Gladstone Papers, MS 44, 213, fols 5–8, Hook to Gladstone, 26 Mar. 1838; *LI*, 2 Mar. 1839.
54. BL, Gladstone Papers, MS 44, 213, fols 5–8, Hook to Gladstone, 26 Mar. 1838; PH, fols 103–16, Hook to Pusey, 9 June 1840; Steele, p. 188.

At interview Sinclair probably satisfied the trustees that he held Evangelical beliefs tenaciously and would proclaim them with conviction if elected.

Completion and Consecration of St George's, 1836–38

St George's completion occurred later than originally expected, because the committee revived a plan for extra revenue by constructing burial vaults under the edifice.[55] By the autumn of 1838 the church was ready for consecration, fixed for 7 November.[56] Though built of stone the church was nevertheless planned with the greatest economy in construction, 'consistent with giving a Church-like character to the exterior'.[57] The exterior therefore conformed to the reproduction Gothic architectural style then considered ecclesiastically appropriate, but inside there was not the slightest evidence of nostalgia for the pre-Reformation Church. St George's was designed for preaching the Gospel. Apart from a five-sided projecting apse at the east end, accommodating the communion table, the interior was rectangular. The minister was audible and visible to the entire congregation. In this St George's resembled many eighteenth-century churches. Of the nineteenth century were its gaslighting and central heating hot water pipes underneath the aisles, and covered by ornamental pierced ironwork.[58] There were 1655 sittings, 1046 being for rent, 609 free, with the latter including 246 for children. The free pews resembled the rented in appearance, but were less roomy, a feature much criticized in a Leeds pamphlet in 1842. The churchwarden T. T. Dibb in reply declared that the free seats were in fact much appreciated and regularly filled on Sundays.[59]

For the consecration there was again a procession, though less elaborate. To show his respect for the Established Church, the Unitarian Mayor, T. W. Tottie made his attendance an official occasion.[60] Inside St George's the packed congregation included fifty-five clergymen and many influential local people. Following the customary pattern the Bishop consecrated the church and graveyard, with his Deputy Registrar ensuring the legal necessities.[61] The consecration collection realized £282; two months later, even with an appeal, the committee's debt stood at £540.[62] In January 1839 a hurricane badly damaged St George's and Christ Church. To pay for repairs costing £500

[55] *LI*, 17 Dec. 1836, 10 Nov. 1838.
[56] *LI*, 11 Aug., 6 Oct., 3 Nov. 1838; *LM*, 3 Nov. 1838.
[57] *LI*, 17 Dec. 1836; Webster, *Chantrell*, pp. 45, 59.
[58] *LI*, 10 Nov. 1838; D. Linstrum, *West Yorkshire Architects and Architecture* (1978), p. 185.
[59] *LI*, 10 Nov. 1838; 26 Feb. 1842; *JSS* II: 'Report on Leeds' p. 415; *Parochial System*, pp. 16–18.
[60] *LM*, 3 Nov. 1838.
[61] *LI*, 10 Nov. 1838; *LM*, 10 Nov. 1838.
[62] *LI*, 10, 17 Nov., 1 Dec. 1838, 5 Jan. 1839; *LM*, 10, 17 Nov. 1838.

each, a joint Whitsuntide bazaar was arranged.[63] Extinguishing the debt on St George's became also an objective. The bazaar was a huge success. The proceeds cleared all liabilities and provided a surplus for new schools.[64]

The Significance of the Leeds Church Extension Scheme, 1836–38

The Leeds Church Extension Scheme marked a new approach to church provision in the town. Anglicans there had in effect recognized the diminished importance of the Established Church in the State. Parliaments since the Reform Act contained a handful of Dissenters, but far more Catholics from Irish constituencies. However fervently many Anglican Members desired the legislation, political constraints operated against Parliament voting more funds for the denominational objectives of England's State-Church. The *Leeds Mercury* perceived that Leeds Churchpeople had fully grasped the political realities of their Church's changed situation. Writing of the new scheme, it hailed 'with sincere pleasure this distinguished concession to the Voluntary Church Principle in Leeds'.[65] For local Dissenters the scheme removed an old grievance about contributing towards new Anglican churches through general taxation. Probably it was this, as much as respect for the Bishop's office, or common evangelicalism, which prompted the Council to make Dr Longley's visit on foundation day a civic occasion. At Christ Church, the Dissenting stalwart Edward Baines was deeply impressed by the Bishop's generous attitude towards Dissenters. Hence, although Baines's influential Dissenting *Leeds Mercury* would still bitterly attack the Established Church and its clergy, Bishop Longley personally was never its target.

Leeds Churchpeople's wholehearted response to the scheme showed that they recognized the urgent need for parishioners to receive better spiritual care through additional churches and clergy for unprovided areas. From then on this awareness enabled them to sustain many similar schemes among the poor in Leeds working-class districts.[66] Although the scheme of 1836 recorded subscriptions from workpeople, their financial resources were indeed limited. At Hirst, Bramley and Co., locally renowned as a caring employer, woollen handloom weavers, making top-quality cloth for the highest district wages, received 18s. 9d. per week in 1840.[67] Availability of employment in typical occupations varied between nine and twelve months of the year, and average adult wages ranged from 18s. 5d. to 23s. 8d. per week. In this perspective the immense purchasing power of the amount subscribed for the extension

---

63. *LI*, 12 Jan. 1839; *LM*, 12 Jan. 1839.
64. *LI*, 25 May, 22 June 1839; *LM*, 25 May 1839.
65. *LM*, 17 Dec. 1836.
66. See Chapter 7.
67. *LI*, 5, 12 Mar. 1836; Morris, pp. 86, 103.

scheme, in terms of goods and services obtainable, can readily be appreciated.[68] For Church life in Leeds the appointment of William Sinclair as minister of St George's was not the least of the benefits conferred by the scheme. He was a man of rare quality, providing the leadership for a continuing Evangelical presence from 1837 in a town showing increasingly High Church tendencies. The fact that he also 'took the patriciate and good Anglican relations with Dissent for his distinctive work' was an important element in the gradually improving relations between Church and Chapel from the late 1840s.[69] By 1852, he was held in such regard that he was publicly referred to as one 'against whom no man breathing could say a single word'.[70]

[68.] 'Report 1839', p. 422; Morris, p. 105.
[69.] Steele, p. 188.
[70.] *LI*, 7 Feb. 1852; Mayhall, pp. 686, 690–91.

CHAPTER 3

Churchwardens and Trustees, January–April 1837

On 22 January 1837 the Vicar of Leeds, Richard Fawcett (b. 1760), succumbed to influenza. His death created a vacancy in the Vicarage of Leeds. Until Fawcett's successor arrived, the churchwardens were required to arrange for the day-to-day running of the Parish Church, especially the Sunday Services and the conducting of baptisms, weddings and funerals. The trustees of the Vicarage, for their part, as patrons of the living, were charged with the longer term objective of finding a successor. In Leeds the number of churchwardens and patrons was unusually large. By old custom the Parish Church possessed eight churchwardens, whilst the regulations governing the trustees required the full complement of twenty-five to exist, before an election could proceed.[1] Although Fawcett was not in good health, his death was unexpected. He had recently accompanied the Bishop on his first engagements in Leeds. Even on 31 December 1836 he could examine and sign the Leeds National School's accounts in a firm, clear hand.[2] Local obituaries focused on Fawcett's good nature, kind heart and charitable disposition, but did not attempt any assessment of his tenure of the incumbency.[3] In Council the Mayor, Dr James Williamson, paid tribute to Fawcett's desire to serve the town. Common evangelicalism had made Fawcett esteemed by the influential Dissenters present, as well as Churchmen. All cordially endorsed these remarks, and influenced the Mayor, himself an Independent, to attend Fawcett's funeral officially instead of privately.[4] Civic dignitaries therefore joined Fawcett's funeral procession to the Parish Church on 28 January. People lined the streets and shops closed to mark their respect for the deceased.[5] Even before the funeral the mechanisms of continuity had commenced. By 26 January the Bishop had signed the legal deed of sequestration and appointed the churchwardens to administer parish affairs.[6] Earlier still, Henry Hall and Christopher Beckett, as senior and second resident trustees respectively, had jointly called a trustees' meeting for 9 February, to

---

[1] WYASL, LPC24/1, Lord Hardwicke's Decree, 23 Feb. 1749, MS 'Office Copy of Decree', dated /3 1749 and endorsed fo 221, pp. 168, 174–78.

[2] WYASL, LCP70/1, Leeds Dist. Natl Society Account Book, 1822–47; *LI* 17, 24 Dec. 1836, 28 Jan. 1837; *LM*, 17 Dec. 1836; Taylor, pp. 368–70.

[3] *LI*, 28 Jan. 1837; *LM*, 28 Jan. 1837.

[4] *LM*, 28 Jan. 1837.

[5] *LI*, 28 Jan., 4 Feb. 1837; *LM*, 4 Feb. 1837.

[6] WYASL, LPC49/1, Sequestration Papers, Bishop's Deed of Sequestration, 26 Jan. 1837.

elect sufficient new trustees to make up the number legally required.[7] The churchwardens and the trustees were entirely separate bodies. Their functions did not interlock in any way and are now considered separately.

Functions and Role of the Churchwarden-Sequestrators

In the sequestration deed the Bishop addressed the churchwardens by name, and outlined their responsibilities during the interregnum for the spiritualities and temporalities of the Vicarage. For the parishioners their most important duty was 'to cause the Cure of Souls . . . to be well and sufficiently served', by ensuring that funds were available for Sunday and other services, and for the expenses of the sacraments or visiting preachers. It may seem anomalous that the Parish Church's lay officers should be entrusted with such arrangements, rather than the senior curate. At that time, however, unbeneficed curates possessed no security of tenure, being employed by the incumbent personally. Sometimes they were dismissed immediately the incumbent died. Church-wardens, on the other hand, were 'admitted' to their duties by the diocesan Archdeacon or his Official, so had a recognized legal status. Regarding the temporalities of the Vicarage, the Bishop demanded careful husbanding of resources. All dues must be collected, and only absolutely necessary expenditure incurred. The sequestrators would be required in due course to render a full account of their conduct as fiduciaries to the Bishop or his agent. Their immediate duty, however, was to 'publish the sequestration in the way lawfully required'.[8]

The recipients of the sequestration deed must have regarded their mandate as interregnum caretakers as highly unusual, since for this office Anglican membership was not required. Churchwardens were elected annually by the ratepayers at a special vestry meeting held in Easter week, apart from one, always an Anglican, chosen by the Vicar to represent Kirkgate ward, where the Parish Church was situated. The remaining seven were elected singly for each of the other seven wards of Leeds township, but often they were elected *en bloc* from political party lists. Since 1828 Liberals had constituted the majority, pledged to economy and to keeping down or preventing Church rates. In any year they were mostly or entirely Dissenters.[9]

During the interregnum, therefore, the churchwardens carried out two distinct financial functions. As churchwardens they kept the Parish Church running expenses to the minimum commensurate with their legal responsibil-ities; as sequestrators they collected and banked the Vicarage's revenues. In their dual capacity they walked in the procession following the Vicar's

7. WYASL, LPC26, Election Papers, MS notice of 24 Jan. 1837.
8. WYASL, LPC49/1, Sequestration Papers, Bishop's Deed of Sequestration, 26 Jan. 1837.
9. Fraser, 'Politics and Society', pp. 273–74.

cortège — a gesture of respect undoubtedly acceptable to Churchpeople. Possibly with an eye to future problems they kept and preserved records of their proceedings, the only wardens to do so before 1847. The first sequestrators' meeting took place on 2 February 1837. George Nussey, Jr, presided. A man of standing and a dyemaster, he was deputed to receive the funds of the benefice as they accrued, and to deposit them with Beckett and Co. The sequestrators' choice was financially sound and religiously tactful, since Beckett's bank was highly successful, and its partners were well-known Churchmen. The knottiest point in this first meeting proved to be the interpretation of the Bishop's instructions to publish the sequestration. Edward Johnson, a leading churchwarden, was delegated to obtain legal advice. Details consequently appeared in the local press two days later. The Liberal *Leeds Mercury* highlighted for its readers, mainly Dissenters, that the sequestrators were custodians of the temporalities — the church keys and the Vicarage income. For its Anglican readers the *Leeds Intelligencer* stressed, perhaps as veiled advice to the sequestrators, that the Bishop had released Vicarage funds for them to ensure the proper performance of services at St Peter's.[10]

To provide continuity at the Parish Church the sequestrators sensibly retained Robert Taylor, Fawcett's curate, at a stipend of £130 per annum. With the idea of raising funds to defray the cost of refitting and altering the church's gaslighting, they invited the celebrated Hugh Stowell, of Manchester, to preach two sermons, with collections following. Stowell declined, without explanation. John Hugill, of Earlsheaton, was more accommodating. The sequestrators were so eager for his concurrence that three made the eight-mile journey to secure his acceptance personally. Paid advertising in the *Leeds Intelligencer*, the *Leeds Mercury*, and the *Leeds Times* ensured wide publicity. Hugill received his expenses and the cost of a substitute. Total expenditure amounted to £4 12s. 2d. — the two collections realised £33 8s. 11d. On each of the three Sundays in March preceding the actual election to the Vicarage, the sequestrators permitted a different candidate to occupy the Parish Church pulpit, 'to give the congregation the opportunity to estimate their qualifications'. They also countenanced, but did not arrange, a course of midweek Lenten sermons at the Parish Church, given by local clergy.[11]

By the terms of Bishop Longley's deed of sequestration the churchwardens received full possession of the revenues and finances of the benefice.[12] With the deed as their authority they were thus able to undertake a delicate but necessary task. This was to visit Fawcett's executors, to require them to give

[10.] WYASL, LPC49/1, Sequestration Papers, Churchwardens' minute book, 2 Feb. 1837; *LI*, 4 Feb. 1837; *LM*, 4 Feb. 1837; Grady, 'Commercial Amenities' p. 180.

[11.] WYASL, LPC49/1, Sequestration Papers, Churchwardens' minute book, 2, 7, 22 Feb. 1837; *LM*, 4 Feb., 4 Mar. 1837.

[12.] WYASL, LPC49/1, Sequestration Papers, Bishop's Deed of Sequestration, 26 Jan. 1837.

up all property belonging to the Church. Probably the most important matter was to secure an agreed date for vacating the Vicarage house. The executors were Fawcett's sons-in-law, the Revds F. T. Cookson, of St John's and W. C. Wollaston, second master of Leeds Grammar School. For their delegation of three the sequestrators made an admirable choice in selecting John Garland, master builder and Churchman, whom Fawcett had personally appointed as his warden for Kirkgate; William Gregory, a Briggate draper, and George Nussey. The delegation found the executors co-operative. For their purposes the sequestrators apparently needed the amounts of the different types of income accruing to the Vicarage, and also Fawcett's personal expenditure on curates. At any rate, Cookson and Wollaston allowed these various details to be copied by the delegation from the late Vicar's private books from 1834 to 1836 inclusive.[13]

Hook's induction on 15 April 1837 simultaneously gave him immediate access to Vicarage funds and removed it from the sequestrators. The Bishop, however, did not release them officially from their responsibilities until 24 April. During this interim period the sequestrators found themselves with insufficient funds for outstanding obligations. On 20 April they resolved that payment of £37 10s. to Robert Taylor for curate's duties had first call. This left them five or six pounds short of meeting the gas refitting account in full. They resolved to request Hook's assistance at a forthcoming meeting to settle sequestration business. As with Fawcett's executors, they similarly smoothed their way by including the Anglican Garland with the two leading Dissenters, Nussey and Johnson, in their delegation.[14] This interview probably constituted the full account of the sequestration enjoined by the Bishop. Some evidence exists that Nussey kept detailed accounts of Vicarage income and expenditure, presumably for a final statement to be presented by the delegation.[15]

The interregnum of 1837 in the parish of Leeds possessed some unusual features. On previous occasions all the churchwardens appointed as sequestrators were Anglicans. From the 1820s Dissenters were increasingly elected as churchwardens. By 1837 this was so usual that the Bishop showed no hesitation about naming Dissenting churchwardens as sequestrators. They applied themselves conscientiously to their duties, especially in ensuring the cure of souls was maintained. Equally striking, perhaps, their responsible approach seemed taken for granted in early Victorian Leeds. Not even the Anglican *Leeds Intelligencer* disputed the propriety of the arrangement. Probity

13. WYASL, LPC49/1, Sequestration Papers, Churchwardens' minute book, 2 Feb. 1837; Surplice Fees of Revd R. Fawcett, cash book, p. 1; *LPB, 1834*.
14. WYASL, LPC25, Vicarage Book, MS note of 15 Apr. 1837; LPC49/1 Sequestration Papers, Churchwardens' minute book, 20 Apr. 1837; Bishop's Deed of Relaxation of Sequestration, 24 Apr. 1837; *LI*, 22 Apr. 1837; *LM*, 22 Apr. 1837.
15. WYASL, LPC49/1, Nussey Sequestration Papers, Churchwardens' cash book, 'Daily dues received for Vicar of Leeds', 23 Jan.–8 Apr. 1837, pp. 1–12.

in matters of trust was expected of reputable Dissenting businessmen acting as churchwardens, who were often chapel officials in their own right. This attitude was symptomatic of the respect and goodwill which Church and Chapel folk felt for each other in daily life, and which were so often obscured by blown-up reports of interdenominational conflict. From 1847 the old custom of eight Anglican churchwardens was restored. Hence the interregnum of 1837 administered by Dissenting churchwardens has continued unique in Leeds Church life.[16]

Functions and Role of the Vicarage Trustees

The advowson for the Vicarage of Leeds was held by a patronage trust of twenty-five influential Churchmen. Since moneyed parishioners purchased the advowson around 1588, election procedures had been refined following litigation over the choice of new Vicars. A self-perpetuating trust was ordered in 1615, whilst Lord Chancellor Hardwicke in 1749 laid down strict procedures for future elections. They must be held within a specified time of a vacancy occurring, with trust membership at full strength.[17] By the eighteenth century the Leeds Vicarage trustees apparently regarded presentation to St Peter's as an appropriate reward to merchant families with near relatives in holy orders — as did the trustee bodies for neighbouring St John's and Holy Trinity. For St Peter's the only Vicar not born in the West Riding of Yorkshire was Peter Haddon, of Warrington (1786–1815). He was one of the three Vicars elected under Hardwicke's regulations, the others being his predecessor, Samuel Kirshaw (1751–86), and successor, Richard Fawcett (1815–37).[18]

Selecting a Candidate

Hardwicke's provisions were still applicable in 1837. The senior trustee, Henry Hall, called a meeting for 9 February, to fill the vacancies then existing. Before this meeting a pseudonymous 'Churchman' circularized all the trustees, deploring the monopolization, by a few families of the old Tory corporation, of the trust's membership. These men, he asserted, were readier to make the wishes of friends their first concern, rather than the spiritual needs of parishioners. Their appointment of Fawcett, 'Churchman' roundly

16. *LI*, 1 Apr. 1837; *LM*, 1 Apr. 1837; Fraser, 'Politics and Society', pp. 273–74; Fraser, 'Churchwardens', p. 21.
17. WYASL, LPC24/1, Lord Hardwicke's Decree, 23 Feb. 1749, MS 'Office Copy', pp. 174–78; Forster, 'Foundations', p. 15; Mayhall, p. 130; Taylor, p. 184; Wilson, p. 33.
18. Taylor, pp. 183–85, 259–60, 268–70; R. G. Wilson, *Gentleman Merchants: The Merchant Community in Leeds 1700–1830* (Manchester, 1971), p. 183; Wilson, 'Georgian Leeds', p. 33.

declared, was injudicious, and injurious to the Church. Most of Fawcett's own appointments were similar, in his view, giving the parish 'mere trading ministers', and churches with small congregations and little devotion. To counter this depressing picture 'Churchman' envisaged that if the trustees kept faith with Leeds parishioners they would appoint 'such a skilful workman' that he would restore the Church's fortunes in the town.[19] The writer was preaching to the converted. Two days before receiving his circular the trustees' had announced their intention of appointing a 'clergyman of distinction', a course of which the Bishop, on meeting them, thoroughly approved. Influential Churchpeople locally asked for 'a first-class man' of proved ability as preacher and pastor. An anonymous correspondent in the *Leeds Intelligencer* urged the trustees to look for a godly Evangelical minister. For preserving interdenominational peace the *Leeds Mercury* hoped for someone amiable and co-operative towards Dissenters.[20]

On 9 February the trustees available elected George Bischoff and J. R. Atkinson to complete their number. Atkinson's appointment was significant for more than one reason. He was a leading flax manufacturer, and his admission to this élite body, over-dominated by merchants and under-represented by manufacturers, implied a belated recognition of the changed pattern of the local economy over many decades. Atkinson's chairmanship of the local Church extension scheme was probably also a factor. Five trustees were already on this committee, T. Blayds, R. Bramley, J. Gott, W. Hey, and R. Hall. The election of Atkinson as a trustee implied a similar commitment to Church efficiency in the search for the new Vicar. For the ensuing election the trustee strength was as follows: merchants (nine); manufacturers (two); ironmaster (one); bankers (two); barristers (two); physician (one); surgeons (two); independent (four); unspecified (two). Two-thirds of this upper-middle-class élite had been members of the old Tory Corporation until its abolition. The family connections to which 'Churchman' also objected were also well to the fore: two Halls; two Heys; two Gotts; two Becketts. There may have been other trustees related but with different surnames.[21]

At this meeting the trustees reaffirmed their determination to secure the best man possible. The yardstick in future would be personal qualities and achievements, not kinship or 'connection'. This approach signified conversion to a principle of merit unthought of when Fawcett was elected Vicar of Leeds in 1815. He was then aged fifty-five, still a curate, after thirty-two years' ministry in his birthplace. For this major parish the trustees had appointed someone who had never held even a small independent cure of souls. He was

[19.] WYASL, LPC49/1, Sequestration Papers, Circular Letter, dated 6 Feb. 1837.
[20.] *LI*, 11, 25 Feb. 1837; *LM*, 4 Feb. 1837.
[21.] *LI*, 28 Jan., 11, 25 Feb. 1837; *LM*, 4 Feb. 1837; *LPB 1834*; Mayhall, pp. 427–29; Morris, p. 165; Taylor, pp. 30–31.

Leeds-born and the local connection proved sufficient. It was a very inadequate preparation for becoming the parish priest of a town already one of the largest in England. Although Fawcett possessed an estimable character, leadership and initiative were beyond him at a time when both were required. During his vicariate the Church lacked impact and Dissent flourished.[22]

As the trustees hoped, their intentions were sufficiently novel to obtain wide press publicity. Many applications resulted. Meanwhile the trustees were sounding Samuel Wilberforce, the well regarded and successful High Church Rector of Brighstone, Isle of Wight and a former Evangelical. Wilberforce was attracted by the prospect of industrial but grimy Leeds. His Bishop was against it, saying that Wilberforce and his wife Emily would be 'choaked with coal smoke'. Ultimately Wilberforce declined consideration, but only on medical advice, as he later informed Hook. From the start of their search, therefore, the trustees did not commit themselves to appointing a further Evangelical Vicar.[23] In fact, as Hook later discovered, there existed in Leeds an 'undistributed middle' of Churchpeople uncommitted to High Church or Evangelical beliefs, who regarded enthusiasm and warmth of personality in clergy as more important than particular doctrinal emphases. Because some trustees were of like mind, a formal approach was made to Hook, through Dr Barnes, sub-dean of Christ Church, Oxford, enquiring whether he would accept the Vicarage, if offered.[24]

The trustee Robert Hall was responsible for the approach. He was a barrister, formerly of Leeds, now living in London; Henry Hall, the senior trustee, was his father.[25] Some months before Fawcett's death Hall had heard about Hook's work at Coventry from Mrs W. P. Wood, the wife of a fellow barrister who was Hook's oldest friend. Hall was greatly impressed. Following Wilberforce's refusal Hall visited Hook's parish at Coventry to see for himself. Earlier he had been to Canterbury, to assess the Revd J. E. N. Molesworth also regarded as a strong candidate. Hall decided that Hook was much more fitted to be Vicar of Leeds. After the formal approach Hall asked Wood to request Hook not to delay consenting, so that testimonials representing various shades of Church opinion could be obtained.[26] Taken by surprise, Hook consulted his wife by post. Within three days, however, he had informed Barnes that, if the Vicarage were offered, he would regard it as 'a Call of Providence', which he would readily obey; and thereafter serve the parish with all his energy of mind and body. Nevertheless, Hook was not

22. LI, 28 Jan., 11 Feb. 1837; LM, 4 Feb. 1837; Taylor, pp. 368–70.
23. B(odleian) L(ibrary) O(xford University), Wilberforce Papers, d. 38, fols 127–28, Wilberforce to Hook, 14 Aug. 1837, fols 129–30, Wilberforce to Hook, 29 Jan. 1838; A. R. Ashwell and R. G. Wilberforce, Life of the Right Reverend Samuel Wilberforce, 3 vols (1880–82), I, 101–05.
24. Stephens, Hook, I, 296–98, 403.
25. Taylor, pp. 466–71, 474–77.
26. WYASL, LPC25, Vicarage Book, initialled entry, 22 Apr. 1837; Stephens, Hook, I, 295–97.

prepared to offer himself as a candidate, since he made it a rule never to seek responsible office.[27] How would the trustees take this reply? Ever the faithful friend, W. P. Wood, with barrister's foresight, took it upon himself to inform Henry Hall that Hook could 'unquestionably be regarded as a candidate', one of thirty-five for the living.[28]

From 9 February the trustees met weekly to monitor progress, examine testimonials and give names of new candidates to the local newspapers.[29] These weekly updates kept the country's interest sharply focused on the election procedures. Transcripts of Hook's testimonials still exist. His referees, many highly placed, came from ecclesiastics and laity: the Archbishop of Canterbury; six bishops; archdeacons; Oxford professors and dons; past and present clerical colleagues; schoolmasters; politicians (Sir Robert Peel and the Rt Hon. J. W. Croker); members of the nobility and gentry. Hook was clearly well connected and highly respected. Of thirty-four testimonials, half specifically mentioned that they were proffered voluntarily and without Hook's knowledge or request. Purely from his position a testimonial from the Archbishop of Canterbury cannot fail to have impressed the trustees, even though it attested chiefly to the ability and sound doctrine of Hook's publications. For the trustees the most telling testimonial was probably from Hook's diocesan, Bishop Butler of Lichfield and Coventry. Stressing his own impartiality, Butler rated Hook as one of the most deeply learned divines then alive. As a parish priest, he added, Hook was an example to his neighbourhood and far beyond, having filled the immense church of Holy Trinity, Coventry, to overflowing and inspired its large parish to new life. Archdeacon Bayley commended Hook's straightforwardness at Coventry, which had won over all shades of opinion within the Church, and gained the respect of Dissenters outside it. Bayley also confirmed unknowingly Hall's assessment of Molesworth and Hook. Molesworth, he wrote, was the best in Kent, 'but not within a thousand 'Parasangs' of Hook. The term Bayley used was an ancient Persian measure of length. His comparison exaggerated, but made a memorable point. Hook's present clerical colleagues, twenty clergymen of Coventry and neighbourhood, testified collectively to his capacity for leadership. Juniors looked up to him; seniors thought highly of his zeal and industry, and of his powerful advocacy of the Anglican position on faith and order.[30]

---

27. HA, Notebook NB22, fol. 1, Barnes to trustees, fol. 40, Hook to Barnes; WYASL, LPC25, Vicarage Book, Barnes to trustees; Stephens, *Hook*, I, 332.
28. HA, NB22, fols 42–43, Wood to Hall; WYASL, LPC25, Vicarage Book, Wood to Hall, list of candidates showing thirty-six names; Stephens, *Hook*, I, 332.
29. *LI*, 11, 18, 25 Feb., 4, 11, 18 Mar. 1837; *LM*, 18 Feb., 4, 11 Mar. 1837.
30. HA, NB22, fols 1–36, 44–77, esp. fol. 2 (Canterbury), fols 3–4 (Butler), fols 29–31 (Bayley), fols 35–36 (20 Clergymen, 'undersigned', but no names appear on folio); WYASL, LCP25, Vicarage Book; Stephens, *Hook*, I, 303–05.

The trustees probably cast a more wary eye over testimonials from Oxford, Tractarianism's wellspring. That from Dr Barnes was unexceptionable and voluntary. He knew that Hook was unlikely to apply, but his qualifications would be difficult to better.[31] Five glowing testimonials from present or former Fellows of Corpus Christi seem almost like a concerted effort, it is possible they are originated by the Revd T. H. Tragett, a former Fellow and lately incumbent of Christ Church, Coventry.[32] Two or three prominent Tractarians also wrote to the trustees. Keble's commendation of Hook as 'quite fearless and uncompromising in the avowal of his sentiments' might not have struck quite the favourable note intended.[33] Pusey's testimonial covered much ground. Disclaiming 'Panegyric', he cited — often with examples — Hook's energy, application to duty, perseverance, learning and devotion, along with warmth and tenderness towards people. Like Keble, but in different words, he mentioned Hook's firm principles 'tempered with charity'.[34] Whatever the reservations the trustees may have had about the doctrinal stance of those writing from Oxford, the remarks about Hook accorded so well with those of others that they were unlikely to be discounted.

Socially eminent laypeople also wrote favourably of Hook. Taken as a whole, the testimonials of clergy and laity contained a collection of superlatives, from which Hook emerged as a warm and attractive personality, energetic and zealous, a sound theologian, eloquent in the pulpit, firm in his principles, and possessing the ability and confidence to be the parish priest of one of the largest towns in England. Tenacious Evangelicals among the trustees, however, would ponder the implications of Hook's 'Church principles', which differed from their beliefs on such important matters as: the nature of a saving faith; baptismal regeneration; the authority of the Church as against the Bible. Hook's High Churchmanship, combined with his energy and talents, did not augur well for Evangelicalism in Leeds, if he were to be elected as Vicar.

Closing Stages of the Election for the Vicar of Leeds, March 1837

The election for the Vicarage was fixed for 20 March 1837.[35] Robert Hall's advocacy, corroborated by so many testimonials, had inclined many trustees to give Hook their vote, provided they could meet this nonpareil for

---

31. HA, NB22, fol. 1; WYASL, LPC25, Vicarage Book, testimonial 'No. 1', the only testimonial numbered.
32. HA, NB22, fols 17–18 (V. Thomas), fols 46–47 (J. Norris), fols 20–22 (E. Greswell), fols 28–29 (G. L. Cooke, Professor), fols 46–47 (T. H. Tragett); WYASL, LCP25, Vicarage Book; Stephens, *Hook*, I, 291–93, 332.
33. HA, NB22, fols 12–13; WYASL, LCP25, Vicarage Book.
34. HA, NB22, fols 13–16; WYASL, LPC25, Vicarage Book.
35. *LI*, 18 Feb. 1837; *LM*, 18 Feb. 1837.

themselves, whom as yet they knew only by report. Hook, however, proved unwilling to visit Leeds before the election, since he did not wish to give even the appearance of canvassing for himself. Additionally, he abhorred the custom of 'trial sermons'.[36] Henry Hall informed Hook that no wish now existed for a trial sermon, increasingly deemed an impropriety, but the trustees felt it necessary to see him, as some were determined not to vote for anyone they had never seen. Wood cut the Gordian knot. Unknown to Hook he suggested that some of the trustees should put this point of view in person, by visiting Coventry unannounced. Consequently on Saturday, 11 March six trustees arrived in the town: Robert Hall, Christopher Beckett, J. Gott, G. Banks, J. M. Tennant and J. R. Atkinson. That evening four called on Hook to explain their purpose. The following morning they all attended Hook's church to ascertain whether the testimonials accorded with the reality. Hook was engaged on a course of sermons on St Matthew's Gospel. His text that day led him to explain — in terms readily understood by the congregation — that in matters of faith Anglicans looked for guidance on doubtful points neither to the Pope nor the Protestant Reformers, but to the customs of the first churches. Hook's explanation threw light on High Church principles particularly subject to misrepresentation. Afterwards J. R. Atkinson, a well-informed Evangelical, asked Hook whether he believed in transubstantiation — a test question to see if Hook conscientiously rejected this explanation of the change in the eucharistic elements at consecration, formally defined by the fourth Lateran Council in 1215, subsequently repudiated by both Protestant and Anglican Reformers, but retained unaltered by Rome. Hook's decided negative impressed Atkinson by its lack of prevarication.[37] The trustees' visit resolved the impasse. Most felt able to report favourably to their colleagues. Hook himself met nineteen trustees in Leeds on 15 March, informing them he was not there to canvass, but to deny certain charges, if made. He also met most local clergy. They revealed that, if they were to be passed over, they preferred it to be by 'a man of eminence', which Hook gathered to mean himself.[38]

After Hook's candidacy was announced on 4 March, opposition was slow to manifest itself. Surprisingly, the next issue of the *Leeds Mercury* failed to comment. The trustees' visit to Coventry, however, galvanized Evangelicals. They organized a select protest meeting, by invitation, for 15 March. Those attending declared that Hook's appointment would be 'public calamity'; it would divide the Church, and irritate Dissenters. The meeting decided on a memorial to the trustees, and appointed thirty-seven gentlemen of standing to obtain signatures. Robert Perring, editor of the Anglican *Leeds Intelligencer*, being particularly conspicuous. The memorial objected to Hook's denial that

---

[36.] HA, NB22, fols 40–41, Hook to Hall; WYASL, LPC25, Vicarage Book.
[37.] Stephens, *Hook*, I, 299–302.
[38.] *LI*, 18 Mar. 1837; Stephens, *Hook*, I, 312–13.

Holy Scripture of itself was sufficient guide to salvation. It deprecated his unbending attitude not only to Dissenters, but also to the undenominational Bible Society and the Anglican Evangelical societies. For information the memorialists appended a copy of Hook's remonstrance to his then diocesan, Bishop Ryder, for presiding in 1830 at the Bible Society's meeting in Coventry. This memorial attracted about three hundred and seventy signatures. On presenting it to the trustees on 18 March, the memorialists' deputation of three were quite discomfited when asked to name a suitable person, in their eyes, for whom a vote might be given.[39]

On 18 March the *Leeds Mercury*, citing and selectively summarizing an article from the Anglican Evangelical *Record*, belatedly declared that Hook would be a disastrous choice. Accusing him of the 'modified Popery' of the *Tracts for the Times*, it also likened him to 'a Jesuit in disguise' for working mischief to the Establishment.[40] Its protests came too late. The memorialists' deprecatory terms rallied Hook's supporters. 'A Parishioner' published on 17 March a defence of the trustees' actions. For the memorialists it was uncomfortably candid. They were characterized as a 'monopolising minority' of bigotry, intolerance and pride, impudently attempting to bully the trustees. 'Parishioner' alleged that some persons supporting the memorial had been duped into signing — the prime 'Cat's Paw' was allegedly Robert Perring, because of his editorship of the *Leeds Intelligencer*.[41] On 18 March a counter-memorial, expressing confidence in the trustees' Anglican loyalty and judgement, was also presented to the trustees. It censured the other memorialists' attempt to coerce the trustees' choice. By implication this form of wording supported Hook. With three hundred signatures the counter-memorial was sufficiently weighty to encourage the trustees to give him consideration.[42]

The Election of Hook and Reactions to it

On 20 March the election was held in the Parish Church vestry, with sixteen of the twenty-three trustees present voting for Hook. An indication that feelings had run high was that voting for the first time was by secret ballot. If the first ballot produced a candidate with a majority, the total of his votes alone would be declared. Those voting for Hook seem to have disclosed the fact. The trustee Griffith Wright's list showing sixteen names for the candidate has the mark of authenticity: H. Hall; C. Beckett; J. Hill; G. Banks; M. Hind;

39. WYASL, LPC25, Vicarage Book, printed list of *c.* 370 names, with initialled comment by the trustee Griffith Wright; Stephens, *Hook*, I, 184–87, 314–16.
40. *LM*, 18 Mar. 1837; Stephens, *Hook*, I, 307.
41. WYASL, LPC25, Vicarage Book, printed sheet, 'To the Parishioners'.
42. *LI*, 25 Mar. 1837; Stephens, *Hook*, I, 316.

T. Beckett; R. Markland; J. Gott; R. W. D. Thorp; R. Hall; J. M. Tennant; R. Bramley; G. Wright; J. W. Rhodes; W. Gott; J. G. Uppleby. The following were present and did not vote for Hook: W. Hey; T. Blayds; J. Wilks; C. Smith; W. Hey, Jr; G. Bischoff; J. R. Atkinson. Absent: P. Rhodes; J. Hardy. Informing two hundred writing parishioners of the result, Henry Hall told them of the exhaustive enquiries made, and hoped they would receive the new Vicar in a good spirit.[43]

Though a memorialist against Hook, Robert Perring decided it was now time to close Anglican ranks. In the *Leeds Intelligencer* he reprinted both the *Coventry Standard*'s pre-election view that Hook was eminently qualified, and also a very complimentary post-election assessment of him from the *York Chronicle*. Perring refrained, however, from penning a leading article himself. The anti-Hook memorialists' committee similarly discontinued adverse activities, to give the new Vicar the opportunities which his talents and high character justified.[44] The *Leeds Mercury* saw the election result in political terms — an expression of party spirit by the old Corporation's High Church Anglican Tories. It reprinted the *Record*'s famous comments lamenting the result and requesting prayers that such an unpropitious result should ultimately work to the spiritual benefit of Leeds. The *Mercury*'s disclaimers of attempting to prejudice parishioners or impugn the trustees' integrity sounded a very hollow note.[45]

The Significance of Interregnum Roles for Churchwardens and Trustees

The actions of the churchwardens during the interregnum demonstrated how the forces of religion and politics then operated simultaneously within the same process. These years of reform brought opportunity to Dissenters, uncertainty to the Church, and changed attitudes for both. Leeds churchwardens were elected to keep down St Peter's running expenses and prevent Church rates being imposed. Dissenters' ability to do this indicated their rising political power locally and nationally. Leeds churchwardens' actions as sequestrators, however, showed that they fully accepted their sequestration duties, for which they were directly accountable to the Bishop. Financial matters were conducted with probity, and the cure of souls unobtrusively but efficiently maintained. Probably having exercised similar functions for chapels they readily perceived the necessity at St Peter's. Churchpeople and Dissenters (except the militant) often liked and respected each other, and worked

---

[43] WYASL, LPC25, Vicarage Book, Griffith Wright's list; *LI*, 25 Mar. 1837; *LM*, 25 Mar. 1837; Stephens, *Hook*, I, 316–17, 332; cf. Mayhall, p. 444.

[44] *LI*, 25 Mar. 1837; *Coventry Standard*, 18 Mar. 1837, cited in *LI*, 25 Mar. 1837; *York Chronicle*, 22 Mar. 1837, cited in *LI*, 25 Mar. 1837.

[45] *LM*, 25 Mar. 1837; *Record*, cited in *LM*, 1 Apr. 1837; Stephens, *Hook*, I, 326.s

together in undenominational and charitable societies, and when crises struck the local community. Perhaps the highest praise for the Leeds churchwardens as sequestrators is that their performance in this role attracted no adverse comment.

In assessing the role of the trustees similar political and religious forces applied. Political reform had not lessened the Established Church's ecclesiatical standing, but Churchmen nevertheless perceived that changes were needed to enable it to fulfil its spiritual responsibilities to the nation. Among the clergy signs of reviving zeal were apparent by the 1830s, as the ministries of Hook (Coventry), Stowell (Manchester), McNeile (Liverpool), and others testified. In 1837 circumstances required local laity — the trustees of the Vicarage — to occupy a pivotal role in the Anglican revival at Leeds. It was clear from the outset that they recognized the need for a change of approach when selecting the new Vicar. Local mediocrities were not to be considered; merit would be the sole criterion. Knowingly or unknowingly they invoked Benthamite ultilitarianism — the greatest good of the greatest number. The presentation would be to the man considered best for Church and parishioners. By selecting Hook the trustees provided the finest 'gift' in their power to Church and town.

CHAPTER 4

Walter Farquhar Hook (1798–1875)

Professional Development and Career to 1837

Walter Farquhar Hook was born in London on 13 March 1798, the son of the Revd James Hook (1771–1828) and his wife Anne, the daughter of Sir Walter Farquhar, Bt, the Prince of Wales's physician and friend. After various private schools, Walter attended Winchester from 1812 to 1817. His academic progress was unremarkable. By 1816, however, he possessed the quality of voice which could captivate and enchant others, gaining him a silver medal at Speech Day. When Hook repeated this success the following year, his father described him as displaying 'the Nerve, the Dignity and the impressive Tone of that great Master', William Pitt. This full, melodious voice was to prove a great asset in Hook's chosen career. Through Farquhar's royal connection Hook was accepted at Christ Church, Oxford in 1818, graduating in 1821. Though not attempting honours, he did better than he expected, especially in divinity. Given a free choice of profession after graduating, Hook decided to take holy orders. This decision fulfilled his mother's hopes and early training. 'By her I was dedicated from the womb to God's service', he told E. B. Pusey later.[1]

Hook's decision solved a problem for his father. As pluralist Rector of Whippingham, in rural Isle of Wight, he needed a resident curate. By appointing Hook he provided his son with a 'title', or place of duty, the canonical prerequisite to ordination. This gave Hook's career a flying start. Titles at this time were difficult to obtain, as Alan Haig reminds us, citing Samuel Wilberforce's dismaying experience. Examined and presented by his father, Hook was privately ordained deacon on 30 September 1821, by the Bishop of Hereford, Warden of Winchester, in the College chapel. At Whippingham where Hook was effectively the curate-in-charge, habits of ministry were formed for a lifetime. In such a small parish he was in constant touch with its inhabitants, delighting in their company, and becoming for many an intimate friend. The poor were Hook's special concern. Every Sunday, after services at Whippingham, he walked two miles to East Cowes, to conduct evening service for the impoverished seafaring population, and to catechize their children in a sail loft he had borrowed.[2]

[1.] HA, J8, G. Nott to J. Hook, 3 May 1816; J9, J. Hook to Sir W. Farquhar, 16 July 1817; PH, fols 135–38, Hook to Pusey, 10 Oct. 1840; Stephens, *Hook*, I, 1, 4–39, 49.
[2.] A. Haig, *The Victorian Clergy* (1984), p. 86; Stephens, *Hook*, I, 50, 58–62.

At Whippingham Hook also equipped himself by intensive private study. The theological knowledge he acquired later impressed his congregations. Initially he asked his father's friend, Prebendary G. F. Nott, of Winchester, for a reading list, probably some time before being priested at Christmas 1822. A later course of reading is better known, comprising Church history, doctrine and apologetics, with emphasis on patristics and Reformation studies. According to E. B. Pusey, no mean judge, Hook's range of reading was 'deeper than is ordinary'. When completed it enabled Hook to preach and teach with clarity and assurance to people of all ages and attainments. The depth and rigour of Hook's course was possibly exceptional, but such self-devised reading programmes were not unusual, as clergy in the 1820s received little theological education.[3]

Whippingham's parishioners regretfully witnessed Hook's departure in 1826. His father exchanged the living when he was appointed Dean of Worcester. As pluralist Vicar of Bromsgrove and King's Norton, Dean Hook then appointed his son to the stipendiary curacy of Moseley, near Birmingham, at £150 yearly. Moseley represented a step nearer a fully independent cure. Hook made the most of this opportunity, and became known further afield. His principal pastoral concerns were again for the poor. To enable their funerals to take place in church, he discontinued the half-guinea fee previously required. For the children of the needy Hook established a National School. Initially he tramped Birmingham to purchase a site, eventually persuading his local squire, James Taylor of Moseley Hall, to lease ground for a guinea annually. He then cajoled funds from the local laity to run the school. Even though engrossed in parish work, Hook kept up his studies. In 1827 he was reading Athanasius and Bishop Horsley, the better to explain the doctrines of the Holy Spirit and the Holy Trinity to Unitarians beginning to attend Moseley church.[4]

Hook's growing reputation at Moseley led Dr Gardener, Rector of St Philip's, Birmingham, to offer him a lectureship there. As at Moseley, this carried tenure. The remuneration of £250 yearly enabled Hook to maintain a curate at Moseley, and to divide his own time between both places. St Philip's gave Hook an influential pulpit and endeared him to a large congregation. At Birmingham Hook involved himself in the education of the poor, by superintending pupils' progress at the Blue Coat and National Schools. Industrial Birmingham determined the direction of Hook's future career. It enlarged the scale of his pastoral experience, introducing him to the

3. HA, NB22, fols 9–10 (G. Nott), fols 13–16 (Pusey); WYASL, LPC25, Vicarage Book, Nott, Pusey; Stephens, *Hook*, I, 62–66; Stranks, pp. 24, 118–19.
4. HA, NB22, fols 6–7 (J. Taylor), fols 27–28 (Sir G. Seymour), fols 29–30 (Archdeacon H. V. Bayley); WYASL LPC25, Vicarage Book, Taylor, Seymour, Bayley; C. Gill, *A History of Birmingham, I: Manor and Borough to 1865* (1952), p. 374; Haig, p. 218, 337, notes 88, 98; Stephens, *Hook*, I, 118–19, 121; P. Virgin, *The Church in an Age of Negligence: Ecclesiastical Structure and Problems of Church Reform 1700–1840* (Cambridge, 1989), pp. 35–36.

special requirements of ministry in a large manufacturing town, where the grime and squalor were of a different order from Whippingham or even Moseley. In February 1828, however, Hook's circumstances changed. His father died, leaving Hook's mother and sister in poor circumstances. It became imperative for Hook to seek a better living. One Birmingham resident suggested a public subscription to augment Hook's stipend to enable him to stay at St Philip's. Forbidding his mother to approach any patrons, Hook wrote to his father's old friend, Lord Chancellor Lyndhurst, from whom he received the Crown living of Holy Trinity, Coventry. Hook's mother attributed the professional esteem coming his way to his father's careful direction, but Hook's remarkable talents probably counted even more.[5]

From 1828 as Vicar of Holy Trinity, Coventry, Hook enjoyed the freedom of action accorded to Anglican parish priests. His new cure became the proving ground for his ideas of working an industrial parish. The proper performance of the liturgy was Hook's personal priority, but his preaching and personality so filled the church that in the summer of 1830 a Sunday evening service was instituted to supplement the morning and afternoon services. As it attracted nearly two thousand people, gas lighting was installed, so that it could become a permanent feature. Hook's ability to attract and hold congregations was impressive. The Rector of the neighbouring parish of St John's and many of his congregation delighted to attend Hook's services on Sunday afternoons. In November 1830 Hook preached his first sermon before the King and Queen at the Chapel Royal, following his appointment as one of the King's Chaplains.[6] Whilst at Coventry Hook also became notable as one of Oxford University's Select Preachers. By March 1836 he was so admired by the undergraduates that he was cheered on leaving the Sheldonian Theatre. Keble amongst others testified to Hook's power to draw crowded congregations to the University Church.[7]

At Coventry Hook identified ways to promote the intellectual and social well-being of working-class people. He opened an infant school in 1831. Under his guidance the Sunday schools flourished, increasing in numbers from one hundred and twenty in 1829 to twelve hundred in 1837. Many

5. HA, K6/18, MS note by Mrs Anne Hook, n.d.; NB22, fols 2–3 (Bp of Rochester), fols 6–7 (J. Taylor); WYASL, LPC25, Vicarage Book, Bp of Rochester, Taylor; B. Heeney, *A Different Kind of Gentleman: Parish Clergy as Professional Men in Early and Mid-Victorian England* (Hamden, Conn., 1976), p. 112; Stephens, *Hook*, I, 120–27, 217.

6. HA, NB22, fols 3–4 (Bp of Lichfield and Coventry), fols 13–16 (Pusey), fols 32–34 T. Sheepshanks to J. Gott; WYASL, LPC25, Vicarage Book, Bp of Lichfield, Pusey, Sheepshanks to Gott; Stephens, *Hook*, I, 144, 168–70, 210–11.

7. HA, K6/14, Hook to Mother, 23 Mar. 1836; NB22, fol. 3 (Bp of Lincoln), fols 11–12 (W. Palmer), fols 12–13 (J. Keble), fols 19–20 (J. Norris), fols 20–22 (E. Greswell), fols 28–29 (G. L. Cooke, Prof.), fols 32–34 T. Sheepshanks to J. Gott; WYASL, LPC25, Vicarage Book, Bp of Lincoln, Palmer, Keble, Norris, Greswell, Cooke, Sheepshanks to Gott.

scholars became teachers. A Sunday School Teachers' Society was formed, which virtually ran the schools under Hook's light but firm clerical rein. In 1835 the teachers initiated 'a sort of Mechanics' Institute on a religious principle', entitled the Religious and Useful Knowledge Society. Its lectures, classes, library and reading-room soon presented stiff competition to the existing Mechanics' Institute. Hook was also largely instrumental in establishing a 'penny-weekly' dispensary for medical care. Leadership accompanied by delegation became Hook's pastoral method.[8]

From his earliest days as a curate Hook developed steadily, displaying self-motivation and self-reliance. His warm personality, leadership and pastoral zeal appealed to successive parishioners. As twenty Coventry and district clergymen testified, these qualities also impressed his clerical colleagues. Capable Evangelical incumbents elsewhere earned similar regard. The likelihood is that personality and pastoral zeal were the qualities, as much as particular Churchmanship, which attracted congregations. Nevertheless, Church principles were integral to Hook's own religious development.[9]

Religious Development to 1837

Hook's earliest impressions of religion came in childhood through his mother's careful training in moral virtue and scriptural knowledge. As schoolboys at Winchester, Hook and his friend W. P. Wood 'worked out [their] Church principles together', coming to an ardent belief in the Catholicity and Apostolic ministry of the Church of England and its sister Churches. Hook's mother recorded, when he was beginning to be noticed as a parish clergyman, that Walter as a Churchman was walking in his father's path. Perhaps in this he resembled Keble, who avowed that his beliefs were those of his father. Doctrinal consistency proved to be the outstanding characteristics of Hook's life. For him and like-minded others the Oxford Movement widened support for previously held convictions of Anglican Catholicity. In his consistency Hook differed from his sometime friends, Newman and Manning, who entertained Evangelical convictions before arriving at Tractarianism, and later went over to Rome. In 1847, after secessions at St Saviour's, the Tractarians' church in Leeds, Hook warmed to

---

8. HA, NB22, fols 13–16 (E. B. Pusey), fols 32–34 T. Sheepshanks to J. Gott; WYASL, LPC25, Vicarage Book, Pusey, Sheepshanks to Gott; *LI*, 13 May 1837; Stephens, *Hook*, 1, 176–83, 281–82.
9. HA, NB22, fols 35–36 (20 Clergymen of Coventry and Vicinity); WYASL, LPC25, Vicarage Book, 20 Clergymen.

the Evangelicals' common Anglicanism, but his core conviction of Anglican Catholicity remained.[10]

Church principles, in Hook's understanding, were based on acceptance of the claim of full Catholicity for the English Church, as maintained after the Elizabethan settlement by Bishop Jewel (1559), Richard Hooker (1593, 1597), and others subsequently. Thomas Sikes (1767–1834), Vicar of Guilsborough, wrote that neglect of teaching on the article in the Creed affirming belief in the Holy Catholic Church had led to an unbalanced faith, for which catechetical teaching was necessary to restore the balance. Such teaching, F. W. Cornish asserted, implied instruction in the whole theory of apostolic succession, divinely appointed pastors, authoritative guidance on Scripture and morals, and an obedient laity.[11]

For nineteenth-century Anglicanism Sikes's propositions were far-reaching. He was part of a High Church circle of clergy and wealthy laity, whose focus was William Stevens, a Southwark hosier. Like the Evangelical Clapham Sect they were people with the funds and status to give effect to their beliefs, perhaps especially Samuel Horsley (1733–1806), the leading bishop of his generation. By 1796 the circle included vigorous younger men: William Van Mildert (later Bishop of Durham); Joshua Watson, wine merchant; his brother John James Watson, Rector of Hackney; Henry Handley Norris, the latter's brother-in-law, incumbent of South Hackney. Sikes and the Watsons were connected by marriage; other relationships of friendship or marriage also existed. By apt analogy this High Church counterpart of the Clapham Sect became best known as the Hackney Phalanx, a close-knit band supporting the high doctrine of the Church. To advance their principles Stevens and William Jones, a curate of Nayland launched the monthly journal the *British Critic* dedicated to High Church principles in 1787. Eventually changes in ownership altered its doctrinal complexion. To restore its original function, Joshua Watson and Norris bought the *British Critic* back around 1811, Watson having become the Phalanx's mentor in 1807 after Stevens's death. If challenged on their beliefs by Evangelicals on issues such as the role of the Church as against Scripture in the scheme of salvation, the Phalanx would put the High Church view, but controversy was not their priority. More pressing concerns were: extending the Church through 'sound doctrine'; educating poor children; more churches for poor people. To promote these purposes Phalanx members were to the fore in

---

10. BL, Gladstone Papers, MS 44,213, fols 119–21, Hook to Gladstone, 25 June 1851; BLO, MS Eng. Lett., d. 368, fols 35–36, Hook to J. W. Croker, 3 Apr. 1839; HA, K6/18, MS note, Mrs Anne Hook; PH, fols 135–38, Hook to Pusey, 10 Oct. 1840; Chadwick, I, 211, 300; Cornish, I, 214–15, 293, 334; Hylson-Smith, p. 119; Stephens, *Hook*, I, 5.
11. Cornish, I, 66; Moorman, pp. 215–16, 224–25, 230, 233–37, 309–10; Stephens, *Hook*, I, 141–42.

reviving the Society for Promoting Christian Knowledge (SPCK), and in founding the National Society and the Church Building Society.[12]

This patient, almost Fabian, advocacy of high doctrine in time prepared the ground, both in universities and parishes, for High Church Catholicity. Without High Churchmanship of this type the Oxford Movement from 1833 onwards would have received a less ready acceptance. It seems clear that the Church principles which Hook and Wood adopted in their schooldays were those of the Hackney Phalanx, which they held ever after. It was to a Phalanx sympathizer Charles Lloyd (later Bishop of Oxford) that Hook went for divinity lectures whilst a deacon. From 1823, through his father, Hook became on friendly terms with H. H. Norris, a central figure in the Phalanx. Thereafter Norris was for Hook a mentor, confidential friend and sounding-board.[13] When a deacon Hook delivered a remarkable Visitation sermon in 1822. Like the great Bishop Horsley (1790) he maintained that the Church of England in its essential being possessed Catholicity and apostolic ministry, irrespective of establishment. From this cornerstone of High Anglican doctrine Hook never swerved.[14]

Strictly interpreted, Anglican Church principles unchurched all Protestant Dissenters and classed Roman Catholics in England as heretical schismatics. Hook adhered to this strict interpretation. Hence at Whippingham he christened two boys already baptized by the Baptists, whose rite he considered invalid. He also politely declined to act with the undenominational Religious Tract Society. At Moseley, Hook personally subsidized SPCK publications to undersell those of the undenominational British and Foreign Bible Society (BFBS). When at Coventry, Hook roused the wrath of Dissenters for insisting on an Anglican master for his new infant school in 1831. A year earlier Hook's remonstrance to his diocesan, for co-operating with Dissenters in Coventry against Hook's wishes as parish priest, had rapidly become notorious. It was remembered against him by Leeds Evangelicals in their memorial opposing his election in 1837. Bishop Ryder, however, was a fair-minded man, who made no secret of his regard for Hook as an outstanding parish priest. Hook's approachability, wide human sympathies, sense of humor, and capacity for hard work made him more friends and followers than enemies. The man who in 1837 faced the challenge of leading a minority Church in the Dissenting

12. Cornish, I, 70–73, 102; Port, pp. 2–5; E. A. Varley, *The Last of the Prince Bishops: William Van Mildert and the High Church Movement of the Early Nineteenth Century* (Cambridge, 1992), pp. 7–10, 30–31, 48, 63–88.
13. BLO, MS Eng. Lett., *c.* 789, fols 194–95, 11 Sept. 1829, *c.* 790, fols 57–58, 10 Nov. 1832, *c.* 790, fols 63–64, 8 Apr. 1835, *c.* 790, fols 107–10, 11 Mar. 1843, *c.* 790, fols 112–15, 17 Mar. 1843 (all Hook to Norris); Cornish, I, 70, 72, 75; Stephens, *Hook*, I, 52, 69, 101–02; Varley, pp. 56–57.
14. W. F. Hook, 'The Peculiar Character of the Church of England', in *The Church and its Ordinances*, ed. by W. Hook, (1876), I, 1–13; Stephens, *Hook*, I, 67–69; Varley, pp. 29, 210, note 52.

stronghold of Leeds was alert, confident and energetic, well equipped by learning and personality for the task.[15]

Arrival at Leeds and Inaugural Sermon, April 1837

On 4 April Bishop Longley instituted Hook into the spiritualities of the benefice. A brief induction ceremony by the Revd Robert Taylor subsequently conveyed, on the Bishop's behalf, its temporalities—churches, churchyard, house, and emoluments.[16] Hook's first public test at Leeds was his inaugural service on 16 April. It would introduce Hook to his new community, where Dissent since 1800 had become predominant. A similar situation had obtained at Coventry, which soon came to value Hook's endeavours exceedingly. This ability to earn the good opinion of others without surrender of principles was known to Dr Longley, who nevertheless told Hook that in Leeds the attitude of Dissent posed a far more difficult task. Bishop Blomfield of London felt that Hook would be more than ever in need of Heaven's guidance and support, because of 'an active & not very placable party' probably waiting to oppose him. For Hook, Leeds was a place where, as he told his wife, 'there is no Church feeling, no Catholic feeling . . . People there do not know what the Catholic Church is, and if I may be honoured as an instrument to introduce Catholicism there, . . . I should feel that I have not lived entirely in vain'.[17]

Hook's inaugural sermon was eagerly awaited. The *Leeds Intelligencer* declared that even standing-room would be worth having. St Peter's began to fill at 9 a.m., all seats being occupied within forty-five minutes, and standing places by service time. On this occasion the Independent Mayor, Dr Williamson, took his place in the Corporation pew, though conscientiously refusing civic attendance previously. In Hook's conduct of the service the *Leeds Mercury* perceived a solemnity and energy which powerfully enhanced 'the simple beauty of the prayers and liturgy' — a Dissenting testimony of singular value.[18]

The text of Hook's sermon signalled his aspirations as Vicar of Leeds: 'To declare unto you all the counsel of God'. Carefully structured, the sermon demonstrated the central place of Church principles in Hook's preaching,

[15] HA, NB22, fols 44–45 T. Sheepshanks to R. Hall; WYASL, LPC25, Vicarage Book, Sheepshanks to Hall; J. H. Markland to R. Markland, 10 Mar. 1837; Cornish, I, 73–74; Stephens, *Hook*, I, 108–12, 117, 177–78, 184–87, 208, 214–25, 314–16.

[16] WYASL, LPC25, Vicarage Book, MS entry 15 Apr. 1837; *LI*, 8, 22 Apr. 1837; Stephens, *Hook*, I, 319.

[17] HA, LI/8, Blomfield to Hook, 29 Mar. 1837, NB22, fols 3–4 (Bp of Lichfield), fols 5–6 (Blomfield to R. Hall); WYASL, LPC25, Vicarage Book, Bp of Lichfield, Blomfield to R. Hall; Stephens, *Hook*, I, 298, 332, II, 1.

[18] *LI*, 8, 15, 22 Apr. 1837; *LM*, 22 Apr. 1839; Mayhall, p. 440.

pastoral care, relations with fellow Anglicans and other Christians. He introduced himself as fallible and sinful, like his parishioners, but nevertheless anxious to do his duty. As chief minister he would engage in every public activity for promoting the temporal, intellectual, moral and religious welfare of Leeds inhabitants. He was willing to visit the sick, dying or bereaved, rich or poor — but especially the poor — to assist in their distress, according to his means. Hook's authority for his ministry, he told the congregation, came from Christ himself, transmitted in unbroken succession to bishops, priests, and deacons. The doctrine of apostolic succession could not have been more clearly stated. Believing that the Church of England was not infallible, but not in error as then existing, Hook placed its apostolate within the Catholic Church of Christ, and equally firmly, without using the term, in the context of the Reformation. He would teach in conformity with the doctrine of the Old and New Testament as understood by the Catholic Fathers and ancient bishops, and would always act in 'the spirit' of the English Reformation. It was through the teaching of the early Church, he explained, that such matters of contention as the Trinity, the Christian Sabbath as Sunday, and infant baptism had been settled. When the text of Scripture was obscure, the Fathers were 'lighthouses for guidance' for the English Church, with a prayerful study of the Scriptures being the best guide throughout life.[19]

In his discourse Hook explained what he intended by his sermon text. His teaching would cover the entire span of Christian doctrine: Creation and the Fall; the Incarnation, Atonement, and Resurrection of Christ; the work of the Holy Spirit; and the four last things, Death, Judgement, Heaven, and Hell. Citing each in turn, Hook revealed his mastery by conveying the essence in a few well-chosen, easily grasped words. Good works, he reminded the congregation, were a necessary corollary of Christian life, but always to be based solely on faith. Renewal of individual nature should be sought through the Holy Spirit, prayer and Bible reading, hearing the Scriptures expounded; and above all by grace, given at baptism, and continually 'stirred up', to make one's calling and election sure. Hook also urged frequent attendance at Holy Communion as the other due and proper use of the sacraments.[20]

Hook's doctrinal scheme indicated that he would not be restricting his preaching to the Fall, the Atonement, Justification, Sanctification. These doctrines were sometimes regarded as too intensively covered by Evangelicals, to the exclusion of others which were by no means peripheral. When discussing the Scriptures, Hook signified his preference for the editions of the SPCK, because it was under proper episcopal superintendence, like its sister Society for the Propagation of the Gospel (SPG). In practical terms for Churchpeople the reason given meant that Hook would not countenance

[19] Acts 20.27; *LI*, 22 Apr. 1837; *LM*, 22 Apr. 1837.
[20] *LI*, 22 Apr. 1837; *LM*, 22 Apr. 1837.

Evangelical organisations like the Church Missionary Society (CMS), which had no equivalent role for bishops. For Leeds Dissenters Hook was indicating that he would not be co-operating in undenominational institutions like the Bible Society. He did, however, make plain his readiness to engage with Dissenters in personal friendships or civic or charitable affairs, but not in specifically religious undertakings. Hook felt sure that Dissenters would not take offence at any implied religious error on their part, since their position implied the same about the Church. Though softly worded these remarks validated the indications elsewhere in the sermon that it was an undisguisedly partisan High Church manifesto, pointing to imminent changes in the parish of Leeds. For Church life in Leeds this sermon proved the key to Hook's ministry in the town.[21]

With a revealing humility Hook regarded his inaugural sermon as a total failure. Henry Hall as senior trustee nevertheless persuaded him to have it printed. The *Leeds Mercury* considered Hook's remarks to Dissenters as candid and liberal. It refrained from comment about doctrine, but confessed itself puzzled by Hook's refusal to cooperate with Dissenters in religious matters. Robert Perring, prominent in the memorial against Hook, decided as editor of the *Leeds Intelligencer* that the new Vicar had already made a strong and favourable impression on his parishioners. On 22 April the trustee Griffith Wright, who had voted for Hook, recorded that Robert Hall had secured 'such a Vicar as the Parish of Leeds has, too long felt the want of!'. After his inaugural service Hook attracted even larger congregations.[22]

The Scene of Hook's Labours

Hook's ministry from 1837 took place in an environment unlike anything that traditional Anglicanism had envisaged a generation or so earlier. Early Victorian Leeds was 'one of a new type of urban place created by the Industrial Revolution, the 100,000 provincial city'. In 1831 half the in-township houses were less than twenty years old, their raw red brick already blackening with smoke even more harmful to lungs. Factories and warehouses were scattered haphazardly among rows of mean, insanitary, back-to-back houses. Mains sewerage was largely absent. Black furnace ashes paved the funereal streets; grit blew in summer; quagmires formed in winter. The Council ignored these nuisances until 1845, when it was forced to

---

21. *LI*, 22 Apr. 1837; *LM*, 22 Apr. 1837; Stephens, *Hook*, i, 321–22.
22. WYASL, LCP25, Vicarage Book, Anti-Hook memorial, list of names printed by Perring, Leeds; printed sheet, 'To the Parishioners'; copy of *An Inaugural Discourse preached in the Parish Church of Leeds, on the 16th Day of April, 1837, Being the third Sunday after Easter, by the Rev. Walter, Farquhar Hook, MA, Vicar* (1837); initialled comment by the trustee Griffith Wright, dated 22 Apr. 1837; *LI*, 18 Mar., 22, 29 Apr. 1837; *LM*, 22 Apr. 1837; Stephens, *Hook*, i, 334–35.

acknowledge that Leeds was one of the dirtiest towns in the kingdom, far worse than Manchester.[23] Nevertheless, nuisances still abounded. In 1847 animal slaughter in open shambles near the principal streets attracted outraged comment. Environmental drawbacks notwithstanding, the flow of migrants seeking employment never ceased in these mid-century decades.[24]

Hook's residence in the west of Leeds township was more fortunately placed. Here and in localities to the north-east and north-west were the better quality houses of the more prosperous. The Vicarage in Park Place, where the Hook family were delightedly settling in July 1837, was situated in the still pleasant West End, which had been gradually developed since 1767. Of this house Hook said that he could not wish for a better. It was large, airy and comfortable, with a long garden across the street giving a view of riverside meadows. This domestic refuge was ten minutes' walk from the Parish Church on Kirkgate. Immediately west of the Parish Church, it was a street which had seen better days. Formerly containing merchants' houses, it was now the thoroughfare for adjoining insanitary yards and closes, such as the overcrowded Boot and Shoe Yard, notorious for pestilence. At the town's East End, beyond the Parish Church, a more extensive warren of dingy, unsubstantial housing existed. In the area known as the Bank, terraces of cottages, built as a speculation for letting, had then been auctioned in blocks. Similar high densities existed in nearby Quarry Hill, where an acre of ground could be made to hold eighty dwellings, by means of back courtyards and limited access ways. From 1832, when cholera appeared, criticism of such conditions began to mount, but more because of the noxious effects of smoke and the dangerous impurities of water supplied from a polluted river. This fearful result of uncontrolled and haphazard development was graphically described in the *Artisan* during Hook's incumbency, and cited and endorsed from experience by Engels. It was also the scene of Hook's labours — his personal ministry to the poor, the sick, the dying, and the bereaved. Here was the place where Hook in his own eyes fulfilled the prime responsibility of his pastoral calling.[25]

---

23. *LI*, 22 Sept. 1838, 10 Dec. 1842, 29 July 1843, 11 Jan., 16 Aug. 1845, 25 Apr. 1846; 'Report 1839', pp. 397–424; Beresford, 'The Face of Leeds', pp. 72–74; Morris, p. 37.

24. *LI*, 4 Dec. 1847; Morgan, pp. 48–49.

25. *LI*, 13 June 1840, 27 Mar. 1841; Beresford, *East End, West End*, pp. 125, 137, 188, 262–64, 305, 381–405, 393, 476; *Artisan*, cited in Stranks, pp. 33–34, as quoted and endorsed from experience by F. Engels, *Condition of the Working Classes in England in 1844* (1926), pp. 39–40; Morris, p. 40; Stephens, *Hook*, 1, 369, 408.

CHAPTER 5

Hook's Influence on Anglican Renewal in Leeds, 1837–51

Religious Leadership and Jurisdiction

With Hook as its parish priest Leeds gained a natural religious leader. He was a man whose example and behest many would willingly follow. Until Hook arrived in 1837 there had been few signs of religious leadership from successive Vicars of Leeds since the reign of George I. Between 1837 and 1851 Hook's powers reached their height, both for the Church and the wider community. He was not an isolated phenomenon of an active and energetic priest. The zeal of English clergy had been observed in the 1830s, and remarked upon even as far away as New York.[1] Hook's work for the Church and the wider community is therefore best seen as a prime example of what parish clergy could achieve in the early Victorian period. Other industrial towns comparable to Leeds also possessed extremely able incumbents, such as J. C. Miller (Birmingham), Hugh McNeile (Liverpool); Hugh Stowell (Salford); Thomas Sutton and Thomas Sale (Sheffield). All this distinguished company did great things in their localities, and all were Evangelicals,[2] apart from Hook, whose manifestly High Church ministry was based on principles predating the Tractarians of 1833. In Leeds Hook's reputation locally shone the more brightly because he succeeded an unimaginative run-of-the-mill Evangelical Vicar. For High Churchmen in the England of the 1830s Hook was the outstanding exponent of Church principles. No incumbent with similar views possessed a comparable cure or jurisdiction as Hook in his early years at Leeds.[3]

In 1837, however, Hook succeeded to a diminishing jurisdiction. National legislation to modernize the Church's medieval parochial system had already made inroads into the responsibilities of the Vicar of Leeds. From 1818 Church Building Acts had enabled new churches to be built with the aid of Parliamentary grants. Since then four new churches had been erected within the ancient parochial area. Two received their own parish districts from the

---

[1.] *New York Review*, April 1838, cited in Stoughton, II, 59.
[2.] Gill, I, 374–75; A. Briggs, *History of Birmingham, II: Borough and City 1865–1938* (1952), 3, 351; S. C. Carpenter, *Church and People 1789–1889* (1993), pp. 26, 194–95; Cornish, I, 31–32; Hylson-Smith, pp. 147, 150; M. Walton, *Sheffield: Its Story and Its Achievements* (Sheffield, 1948), pp. 216–17.
[3.] Virgin, p. 23.

Church Building Commissioners: St Mark's, Woodhouse (1826); and St
Stephen's, Kirkstall (1829). Both these were entirely independent, with
patronage of each vested in the trustees of the Vicarage of Leeds. The other
two, Christ Church (1826) and St Mary's, Quarry Hill (1827), remained
under the jurisdiction of the Vicar of Leeds, who as parochial incumbent
received the power of appointment. In 1838, the year after Hook's arrival, St
George's was consecrated. Although it constituted a district church within
the parish of Leeds, its erection under the Church Building Act of 1831
allowed its patronage to be vested in five trustees, initially of the subscribers'
choice in 1836, but thereafter self-perpetuating.[4] Peel's Act of 1843 for the
Spiritual Care of Populous Parishes continued the legislative trend for
diminishing the jurisdiction and patronage of the incumbents of mother
churches of extensive ancient parishes.[5] Hook's own Leeds Vicarage Act of
1844 continued the process, by making it possible to create parishes for
churches not covered by previous legislation.[6] In substance, however, until
6 December 1844, when St Andrew's district was gazetted under Peel's Act,
Hook presided over the same parochial area and organization to which he had
succeeded in 1837. During these years, though Evangelicalism in Leeds by no
means disappeared, much of the parish veered towards the High Anglicanism
of Church principles and sacramental doctrine advocated by Hook.[7]

Proclaiming Church Principles

Hook's early years at Leeds provided some notable occasions when he
expounded the implications of Church principles, the first being at his
inaugural sermon in April 1837. Some months later, again at Leeds Parish
Church, he preached so cogently on the apostolic succession that three
Methodist local preachers — non-stipendiary unordained laymen — indicated
to Hook that they were prepared, along with some of their week-night class
members, to accede to the Church of England, provided they could continue
with their class meetings. After consulting Bishop Longley, Hook agreed. He
modified their procedure to accord with Anglican usage, by appointing
clerical leadership. At the time, and even forty years later (by Hook's
biographer W. R. W. Stephens) these relatively few accessions were seen as a
powerful vindication of Church principles. More important in the long term,
however, was the incorporation of weekly devotional meetings into the

4. Mayhall, pp. 300, 320, 323, 440–41; Port, pp. 24–28, 35–37, 93–94, 107–12, 138–39,
   168–69, 191; Wood, *Church Extension*, pp. 6, 29.
5. Port, pp. 117–18.
6. Wood, *Church Extension*, pp. 9–15.
7. Cornish, I, 62–76.

Leeds parochial organisation.[8] Hook's own jurisdiction soon gave signs of active dissemination of Church principles. Five extra curates were appointed in Leeds by 1838, all funded by the Additional Curates Society (ACS), a High Church society to which Hook had subscribed since its inception in 1837.[9] Before the end of 1839 Hook had preached in many big towns in the North (York, Wakefield, Bradford, Liverpool, Huddersfield and Manchester) and also smaller places in the West Riding. The Evangelical Vicar of Bradford made Hook welcome. In contrast the Evangelical Vicar of Sheffield politely warned him off, but solely on account of Hook's High Churchmanship.[10]

Three occasions when Hook expounded aspects of Church principles in 1838 reached wider attention than church congregations. At a grand Conservative Festival at Leeds in April, in support of Peel, he made the speech of the evening. He consented to participate because he suspected that the Church was in danger from 'an essentially infidel ministry'. In doing so, he mounted a stirring defence, 'as an Englishman', of the Church of England. His particular concern was to defend the Church's special role in religion and education, and to make it clear that any suggestion of expropriating Church property to fund a national education system would meet vigorous opposition. For Hook the Church's right to its property carried the obligation that it must be used to benefit the English people spiritually and educationally. This was no inward-looking ecclesiastic concerned for his own privileged existence. Hook's disquiet about the ministry's attitude to the Church prompted him in June 1838 to broach the matter in the Chapel Royal, before the highest in the land. As an antidote to possible Erastian influences round the young Queen, he explained that the Church's ecclesiastical status was intrinsic to itself, and dependent in no respect on the fact of its Establishment. The sermon, ever after known as *Hear the Church*, had been preached before, without exciting particular comment. Because of the occasion, it now attracted great attention. A hundred thousand copies were sold in printed form. Bishop Longley's primary visitation, at Leeds Parish Church in August 1838, afforded Hook another opportunity to reach an influential group, when he preached the visitation sermon before the assembled district clergy. He called for union on the basis of the principles of the English Reformation. Subsequently printed and copiously referenced, the sermon included an extended treatment of Church principles.[11]

---

8. PH, fols 33–41, Hook to Pusey, 7 Sept. 1837, fols 48–51, Hook to Pusey '2 in Advent 1837'; *LI*, 19 Aug., 21 Oct. 1837; *LM*, 14, 21 Oct. 1837; Stephens, *Hook*, I, 391–401, 406, 408, II, 12–13.

9. WYASL, LPC112/1, Parish Church Record, Clergy List; *LI*, 4 Nov. 1837; 10, 17 Nov., 22 Dec. 1838; *LM*, 27 Jan., 10 Feb., 10 Nov. 1838; Wood, *Church Extension*, p. 29.

10. *LI*, 21 Oct., 4 Nov. 1837, 21 Apr., 5 May, 11 Aug., 8, 22 Sept. 1838; *LM*, 28 Apr., 11 Aug. 1838; Jowitt, pp. 37–61; Stephens, *Hook*, I, 425–35.

11. *LI*, 18, 21 Apr. 1838; *LM*, 21 Apr. 1838; Stephens, Hook, I, 403–04, 416–24.

Parish Church Worship: St Peter's and St John's, 1837–41

In 1837 Hook wrote to Samuel Wilberforce of his plans for Leeds: 'I shall hope that God has called me to this post to be the instrument of a great change . . .'. Hook's immediate challenge was the conduct of services at St Peter's. From his arrival he set the tone. There was to be reverence and decorum, to convey the importance and solemnity of the occasion. Hook's purpose registered with the *Leeds Mercury* from the very first. It reported that Hook's style for the prayers and liturgy was admirable, and recorded the universal opinion that Hook was incomparably the best reader to occupy the pulpit in living memory. Hook's insistence on reverence owed much to his sense of the numinous. At Coventry, for example, he rearranged the prayer reading desk so that it faced the altar instead of the congregation, to emphasize that prayer was directed to God. Hook had long held that justice was seldom done to the Anglican liturgy, but when he arrived at Leeds he saw that more than minor adjustments were necessary. The dirt, slovenliness and indecorum he found quite distressing. Daily services were neglected, whilst baptisms, weddings, and funerals were gabbled mechanically, without thought to the effect on those most nearly concerned. As Hook believed that example must precede precept, he initially took all these services himself, to demonstrate the standard he required. From July 1837 Hook had the assistance of the Revd J. W. Clarke, whom he had appointed to the vacant post of lecturer, in raising standards. By 1838 these standards had been achieved, with St John's functioning as the Parish Church, whilst St Peter's rebuilding was in progress. Worship at St John's was described by the *Leeds Mercury* as 'Cathedral Service' and others remarked on the music, the prayers, and the impressive Holy Communion celebrations.[12]

Within the context of the liturgy Hook regarded sermons in public worship as an excellent means of instruction in the faith. Shortly after arrival in Leeds he became aware of a 'Methodistic' emphasis — by all Dissenters and even among the most pious of Churchpeople — on the related doctrines of Justification and Sanctification in preaching. It conflicted with his own declared aim of expounding the Catholic faith in its entirety. Because Hook wished to gather a regular flock, he was much annoyed by 'sermon-tasters' on Sundays, in quest of 'that most detestable of all characters, a popular preacher'. In September 1837 Hook told Pusey that everything at St Peter's had exceeded his most sanguine expectations: 'Catholicism is such a novelty that it takes wonderfully from that very circumstance.' From November 1837 he was preaching at the Parish Church twice on Sundays and on Friday evenings, and also weekly, by Bishop's licence, to a congregation of poor people in St Peter's, Bank, Sunday school. H. J. Rose, High Church editor of

---

12. PH, fols 132–34, Hook to Pusey, 24 Sept. 1840; *LI*, 15 July 1837, 29 Sept. 1838; *LM*, 22 Apr. 1837, 17 Mar. 1839; Stephens, *Hook*, I, 169–70, 259, 401–02, 404–06, 409.

the *British Magazine*, perceived the wider implications of such zealous proclamation of Catholicism locally. If through sustained teaching of Church principles the richer manufacturers were taught their duty to their workers' souls, and built churches for them, it might serve as an example far beyond Leeds. Provided clergy responded wholeheartedly, the manufacturing districts might then become towers of strength for the Church.[13]

Hook's Effect on Congregations

Hook's congregations in Leeds and elsewhere were drawn by his sincerity of manner at each stage of the service. He possessed natural advantages. His fine voice enhanced the cadences of the Anglican liturgy; his command of words held the congregation's attention, enthralling their minds and enthusing their spirits. More is known of Hook's manner in the pulpit from observers outside Leeds. The Dissenting *Liverpool Albion* remarked on Hook's quiet pulpit manner, and the harmonious construction of his sermon delivered without rhetorical flourishes. The *Nottingham Journal* recorded the powerful effect of Hook's 'affectionate earnestness and soul-subduing exhortations' on a crowded congregation. The effect came from careful composition for Hook disliked extempore preaching. He achieved it, in the *Gloucester Chronicle*'s estimation, by clearness of style, aptness of illustration, and power of putting his prominent points in a striking light. A worshipper from Manchester described Hook's voice as 'of great compass, full, clear, and round, and capable of the greatest modulation'. These perceptive comments from elsewhere appeared between 1839 and 1845, and cannot be matched for analysis in the Leeds newspapers. As early as September 1837, however, the *Leeds Intelligencer* could claim that Hook was winning golden opinions from everyone, except his unco-operative Dissenting churchwardens; whilst the diocesan, Bishop Longley, did not hesitate to describe Hook to his parishioners as 'their talented and beloved Vicar'. Leeds townspeople could recognize a hard and enthusiastic worker. Exhilaration seized the Anglican fold, especially at St Peter's, where it was now essential to arrive early, even for standing-room. In October 1837 it was decided to enlarge the church. The unsafe fabric later discovered led to an entirely new building being consecrated in 1841, different in form and concept of worship from its predecessor. The Parish Church of 1841 is the supreme tangible example of Hook's effect on congregations. Its construction is discussed in Chapter 6.[14]

---

13. PH, fols 33–41, Hook to Pusey, 7 Sept. 1837; Chadwick, I, 170; Stephens, *Hook*, I, 404–06, 408, 411–14.
14. *Liverpool Albion*, cited in *LI*, 29 June 1839; *Gloucester Chronicle*, cited in *LI*, 6 Dec. 1845; *Nottingham Journal*, cited in *LI*, 17 Sept. 1842; *Manchester and Salford Advertiser and Chronicle*, cited in *LI*, 14 Oct. 1843; *LI*, 7, 21 Oct. 1837.

Preparations for Cathedral Service at the New Parish Church, 1841

The architect for the new St Peter's was R. D. Chantrell, who had been responsible for designing several Parliamentary churches locally. Chantrell's brief was to design a church to accommodate a large number of people, and to arrange the interior so that an impressive and dignified service, suitable for the nineteenth century, could take place. For Hook as a Catholic, the heart of divine service was worship, offered with 'the single object in view of promoting the glory of God' — the focus being always on God, never on man.[15] Much of the new church's renown came from its mode of worship. At some stage the idea of 'Cathedral Service' took shape, possibly inspired by a letter in the High Church *British Magazine* of August 1840, regretting that for choral music the Church of England was inferior to the Roman Church; and to the Dissenters for attractive singing. *The British Magazine* was well known to Hook, who may perhaps have suggested the reprint of the letter, which appeared in the *Leeds Intelligencer* under the heading of 'Church Psalmody'. Certainly by February 1841 Hook's plans for introducing Cathedral Service in his new church, when completed, were well advanced. He told W. P. Wood that James Hill, a first-rate trainer, had been secured from Westminster Abbey, at a salary of £120 a year. Hook intended a good choir, whatever the cost. At this stage the proposed choir was involving Hook in great expense personally, he confided to Pusey, as no others were willing to help him. Although Hook declared that he never introduced innovations until parishioners were ready, he knew how to disseminate information to change attitudes. For Cathedral Service this was done on a grand scale. On three successive Wednesdays in March 1841, Hook's friend, Prebendary John Jebb of Limerick Cathedral, gave a course of well advertised open lectures in Leeds on 'Cathedral Service', to Church of England Library subscribers and others interested. These were published in July 1841 in an inexpensive popular series entitled *The Christian's Miscellany*. By then the parishioners of Leeds were reportedly looking forward with pleasure to the introduction of a fully choral service at the new Parish Church, and choir rehearsals were already in progress.[16]

Jebb's lectures created the momentum for change, leading to requests for choral service in the new church. Seizing his moment, plain or choral, Hook replied, it must be the best of its kind. High standards were expected of the choir then formed, consisting of men and boys. Salaried professional singers

[15] PH, fols 158–62, Hook to Pusey, 9 Aug. 1841; W. F. Hook, *The Three Reformations: Lutheran; Roman; Anglican* (1847), p. 72; *LI*, 11 Nov. 1837; Stephens, *Hook*, I, 169–70, 259, II, 133.
[16] PH, fols 147–53, Hook to Pusey, 23 Feb. 1841; *British Magazine*, Aug. 1840, cited in *LI*, 29 Aug. 1840; *LI*, 11 Nov. 1837, 27 Feb., 17 July, 4 Sept. 1841; *LM*, 28 Aug. 1841; J. Jebb, *Three Lectures on the Cathedral Service of the Church of England* (Leeds, 1841); Webster, *Music*, p. 23; Stephens, *Hook*, II, 123–24, 129–30, 133.

formed the nucleus, assisted by volunteers from the Parochial Choral Society. The carefully chosen boys received a small recompense. With three months of practice before consecration day on 2 September 1841, it augured well for the introduction of Cathedral Service in the new church.[17]

The interior of the new church created a splendid setting for choral services. Compared with old St Peter's it gave a sense of spaciousness and height. Stained glass windows and tabernacle-patterned masonry and wood-work added richness. Having overcome all difficulties raised by opponents, Hook expressed himself well pleased with the final result. The new church was 'as nearly right as circumstances would permit' he told Pusey. 'I shall have an altar looking like an altar'. For the congregation Hook had insisted on the altar being well elevated for visibility, and approached by a broad and spacious flight of steps for the benefit of intending communicants. The altar could now be seen by many in the nave, though still not by all but the prayers and discourses could be heard by everyone. The *Leeds Mercury* expatiated on the church's beauty, and recommended parishioners to see for themselves.[18]

The Consecration of the New Parish Church, September 1841

The consecration of St Peter's on 2 September 1841 possessed wider than local significance. Erected by voluntary contributions at a cost of almost £30,000, it was the most expensive church in the West Riding since 1800, and possibly in England. The five most expensive churches built through the first Parliamentary Grant ranged between £22,000 and £25,000; four being situated in London, and one in Ramsgate. The four London churches were overshadowed as churches by Westminster Abbey and St Paul's Cathedral, whilst Ramsgate's church essentially served a small provincial seaport. St Peter's, Leeds, however, was the mother church in a great provincial town, overshadowed by none, with added lustre from its outstanding Vicar.

The new church epitomized the contemporary revival of provincial Anglicanism. It was consecrated by Bishop Longley of Ripon in a brief ceremony before an invited congregation, in the presence of the Archbishop of York and prelates from Scotland and America, along with several hundred surpliced clergy. According to Florence Nightingale there were Puseyites from all parts of England present. The Wesleyan Mayor, William Smith, attended as a civic duty, accompanied by many Council members, whether Anglicans or Dissenters, the latter perhaps in support of common Protest-antism. Once the consecration was concluded, the church doors were thrown

17. WYASL, LPC112/8, 'Rules of Choir', 1 Mar. 1849; *LI*, 4 Sept. 1841, 31 Aug. 1844, 16 Feb. 1850; *LM*, 4 Sept. 1841; S. Dyer, *Dialect of the West Riding* (1970), p. 112, cited in Webster, *Music*, pp. 23–24; Hook, *Duty and Progress*, pp. 25–26; Stephens, *Hook*, II, 129.
18. PH, fols 158–62, Hook to Pusey, 9 Aug. 1841; *LM*, 4 Sept. 1841; Dalton, pp. 36–38 (Plates 3–5); Stephens, *Hook*, II, 87–89; Webster, *Chantrell*, pp. 125–129 (Plates 25–29).

open to the general public, and every seat was quickly filled. Choral morning service then took place, with Bishop George Washington Doane of New Jersey preaching for an hour — twice as long as customary. The first celebration of Holy Communion in the newly consecrated church brought the lengthy ceremonies to a close.[19]

Special services continued the following day. Hook's morning sermon enlarged on the unity of the Reformed Catholic Church exemplified by the presence of the Bishop of Ross and Argyll and the Bishop of New Jersey. For Hook 'the Kingdom of Christ' was to be found in the Holy Catholic Church, of which the 'purest portion' existed in the Church of England and its sister Episcopal Churches in Scotland and America. That evening the new church was completely filled, the ground floor free seats mainly occupied by the working classes. When the service ended, the congregation proved reluctant to leave, so taken were they by the beauty of their surroundings. On Sunday afternoon, 5 September, the poor made the church their own. There was pathos in the amount of the collection, £11 16s. from over two thousand people, in pennies and halfpennies. What they had, they gave, as they had during the rebuilding. The Vicar never forgot their gifts, which he later urged the rich to emulate. From 1837, in fact, the working classes and the poor formed a major element in the congregation, some two-thirds, as in Hook's previous congregations. Nor were the material needs of the poor overlooked at a time of unemployment and distress. On consecration day some one thousand five hundred families received up to 8lb of beef, depending on numbers, at the expense of the Vicar and others. The butcher provided the meat at cost price, to enable more families to be helped.[20]

The Liturgical Arrangement of Interior Space in the New St Peter's

The interior arrangement of the new church accorded with the ecclesiologists' precept of a distinct separation of nave, chancel and sanctuary. By placing the pulpit and reading pew well to the side of the chancel opening, there was an unobstructed view of the altar not previously possible from the nave. There was space for movement: for the clergy and choir to enter and depart in

---

[19.] WYASL, LPC25, Vicarage Book, patron's admission ticket, LPC50/3, 'Sentence of Consecration', parchment dated 2 Sept. 1841; *Church Record of Western New York*, cited in *LI*, 7 Aug. 1841; *LI*, 28 Aug., 4 Sept. 1841; *LM*, 7 Aug., 4 Sept. 1841; Sir E. Cook, *Life of Florence Nightingale* (1913), I, 55, cited in Yates, *Leeds High Church*, p. 15; Fraser, 'Politics and Society', p. 284; Grady, *Georgian Buildings*, p. 39; Mayhall, p. 468; Port, pp. 132–39; *The Seven Sermons Preached at the Consecration and Reopening of the Parish Church, Leeds, with an Introduction*, ed. by W. H. Teale (Leeds, 1841), pp. lxii–lxxii (list of clergy); Stephens, *Hook*, II, 89–90; Webster, *Music*, pp. 25–26.

[20.] *LI*, 16 Nov. 1839, 28 Aug., 11 Sept. 1841, 9 July 1842, 31 Aug. 1844, 28 Apr. 1849; *LM* 4 Sept. 1841; *Seven Sermons*, pp. xliv–xlv, 61–106.

dignified procession; for communicants to come to the altar rail for the sacrament, instead of receiving in pews, as previously. Interior space used in these ways enhanced worship in the new church, and left an abiding impression on visiting clergy and laity. Especially noteworthy, perhaps, was the prominent placing of the lay surpliced choir in the chancel, the first of note where this occurred, and an ideal in Hook's mind since at least 1833. When the opportunity eventually occurred at Leeds to build a new Parish Church, the chancel arrangements reflected Hook's ideal. (The Cambridge Camden Society, founded in 1839, which concerned itself with the interior arrangements of churches, took the same view as Hook about choirs in chancels.) Some years after its consecration the new St Peter's was praised by the *Ecclesiologist* as the first great contemporary instance of 'the Catholic feeling of a church'. From a twentieth-century perspective Addleshaw and Etchells described its design as 'epoch-making', the prototype of Anglican interiors for over a hundred years, and the ideal shape for the grave and ordered beauty pioneered by Hook in parochial worship, whilst for Owen Chadwick, the new Parish Church was 'as grand as any cathedral'.[21]

Cathedral Service

'Cathedral Service' was an innovation which more than fulfilled expectations. The ground had been well prepared by Jebb's lectures, and reinforced by Hook's explanation, in the consecration period, that although intoning prayers might seem unusual, it highlighted the special quality of the church service, compared with all other forms of human activity. Cathedral Service at Leeds conformed to Jebb's view, shared by ecclesiologists, that it was more important to have a service well sung than one in which the congregation could join; it should touch the emotions and the spirit, and move the mind to reverence and awe.

Congregations flocked in their thousands to Leeds Parish Church on Sundays. A factor in such popular acceptance was probably the innate love of choral music in the West Riding, attested by the existence of so many choral groups. In appreciation of Jebb's contribution, St Peter's building committee voted £20 for the Vicar to purchase a present. From September 1841 at the Parish Church there were choral services of mattins and evensong every

---

21. *LI*, 4 Sept. 1841, 5 Feb., 9 July, 3 Dec. 1842, 14 Oct. 1843, 31 May 1851; *LM*, 3 Mar. 1838; G. W. O. Addleshaw and F. Etchells, *The Architectural Setting of Anglican Worship: An Inquiry into the Arrangements for Public Worship in the Church of England from the Reformation to the Present Day* (1948), pp. 206–07, 209–13; Chadwick, I, 213–14; *Ecclesiologist*, VIII, 132, cited in Addleshaw and Etchells, pp. 212–13; J. Le Patourel, 'Medieval Leeds: Kirkstall Abbey, the Parish Church, the Medieval Borough', *P.Th.S.*, LVI (1963), 1–21; N. Yates, *Buildings, Faith and Worship: The Liturgical Arrangement of Anglican Churches 1600–1900*, (Oxford, 1991), pp. 154–55; Yates, *Leeds High Church*, pp. 15–16.

Sunday. At each service versicles, responses and prayers were intoned, and canticles, psalms and anthems sung to the same elaborate settings as in cathedrals, with the purity of tone favoured in English services since the Reformation. On weekdays morning prayer was said daily, with choral evensong at 7.30 p.m., a service greatly appreciated by the poor. When the time was changed to 4 p.m., in August 1847, a Leeds resident protested in the *Leeds Intelligencer* that this denied working men and women the refreshment of mind and spirit which came from the beautifully sung service. Some time later the evening service was reinstated. Evangelicals and Dissenters disliked the new ceremonial worship, but it never disturbed public order, as at St Paul's, Knightsbridge; St Barnabas', Pimlico; and St George's-in-the-East. Few in Leeds could have actually experienced worship in a cathedral. As a term for parochial worship 'Cathedral Service' seems to have brought its own immunity from upset.[22]

In September 1842 Hook told Pusey that no cathedral in England could match the services at Leeds Parish Church for solemnity and grandeur. A 'wonderful improvement' had consequently occurred in neighbouring churches. Some months later the visiting Bishop of Tasmania declared in Leeds that the sublime effect of worship at St Peter's was heightened by the attention and decorum of the crowded congregation. This effect came through the efforts of three distinct groups: the instigators of Cathedral Service; the clergy; and the musicians. On the part of the clergy Hook demanded high standards of himself as well as his curates. The musicians comprised the organist, the choirmaster and the choir. The organist's role was pivotal, both as soloist, accompanist and in selecting the music for the services. Shortly after the consecration the organist's post became vacant. Hook's master stroke was in securing Dr Samuel Sebastian Wesley, the celebrated organist and composer, from Exeter Cathedral. Wesley had recently inaugurated the Parish Church's organ, when he made it 'rain music on the ear'. Wesley arrived in February 1842. St Peter's for him represented the ideal: a magnificent church in a large town, with its music properly performed as an act of worship, in the presence of a congregation of thousands. Wesley came to a choir highly trained by its choirmaster, James Hill. The choirmen were mainly volunteers, with a nucleus of professional singers, whose experience at Leeds often led to cathedral appointments. Boys with good voices were readily recruited. They received a small recompense, but the real attraction was the musical training and assistance in obtaining employment, when choir service ended. In spite of the choir's quickly acquired reputation, financial

22. WYASL, LCP41/8, Rough Min. Bk, 7 Sept. 1841, LCP112/1, Parish Church Record, Notice of Service Times, 6 Aug. 1847, LPC112/8, Notice of Services, 1853; *LI*, 18 Sept. 1847; Addleshaw and Etchells, pp. 209, 219; Chadwick, I, 495–501; Moorman, pp. 352–53; Teale, p. 94, cited in Addleshaw and Etchells, p. 219; Stephens, *Hook*, II, 88; Yates, *Leeds High Church*, p. 74.

support was disappointing. At the end of its first year Hook found the annual expense (£700) greater than expected, and the subscription (£300) less than anticipated. From 1842 congregational collections were also regularly made. Regardless of personal expense, Hook had no regrets. For him the supreme importance of the liturgy demanded that it should be performed supremely well.[23]

Cathedral Service from 1841 drew large congregations to Leeds Parish Church for many decades, both in Hook's vicariate ending in 1859, and those of his successors. However, the revival in the church's fortunes dates from Hook's first months there. He demanded from both himself and his assistant clergy a high standard for conducting services. Contemporaneously there was his remarkable power as a preacher. At Leeds Hook never gave the same sermon twice. Whatever the theme there was always some variation in treatment to meet circumstances then obtaining. Congregations were drawn by the power and tenderness of Hook's message and the unforgettable beauty of his voice. When he left Leeds, he destroyed most of his parish sermons. Those collected posthumously may express their content, but not the impact of their delivery. For Hook's living voice we must look to the speeches printed, often verbatim, in the Leeds newspapers, where his wide human sympathies in matters affecting the community at large were conveyed to audiences in powerful rhetoric and his own special turn of phrase.[24]

Lenten Observances

During Hook's incumbency the observance of Lent at St Peter's became a special event in Church life. His inspiration was the example of Dr Sandford, Bishop of Edinburgh, at whose daily sermons in Holy Week Hook had been present in 1825. At Leeds he continued the practice he inherited of inviting local clergy to deliver Lenten Wednesday sermons. To this end he invited Evangelicals and High Churchmen without differentiation to expound the Passion message. He did, however, put himself down for Good Friday. Hook's special innovation at Leeds was the introduction of evening services with a sermon during Holy Week, to make it possible for the working and business classes to share in the solemn preparation for Easter. Later, with this

---

23. PH, fols 201–05, Hook to Pusey, 29 Sept. 1842; WYASL, LPC112/1, Parish Church Record, Collections for Choir Expenses, 1842–52; *LI*, 9, 16 Oct. 1841, 1 Jan., 5 Feb. 3 Dec. 1842, 16 Feb. 1850; *LM*, 23 Oct., 4 Dec. 1841, 5 Feb. 1842; *Manchester and Salford Advertiser and Chronicle*, cited in *LI*, 14 Oct. 1843; E. H. Fellowes, *English Cathedral Music from Edward VI to Edward VII* (1941), pp. 205–11; Moorman, pp. 363–64; Webster, *Music*, pp. 28–29; S. S. Wesley, *A Few Words on Cathedral Music and the Musical System of the Church, with a Plan of Reform* (1849), pp. 37, 41.
24. W. F. Hook, *Parish Sermons*, ed. by W. Hook (1879), pp. vi–ix.

in view, he instituted four services daily during Lent, at 7.30 a.m., 11 a.m., 3 p.m. and 7.30 p.m.[25]

There was a gradual extension of Lenten practices to other churches, and at St Peter's itself. In 1844 the High Church Thomas Nunns rang the bell at St Paul's to announce morning and evening services instituted daily for Lent. For this he was accused of Tractarianism by the *Leeds Mercury*. As the champion of Dissent, its editor was clearly irritated by such occurrences at a formerly Evangelical bastion. These comments evoked a spirited Anglican claim in the *Leeds Intelligencer* for the Church's right to its customs of worship without incurring derogatory comments from a newspaper which so zealously upheld these rights for all Dissenting denominations. In 1846 further instances of Lenten observances were evident. At St George's, by then the foremost Evangelical church locally, the clergy provided special sermons, weekly on Thursdays in Lent, and daily during Holy Week. In the out-township of Farnley, the High Church curate Henry Jones provided Lenten services daily, except Tuesdays, at varying times, to enable attendence for as many as possible. At Leeds Parish Church the pattern of four daily services continued, with the addition of a sermon by Hook every evening except Saturday, forming an extended devotional commentary.[26]

From 1846 these week-night sermons throughout Lent became for Hook an annual commitment. Each half-hour sermon took at least three hours to compose. Hook bravely published his programme in advance, and wrote a sermon a day. His themes included the Saviour's miracles (1847); the Gospels of St Luke and St John (1849); the discourses of Jesus (1850). In 1847 the increasing observance of Lent was attributed to the gradual division of St Peter's parish. It is more likely, however, that High Church and Evangelical clergy alike recognized the teaching possibilities of a sequence of related sermons. The force of Hook's example was not confined to Leeds. By 1863 he had the satisfaction of knowing that daily sermons in Holy Week were general in all the large towns of England. Hook's own heroic pattern of daily services and sermons throughout Lent continued essentially unchanged at St Peter's from 1846 until he left for the Deanery of Chichester in 1859.[27]

[25] *LI*, 24 Feb., 7 Apr. 1838, 25 Feb. 1843, 17, 24 Feb. 1844, 1 Feb. 1845; *LM*, 4 Feb. 1837, 24 Feb. 1838, 27 Feb. 1841, 5 Feb. 1842; Stephens, *Hook*, I, 72–88, 170–73.
[26] *LI*, 24 June, 1 July 1843, 9 Mar. 1844, 21 Feb., 11 Apr., 17, 24 Oct. 1846, 27 Feb. 1847; *LM*, 2 Mar. 1844.
[27] BL, Gladstone Papers, MS 44, 213, fols 95–96, Hook to Gladstone, 20 Feb. 1847; WYASL, LPC112/1, Parish Church Record, Lenten Services, MS note for 1849, published programme leaflet for 1850; *LI*, 13, 27. Feb. 1847, 13 Feb. 1858; Stephens, *Hook*, I, 172–73.

Confirmations at Leeds Parish Church

Before Longley's appointment to Ripon (1836) confirmations were rare in Leeds. His predecessor as diocesan, Archbishop Vernon Harcourt of York (1807–47), had confirmed once every seven years. The huge gathering of confirmands that ensued were mainly young people. Some had come long distances, were often ill-prepared, and could have gained little understanding of the significance of confirmation from the Archbishop's mode of administration. It was a travesty of the Prayer Book rite. The Archbishop laid episcopal hands on no one. From the pulpit he extended his arms and uttered the confirmation prayer to the congregation in general, pronounced the prescribed concluding prayers, and departed without further ado.[28] Longley approached confirmations far more seriously. From 1837 he instituted triennial confirmations, though railway links from Ripon were non-existent, and still rudimentary from Leeds. By committing himself to travelling round his diocese frequently, Longley was years ahead of Bishop Wilberforce of Oxford, who was consecrated in 1845, yet is often credited as the first to undertake such pastoral journeys. As rail communications improved, Longley confirmed annually from 1847.

With Hook at St Peter's, where confirmations for all Leeds churches still took place, Longley could count on dignity and order. It was obtained by parochial instruction of candidates and Hook's ability of produce an impressive service. For parochial instruction Hook whilst at Coventry had written an inexpensive handbook for candidates entitled *Questions and Answers on Confirmation*, which reached a fourth edition in 1840. Its price of 2*d.* placed it within the reach of individuals, or of churches for distribution. Bearing in mind the long Anglican tradition of confirmations in adolescence, Hook had also written *Pastoral Advice to Young People preparing for Confirmation*. He was not alone in realizing the value of thorough preparation. Four well-known clergyman active in parochial ministry and broadly contemporary with Hook were cited by Brian Heeney as advocating the same careful approach. Two were Evangelical: W. W. Champneys (Whitechapel) and Charles Bridges (Old Newton, Suffolk); and two were High Church: J. H. Blunt (Great

---

[28.] *Confirmation, or the Laying on of Hands* (1926), I, 219–20, cited in Stephenson, p. 95; Heeney, p. 45; W. K. Lowther Clarke, 'Confirmation', in *Liturgy and Worship: A Companion to the Prayer Books of the Anglican Communion*, ed. by W. K. Lowther Clarke (1936), pp. 443–57; Stephens, *Hook*, I, 395–96; Virgin, p. 158.

Oakley, Essex) and J. W. Burgon (Oxford), later Hook's successor at Chichester.[29]

Longley as diocesan fully endorsed the importance Hook attached to preparation. At the Bishop's first visitation in 1838 he commended the Leeds clergy for the evidence of careful preparation observable in the serious demeanour of confirmands assembled at St Peter's in 1837. He stressed that teaching candidates merely to repeat the Catechism, the Creed, and the Lord's Prayer was not enough. Clergy should ensure that candidates were presented only if properly instructed in their meaning. Young people at confirmation, the Bishop declared, were not only professing their faith, but also their resolve to live by that faith for the rest of their lives. Future confirmation dates would be announced in good time, and clergy should inform candidates that, unless extenuating circumstances existed, none could be presented without at least one month's instruction. As A. M. G. Stephenson remarked, a minimum of one month's preparation may not later have seemed much, but in 1838 it represented a significant step forward.[30] Two years later candidates were not presented for confirmation by Leeds clergy without a certificate that Prayer Book requirements were fulfilled. In 1843 Hook's preparation of candidates exceeded three months: weekly preliminary lectures from June; and twice-weekly catechetical lectures from August. In the week before confirmation on 6 September, lectures every evening covered important aspects of Christian belief, character and conduct. On 8 September Hook prepared the newly confirmed for receiving their first communion on the coming Sunday. In 1846 these final lectures depicted the Christian life as a journey on which hindrances could be expected, though divine help was assured.[31]

In keeping with the preparation, Longley's confirmations were dignified and reverent. Patiently, and unhurriedly, he confirmed almost a thousand candidates at Leeds in 1837, in two services, each lasting two hours. We know most about the confirmations of 1840. On the first day in-township's candidates were presented, and the out-townships' the day after. Girls wore white, with caps of uniform design, 'trimmed with white satin ribands'. Candidates in pairs approached the altar, knelt before the Bishop, who laid his hand on each, with prayer. All candidates having been confirmed, he then

29. WYASL, LPC112/1, Parish Church Record, entries for Confirmations, 7 Oct. 1847, 3 Oct. 1848, 5 Oct. 1849, 17 Oct. 1850, 17 Oct. 1851, 28 Oct. 1852; LI, 21 Oct. 1837, 9 May, 3 Oct. 1840, 9 Sept. 1843, 26 Sept., 3 Oct. 1846, 9 Oct. 1847, 7 Oct. 1848, 6 Oct. 1849, 26 Oct. 1850; LM, 21 Oct. 1837, 3 Oct. 1840, 9 Sept. 1843, 26 Sept. 1846, 9 Oct. 1847, 7 Oct. 1848; Chadwick, I, 514–15; Heeney, pp. 45–47, 120; W. F. Hook, Pastoral Advice to Young People Preparing for Confirmation (n. d.); W. F. Hook, Questions and Answers on Confirmation (1834); Lowther Clarke, p. 456; Stephenson, pp. 96–98; R. W. Unwin, 'Leeds becomes a Transport Centre' in Modern Leeds, pp. 113–41.
30. WYASL, RDB18, Visitation Charge, 1838, pp. 19–21; LI, 11 Aug. 1838; Stephenson, p. 97.
31. LI, 3 Oct. 1840, 3 June, 12 Aug., 2, 9 Sept. 1843, 19 Sept. 1846; LM, 3 Oct. 1840.

addressed his 'young friends', adjuring them affectionately to persevere in the Christian life. Longley's benign and handsome presence enhanced the impressive occasion. In 1840, 1019 candidates were confirmed (368 males, 651 females). Of 573 from the main township 256 came from Hook's classes. The *Leeds Intelligencer* accounted for disproportionately fewer boys having been confirmed, by explaining that they generally started work earlier. Here in the factories where conditions diminished parental control, they consequently often grew beyond 'the power of a corrective hand'.[32]

The total of 1800 candidates confirmed in 1843 was evenly divided between the in-township and the aggregated out-townships. It was four-fifths more than in 1840, and reflected the great efforts made by all concerned. It was the highest total in Longley's triennial series. Amongst the out-townships Hunslet's total of 180 owed much to the zeal and personality of the incumbent, John Clark, and his curate J. A. Beaumont. At the last triennial confirmation in 1846, 1400 were confirmed, similarly divided by townships as in 1843. Following the confirmation of 1837 the number of candidates presented in 1840, 1843 and 1846 totalled 4219, a notional yearly average of 469 for the nine years involved. From 1847, when annual confirmations started, to 1850 there were 2396 candidates in total, a yearly average of 599. Hence, annual confirmations increased the ratio of young people going forward, suggesting that in the former three-year intervals a proportion of those eligible were removing themselves annually from consideration. Even so, the disparity between males and females persisted. It was discernible whenever separate figures were available, and occurred irrespective of whether the confirmation was triennial or annual. In early Victorian Leeds, Bishop Longley, Hook and the local clergy all worked in conjunction to make the confirmation service meaningful to candidates. In doing so they produced a joyful and moving event in Leeds Church life and an enduring pattern for succeeding generations.[33]

Hook's Role in Planting Catholicism, 1837–51

The opportunity to introduce Catholicism and Church principles to a district reportedly devoid of both was the deciding factor in Hook's candidacy for Leeds. It was an aim which was to create stress within the Church and alarm among Dissenters. Situated in a vastly more important manufacturing centre than Coventry, St Peter's, Leeds, offered a potentially influential pulpit; the

---

32. *LI*, 21 Oct. 1837, 3 Oct. 1840, 30 Mar. 1844; *LM*, 21 Oct. 1837, 3 Oct. 1840; Stephens, *Hook*, II, 12; Stephenson, p. 98, 1 (note).

33. WYASL, LPC112/1, Parish Church Record, entries for Confirmations, 7 Oct. 1847, 3 Oct. 1848, 5 Oct. 1849, 17 Oct. 1850; *LI*, 9, 16 Sept. 1843, 30 Mar. 1844, 26 Sept. 1846, 9 Oct. 1847, 7 Oct. 1848, 6 Oct. 1849, 26 Oct. 1850; *LM*, 9 Sept. 1843, 26 Sept. 1846, 9 Oct. 1847, 7 Oct. 1848.

emoluments and associated patronage conferred high ecclesiastical status; and the immense population represented a challenge in itself. The prospects for evangelism attracted Hook greatly. The extensive patronage would allow opportunity to appoint like-minded men as curates at St Peter's, or elsewhere within the Vicar's gift. Such appointments would mean that planting Catholicism subsequently would not depend on Hook alone. When explaining the implications of Catholicism for Anglican doctrine and worship, Hook emphasised that only by reference to Christ was any doctrine valuable. The cumulative effect exceeded his expectations and even surprised himself.[34]

The Anglican class meetings in St Peter's district became a powerful means for reinforcing Catholic teaching. After observing a 'trial meeting' of the ex-Methodists, Hook banned further recounting of conversion or related experiences, as encouraging spiritual pride; and appointed clergy as class leaders instead of lay people. At the weekly class meetings the leaders opened with the Litany or other sections of the Prayer Book, rather than extemporary prayer. Instruction in doctrine and Scripture followed. Hook initially used certain Oxford Tracts and Newman's *Sermons* for teaching. General conversation on church matters also took place, so that class leaders and members became well acquainted. Hook delighted in these classes, aimed at poor or rich alike, and appeared more eager to take visitors to those for the poor. When Bishop Doane of New Jersey came for St Peter's consecration in 1841, he was taken to the York Road class. Fifty or sixty poor people were present. Describing the meeting later, Doane praised Hook's manner, inimitable in its naturalness and power to touch hearts. Similarly, when W. E. Gladstone and Lord Lyttelton visited Leeds in 1847, Hook proposed a visit to a class 'of poor Communicants'.[35]

The endeavours of the clergy as class leaders were greatly appreciated. A touching mark of regard came from the operatives of the York Road class in 1840, when Hook was presented with a pocket edition of the communion service. Much moved by the self-denial the gift had entailed, Hook told the donors that, in his chosen role as a servant of the poor, for his 'great Master's sake', the gift would prompt him to his own acts of self-denial. In 1839 the Thursday class at the more affluent St John's, which was temporarily acting as the Parish Church presented a Polyglot Bible. This was followed by a silk gown and cassock in 1840. Other clergy received presentations at various times. In these devotional classes Hook felt himself among friends, whether rich or poor. Together they could discuss the deep things of God, 'Jesus Christ and Him crucified', and explore the privileges of belonging to the

---

[34] PH, fols 33–41, Hook to Pusey, 7 Sept. 1837; *Liverpool Mail*, cited in *LI*, 29 June 1839; Stephens, *Hook*, I, 298.

[35] BL, Gladstone Papers, MS 44, 213, fols 91–92, Hook to Gladstone, 15 Jan. 1847, fols 93–94, Gladstone to Hook, 16 Feb. 1847; PH, fols 33–41, Hook to Pusey, 7 Sept. 1837; Bishop G. W. Doane, *Impressions of the Church of England*, cited in *LI*, 10 Sept. 1842; Stephens, *Hook*, I, 396–400, 408.

Catholic Church. Clergy and laity benefited individually from the inter-change, whilst the Church acquired a band of Catholic-minded helpers, to whose influence Hook attributed much of the decorum of Parish Church services, along with increasing numbers of communicants. Amongst the out-townships, the Revd George Rickards, of Wortley, was one incumbent known to have instituted classes on Hook's pattern.[36]

Hook's aim, once in Leeds, was to encourage existing clergy to adopt Church principles, and also to 'plant a good Catholic', wherever possible. His most immediate opportunities proved to be at St Peters's. Robert Taylor, Fawcett's untenured curate, had maintained the spiritualities during the interregnum. Although he was an Evangelical, Hook retained him, because they found they could work together. Taylor was a special case; he left Leeds in 1839. Edward Brown, tenured clerk-in-orders, proved sympathetic to Church principles, so much so that Hook made him a class leader. In 1840 Hook pointed to him as a model for others. George Wray, the tenured lecturer, clearly preferred not to work with Hook. He resigned in May 1837. His resignation gave Hook the opportunity to appoint his first Catholic, J. W. Clarke, a Warwickshire incumbent, whom he already knew. Untenured curates directly chosen by Hook were all High Churchmen. According to Hook, in a letter to Pusey in October 1841, his 'young men' were 'kind and dutiful', but so influenced by the writings of Newman and Pusey, that they considered themselves more theologically advanced than their Vicar.[37]

Unlike his predecessor, Hook recognized the need for more clergy in the crowded Parish Church district, men who were energetic, practical, and able to relate to the working classes. Before the Additional Curates Society (ACS) provided grants for the support of untenured curates, Hook paid for them from his own resources. Hence in 1838, when perhaps constrained financially by his munificent subscription to St Peter's rebuilding, he asked Pusey if he knew of a hard-working strong young man of 'sound principles', who would accept £20 a year to obtain a title to ordination. Between 1838 and 1850 there were usually four and often five curates at St Peter's, including the lecturer and clerk-in-orders. Hook gave his curates specific districts for pastoral work. Clarke, the new lecturer, received considerable responsibility as the district clergyman for St Peter's Bank, assisted by an untenured new curate, George Elmhirst. Together they gathered a congregation and raised funds for a National School, used for worship from April 1840. Clarke was revered as a devoted pastor. When he left Leeds in 1841 his class selected a farewell gift of works ideally in accord with Church principles — choice

---

[36.] Letters to *LI*, 4 May 1839 (John Clark), 10 Aug. 1839 (R. Ward), 24 Aug. 1839 (Hook), 4 Jan. 1840 (J. W. Clarke, G. Elmhirst), 18 Jan. 1840 (G. Rickards), 18 Apr. 1840 (E. Brown), 13 June 1840 (Hook), 31 Oct. 1840 (Hook), 5 Sept. 1846 (C. H. Burton).

[37.] PH, fols 33–41, Hook to Pusey, 7 Sept. 1837, fols 174–76, Hook to Pusey, 11 Oct. 1841; WYASL, LPC112/1, Parish Church Record, List of Clergy; *LI*, 13 May, 15 July 1837, 4, 25 May 1839, 18 Apr. 1840; *LM*, 3 June, 15 July 1837, 11 May 1839.

editions of Latin and Greek Fathers. Hook appointed George Hills in Clarke's place, presenting him to St Mary's, Quarry Hill, in 1846. Leaving there two years later, Hills referred feelingly to Hook's guidance and training in 'the principles of the Church of Christ'. Between 1837 and 1851 nearly thirty assistant clergy served at St Peter's. Most were trained and pastorally formed by Hook. During the early Victorian Anglican resurgence they represented a significant planting of Catholicism from St Peter's, Leeds.[38]

Patronage of the chapelries and most of the town's district churches gave Hook more opportunities of permanent influence, though vacancies occurred irregularly. His first opportunity came at St James's proprietary chapel which was devoted to Low Church principles but was not Evangelical. In 1837 the Revd John King, the aged incumbent, wished to sell his church for £2000. He was unsuccessful, and because of bodily infirmity ceded all rights to the Vicar, thus putting St James's directly into Hook's control. Hook found a purchaser for St James's, the Revd George Ayliffe Poole, in whose career he had interested himself. Poole took over in March 1839. He was a Tractarian, and 'a very clever supporter of right principles', the author of learned treatises and popular weekly sermons entitled *The Poor Man's Reader*. Poole transformed St James's interior — originally a Dissenters' chapel and octagonal in layout — so thoroughly that Leeds people could scarcely credit that the 'old meeting-house sort of place' could look 'so ecclesiastical'. The church acquired one of the best congregations in town, won over by Poole's eloquence and zeal. In 1840 Poole published several articles in the *Leeds Intelligencer* entitled 'Candles on the Altar', maintaining that ritual and ceremony conveyed truth and religious principles visually, as sermons through the eyes rather than the ears. Equally he rejected the right of Dissenters to make public criticism of Anglican modes of worship. Whilst Poole was proprietor, Hook possessed in Leeds an articulate champion for Catholicism.[39]

Catholicism continued at St James's after Poole's departure. Robert Aitkin, his successor, though holding the evangelical tenet of instant conversion, was Catholic enough for Hook to appoint in 1843. Aitkin indeed established a small ascetic male community, which Hook sanctioned 'as merely a domestic arrangement', without referring to the diocesan. The community did not survive Aitkin's departure in 1846. Hook appointed a former member, Edward Jackson, ordained in 1845, who remained as incumbent until his death in 1892. Similar in churchmanship to Aitkin, though less extreme,

38. PH, fols 33–41, 7 Sept. 1837, fols 48–51, '2 in Advent 1837', fols 60–61, 3 Mar. 1838, fols 103–16, 9 June 1840 (all Hook to Pusey); WYASL, LPC112/1, Parish Church Record, List of Clergy; *LI*, 15 July 1837, 11 Apr. 1840, 31 July 1841, 5 Sept. 1846, 2 Sept., 28 Oct. 1848; *LM*, 15 July 1837, 5 Sept. 1846; Stephens, *Hook*, I, 335, 372.
39. PH, fols 33–41, Hook to Pusey, 7 Sept. 1837, fols 62–69, Hook to Pusey, 24 Apr. 1838; *British Magazine*, cited in *LI*, 14 Sept. 1839; *LI*, 8, 15 Sept. 1838, 2 Mar., 10 Aug. 1839, 22, 29 Feb., 7 Mar. 1840; *LM*, 8 Sept. 1838, 2 Mar. 1839.

Jackson possessed the supreme gift of imparting religious devotion. During his incumbency St James's was a thriving centre of religious life.[40]

On two occasions replacing deceased non-resident incumbents caused Hook some embarrassment. In 1843, following the death of Christopher Atkinson, the Evangelical incumbent of St Paul's, the presentation passed to Hook as Vicar of Leeds. With Atkinson's death the appointment of his curate, John Meridyth, automatically ceased. As an untenured curate employed by Atkinson he had no legal right to the living, nor even a possible moral right through long service. Nevertheless, Meridyth protested vociferously when Hook appointed Thomas Nunns who was a High Church former colleague of Hook in Birmingham. He was of good reputation and ability but Meridyth took exception to the appointment and declared that he had received a 'marked slight' from Hook as patron. He went on to publish acrimonious letters to Nunns, and finally departed in dudgeon. By these actions he gave Hook the chance to explain himself. On arrival in Leeds Hook had retained all curates, irrespective of their ecclesiastical opinions, a practice not always followed elsewhere, and had ejected no one since. Though inapplicable in this instance, curates specifically appointed by Hook were explicitly informed that if they took part against him, they were considered bound to resign. When in post Nunns proved conciliatory, irenic, and very acceptable to St Paul's.[41]

In 1844 the replacement of the non-resident incumbent of Holy Trinity, John Sheepshanks, Archdeacon of Cornwall, lately deceased, thwarted the aspirations of the Revd Joseph Holmes, Headmaster of Leeds Grammar School. An Evangelical, he had officiated as Sheepshanks's curate since 1830, with the school trustees' permission. In 1839 Sheepshanks's death seemed imminent, and Holmes so unwell that resignation from schoolmastering appeared possible. Since becoming Vicar, Hook had been one of three joint patrons of Holy Trinity and ex officio school trustees' chairman. With these dual concerns in mind, he spontaneously offered to support Holmes's appointment to Holy Trinity if the expected circumstances arose. When Sheepshanks died in 1844, Holmes had recovered, but expected the appointment whilst retaining the headmastership. Hook considered both positions were full-time; he would support Holmes for the incumbency, provided he would resign the school. Holmes was unwilling. Thomas Nunns was elected and left St Paul's. Charges of 'party' and 'bad faith' were levied against Hook, but his decision was in the best interests of education and

40. BL, Gladstone Papers, MS 44, 213, fols 51–56, 22 Jan. 1844, fols 57–62, 25 Jan. 1844, fols 67–68, 9 Feb. 1844 (all Hook to Gladstone); PH, fols 219–26, Hook to Pusey, 20 Nov. 1843; *LI*, 11 Mar., 30 Sept. 1843; *LM*, 4 Feb., 2 Sept., 1843, 12 Sept 1846; Stephens, *Hook*, II, 227–28; *Sketches of the Life of Edward Jackson*, ed. by L. and K. Sykes (1912), pp. 11–17, 45; Yates, *Leeds High Church*, pp. 25–27.
41. *LI*, 13 May, 24 June, 1, 8 July 1843, 19 Apr. 1845; *LM*, 20 May, 24 June 1843; *Midland Counties Herald*, cited in *LI*, 19 Aug. 1843; Stephens, *Hook*, II, 324.

pastoral care. Holmes as an incumbent could not have given proper attention to both positions.[42]

The resignation of Edward Cookson, the Evangelical incumbent of St Mary's, Quarry Hill, resulted in a chain of High Church appointments. Following his policy of rewarding outstanding service Hook appointed J. A. Beaumont, curate at St Mary's Hunslet, moving him in 1845 to St Paul's. This meant that four influential churches in central Leeds possessed High Church incumbents: St Peter's, St James's, St Paul's, Holy Trinity — a remarkable change since Fawcett's death. Hook appointed Hills to St Mary's similarly in 1846, and J. Bickerdike, also from the Parish Church, in 1848. Where, however, Hook found a curate publicly against him, he was prepared to require him to leave, in accordance with the understanding agreed at engagement. In 1847 T. B. Ferris, curate at St Luke's since 1841, joined with Evangelical clergy in a memorial to Bishop Longley, censuring Hook, though without naming him, for a 'fundamental error' of doctrine. Hook refrained from public comment, but Ferris himself, on leaving, described his departure as 'removal from pastoral charge'.[43]

Appointments at two further in-township churches require notice. In 1849 the patron of rural Bardsey asked the Bishop to nominate a clergyman to its church. For meritorious long service among the poor of South Leeds, Longley nominated John Holroyd, the Evangelical stalwart of Christ Church. Hook replaced Holroyd by J. D. Hilton, about whom little is extant. When Hilton resigned in 1851, Hook appointed his High Church precentor at St Peter's, W. C. Barwis. In 1851 St Thomas's, Leylands, a new church in a slum district, needed an incumbent. Hook appointed D. T. Gladstone, his senior Parish Church curate, and cousin of the statesman W. E. Gladstone. The new incumbent did well, but Hook knew that he would do even better in a country living. With typical generosity Hook later informed his friend W. E. Gladstone, if he heard of such a living, not to consider his cousin necessarily fixed at Leeds.[44]

Hook also gradually planted High Churchmen in the out-townships. Hunslet received an infusion of Catholicism in 1839, when Hook's York Road district curate, J. Clark, was moved to assist the seriously ill Richard Foster, the chapelry's incumbent. Clark was in effect Foster's locum tenens and received the incumbency after Foster's death in 1841. At Farnley Hook

42. *LI*, 4, 11 Jan. 1845; *LM*, 21 Dec. 1844, 11 Jan., 22 Feb. 1845; Mayhall, p. 360; Stephens, *Hook*, I, 372; Taylor, pp. 454–55.
43. *LI*, 8 May 1841, 30 Mar. 1844, 5 Sept. 1846, 9 Jan., I, 15 May 1847; *LM*, 2 Mar. 1844, 5 Sept. 1846, 9 Jan. 1847, 21 Oct. 1848; Stephens, *Hook*, I, 372, II, 324; Wood, *Church Extension*, p. 6.
44. BL, Gladstone Papers, MS 44, 213, fols 106–07, 7 Aug. 1847, fols 112–13, 9 Feb. 1848, fols 122–23, 29 Jan. 1852 (all Hook to Gladstone); WYASL, LPC112/1, Parish Church Record, List of Clergy; *LI*, 24 Feb., 23 June 1849, 25 Jan., 1 Feb., 1 Nov. 1851, 7 Feb. 1852; Beresford, *East End, West End*, pp. 235, 269 (map), 540 (inset map, ref. 5).

gave two High Churchmen temporary charge of the chapelry, because of the incumbent's lengthy non-residence for health reasons. G. Trevor, a returned East India chaplain, officiated for most of 1846. After Trevor's departure, Hook sent Henry Jones, formerly Fawcett's curate at St Mark's, Woodhouse, who had proved too diligently Catholic for his Evangelical incumbent. In 1848 Hook's still existing patronage enabled him to appoint George Armfield, Chaplain of Leeds Borough Gaol, as incumbent of Armley, following Charles Clapham's death. In similar circumstances J. D. Dixon, St Luke's, replaced Thomas Furbank at Bramley in 1850. None of these High Church appointments caused public comment, since Hook was acting within his rights. Early in his vicariate, however, unfavourable comment occurred when Hook attempted to secure the election of a High Church friend to the independent district parish of St Stephen's, Kirkstall. The patrons, who were also the Parish Church trustees, elected an Evangelical. Hook told his Mother that the Becketts, wishing to placate the Evangelicals for supporting him in 1837, had 'played [him] false'. In 1848, however, one of Hook's High Church curates was elected to St Stephen's, without similar allegations arising.[45].

Hook's own election was the first move in his strategy for planting Catholicism in Leeds. For his large new parish he needed assistants, and with little delay gathered and maintained a gradually changing team of carefully selected curates, drawn from High Church circles. Provided they kept to Church principles, Hook's curates received his loyalty and support, leaving by agreement if their views changed, as occasionally happened. Regular testimonials from parishioners and class members witnessed to the effectiveness of their Catholic instruction. In 1841 the *Leeds Mercury* commented upon the increase of High Church principles in the parish. At that stage this was still mostly due to the Parish Church team. With permanent incumbencies Hook planned ahead, never forcing an opening, but always ready to deal with the unforeseen and the unexpected. Influencing the trustees to elect Sinclair for St George's proved Hook's greatest disappointment. Instead of acquiring a High Church ally, Hook received a skilful and hardworking proponent of Evangelicalism, matching his parish priest in personality and

45. HA, K6/27, Hook to Mother, 9 Feb. 1839; *LI*, 26 Jan., 4 May 1839, 4 Sept. 1841, 10 Jan., 7 Feb., 25 Apr., 24 Oct. 1846, 30 Jan., 11 Dec. 1847, 15 July, 12, 26 Aug., 23 Sept. 1848, 16, 23 Nov. 1850; *LM*, 9, 23 Feb. 1839, 4 Sept. 1841, 15 July, 5 Aug., 2, 9, 23 Sept. 1848; G. E. Kirk, *Farnley, Leeds: Its Chapelry, Chapels and Present Church, with Lists of Local Clergy* (Leeds, 1951), pp. 41–42.

ability. From 1844 legislation diminished Hook's patronage, but by then the predominantly High Church orientation of Anglican Leeds was set.[46]

Hook as Parish Priest

Hook's immediate and lasting success at Leeds Parish Church owed much to his temperament and early career. From ordination Hook had consistently done well in positions of increasing responsibility, where he involved himself in matters affecting the whole community, as well as the Church. At St Peter's, Leeds, Hook made churchgoing attractive. The charm of his manner, the appeal of his voice, his approachability and warmth, all created a favourable first impression. Though Hook's reputation as a preacher initially brought large numbers to St Peter's out of curiosity, they mostly became regular worshippers. Week after week with brilliant clarity Hook expounded the great Christian themes and their applicability to daily life. For Hook preaching was important, but he personally set higher value on the proper celebration of the divine liturgy. On Sundays at St Peter's the dignity of the ceremonial, the decorum of the congregation, the choral settings of the service and the music of the organ blended into a sublime whole, whose effect was remarked upon by parishioners and visitors alike. Within the town, it was in St Peter's district itself that Hook carried out his own self-appointed pastoral work among its poor inhabitants. When the new St Peter's was completed, Hook opened it on weekdays, 'as a place of beauty and stillness', in which they could escape from their crowded homes for private prayer and quiet meditation.

In his early days at Leeds Hook attributed the increasing congregations at St Peter's to the 'novelty' of Catholicism, modestly ignoring the manner of its proclamation. The latter was probably a greater element than Hook was prepared to acknowledge, for High Church doctrines previously had made no headway against Evangelicalism in other West Riding towns apart from Wakefield. However, as soon as the able Sinclair occupied St George's pulpit in 1838 Evangelicalism in Leeds proved a magnet. Even so, Hook's proclamation of Catholicism in Leeds added a new dimension to Anglican religious identity there. He taught his people to see the Church of England as uniquely Catholic, having regained purity of primitive Catholic doctrine at the Reformation, whilst retaining unbroken the apostolic succession of ministry. In Hook's eyes this represented a combination of faith and order

---

46. PH, fols 33–41, Hook to Pusey, 7 Sept. 1837, fols 62–69, Hook to Pusey, 24 Apr. 1838; letters to *LI*, 2 Mar. 1839 (G. A. Poole), 4 Jan. 1840 (J. W. Clarke, G. Elmshirst), 13 June 1840 (R. Ward), 24 Apr. 1841 (G. W. Brameld), 31 July 1841 (J. W. Clarke), 13 Aug. 1842 (T. Rogers), 27 Oct. 1843 (T. Rogers), 30 Mar. 1844 (J. A. Beaumont), 24 Oct. 1846 (H. Jones), 28 Oct. 1848 (G. Hills); *LM*, 13 Feb. 1841; Stephens, *Hook*, I, 298, 396–400, II, 324–25.

unequalled in Christendom. Although for many years it led to difficulties with Dissenters and Anglican Evangelicals, and sometimes with the equally exclusive Roman Catholics, it did not affect the size of St Peter's congregations. At the Parish Church and in St Peter's district Hook was ably assisted by his curates, with whom his relationship was half-brotherly, half-fatherly, but always in the role of chief. When Hook's curates left Leeds Parish Church, they took Church principles and Hook's methods of parish management to many parts of England and beyond.

At Leeds, Hook famously displayed the power of a parochial incumbent to influence local Churchmanship. Brighton in Sussex provided a largely contemporary parallel, achieved in a strikingly different way. Like Leeds in the first half of the nineteenth century, it was the largest town in its county, and rapidly increasing in population. H. M. Wagner, Vicar of Brighton, was its long-serving parish priest from the 1820s. He shared the High Church ideals of his wealthy father-in-law, Joshua Watson, leader of the Hackney Phalanx. By a variety of means, including family money, Wagner encouraged and oversaw an energetic building programme. It provided eight chapels of ease to Brighton Parish Church between 1825 and 1853, with the nomination of incumbents thus remaining firmly with Wagner. He also ensured that it became a High Church town, increasingly more ritualistic and Anglo-Catholic through the influence of his son, A. D. Wagner. Hook, on the other hand, co-operated with the sub-division of his parish under Peel's Act, resulting in new churches with their own patrons, and in his own Act wished to surrender all his patronage to the Bishop. Parliament, however, insisted that some valuable patronage must remain with the office of Vicar of Leeds.

During twenty-two years as Vicar of the town, Hook along with his assistant clergy raised Leeds high in national esteem as one of the most important centres of Anglican life and work in the country. Although the formal jurisdiction of Leeds Parish Church diminished gradually from the 1840s, Hook's personal standing remained high. His title remained Vicar of Leeds, and Bishop Longley made him Rural Dean. Hook's High Churchmanship remained an influence in Leeds for years. As Nigel Yates observed, amongst broadly comparable Yorkshire cities, such as Bradford, Hull and Sheffield (all strongly Evangelical) Leeds was remarkable for the number of 'high' churches which nevertheless fell short of being termed Anglo-Catholic. Hook's most innovative and significant years at Leeds were those between 1837 and 1851, when he reached the peak of his powers. In these years of effort and struggle, Hook suffered setbacks, but still pressed on, and from 1852 onwards enjoyed general respect and approval. By then, however, he was growing steadily more tired, as his energies waned. In 1859, when the Deanery of Chichester was offered, Hook knew that it was time to make way for a younger man. It was as Vicar of Leeds that Hook accomplished, as Stranks has so rightly said, his life's greatest work. He left a far greater position than that to which he succeeded. Hook's predecessors, whether from lack of ability or inclination, had for a hundred years signally failed to respond to the challenge to the Church of the town's increasing population and the growth of Dissent. They had been undistinguished clerical worthies selected from a restricted field. After Hook, and for most of the twentieth century, Vicars of Leeds were men of outstanding talent, more often than not moving on to bishoprics or other high preferment.[47]

47. PH, fols 33–41, Hook to Pusey, 7 Sept. 1837, fols 268–92, Hook to Pusey, 6 Oct. 1845; *LI*, 16 Mar., 28 Sept., 19 Oct. 1839, 15 Feb., 20 June 1840, 23 Jan. 1847; E. P. Hennock, 'The Anglo-Catholics and Church Extension in Victorian Brighton', in *Studies in Sussex Church History*, ed. by M. J. Kitch (1981), pp. 173–88; Port, p. 3; Teale, pp. 78, 84; Stranks, pp. 40, 110; Wood, *Church Extension*, pp. 13, 15; Yates, 'Religious Life', p. 254; Yates, *Leeds High Church*, p. 65.

CHAPTER 6

Rebuilding and Paying for the new Parish Church, 1837–47

Prelude to Rebuilding, 1837–38

When Hook commenced duty at Leeds Parish Church in 1837, he discovered that, because the organ gallery blocked the chancel arch, distribution of the elements at Holy Communion took place in pews (contrary to the Prayer Book's directions) rather than at the altar rail. If one reason could be assigned to the eventual shape of the new Parish Church, it would be Hook's determination to have a building in which the liturgy could be celebrated according to the rubrics. Conditions in the nave, where morning and evening prayer took place, were also less than satisfactory. Pews were crowded together around the three-decker pulpit, and dust and decay were everywhere apparent. The deeply cut fourteenth-century pillars supporting the galleries denoted potential structural danger. This dilapidation was not unique. Examples could be found not far away, at Bradford and Huddersfield. As Bishop Selwyn and the *Ecclesiologist* both noted, some years later, ruinous old churches were common in early Victorian England.[1]

Hook's first weeks in Leeds were spent with Benjamin Gott (1760–1840), a munificent supporter of charitable causes and Yorkshire's leading woollen manufacturer.[2] From Gott's imposing residence Hook described St Peter's to his friend Wood in London as like 'a conventicle built up as a church', adding that he hoped to turn it inside out. Probably Hook had discussed his church's structural shortcomings with his host, for he later gave Gott credit for first suggesting improvement. On 29 April 1837 the *Leeds Intelligencer* reported that the projected gallery and roof alterations, as well as repewing, would cost more than £2000. More ambitious plans were made during July and August, involving an architect, with the possible cost reaching £3000. Trade was poor. Hook therefore made no public move to open a subscription. Experience had taught him that better support came for proposals which laypeople themselves brought forward.[3]

---

1. *LI*, 30 Nov. 1839; *Ecclesiologist*, III (1844), 134, cited in Linstrum, p. 214; Gilbert, pp. 132, 237, note 28; Linstrum p. 214; Stephens, *Hook*, I, 335, 379.
2. Mayhall, pp. 465–66; Taylor, pp. 377–80.
3. PH, fols 163–73, Hook to Pusey, 24 Sept. 1841; WYASL, LPC41/5, Cttee acct book, enc., Committee Report to meeting, 25 Oct. 1841 (printed); *LI*, 29 Apr. 1837; Stephens, *Hook*, I, 335, 401, 403–04, 409.

As Hook hoped, the parishioners themselves took the initiative. They decided to present an address to the Vicar, asking how they could best co-operate with him in remedying the shortage of seating now so apparent at St Peter's. It was 'no secret and no flattery', they declared, that congregations had greatly increased since his arrival. Many people had to stand throughout the service, others could not even get inside. Over six hundred people signed in three days. Hook replied by fixing a public meeting for 8 November.[4] The parishioners' address gave Hook the ideal warrant for maturing his own plans. Proposals from parishioners for enlarging a great church suddenly too small to accommodate all who wished to attend would have greater popular appeal than alterations requested by the Vicar, to meet his idea of an ecclesiastically proper interior.

In the event the enlargement initially envisaged did not materialize. The extension as an option had to be jettisoned and the alternative of erecting a new building adopted. The ancient fabric was found to be unsafe. Derek Linstrum tells us that the aim of Hook and his architect, R. D. Chantrell, was to produce a beautiful copy of an early-fourteenth-century church in a unified style. The brief for the interior was different, not so much a copy, as an adaptation, which would enable the Anglican ritual of the nineteenth century to be performed 'with solemnity and grandeur'. Thus the eventual rebuilding made possible the radical reordering Hook desired, and gave him opportunity to prepare the congregation for a very different style of service for the future. The whole concept of divine worship in the replanned interior of St Peter's probably took shape in Hook's mind even before the parishioners' address of October 1837. It would express his sense of the English Church's mission to its people, for which he also knew himself called. The beauty and dignity of the services in the rebuilt church in time raised standards elsewhere in the Church of England.[5]

Rebuilding a Church for the People, 1837–41

On 8 November 1837 the parishioners' meeting with the Vicar took place at the town's Music Hall. Those present were mainly the more influential, but they were delighted to see some artisans there also. Plans for the nave and new galleries, prepared by R. D. Chantrell (1793–1872) under the direction of the Vicar, were on view, along with a large representation of the proposed interior in colour. Chantrell had been a well-known architect in Leeds since 1819, and had already designed several churches in the West Riding, including Leeds. Trained in Sir John Soane's office in London, he had also

---

4. WYASL, LCP41/6, Committee minute book, p. 3, Parishioners' address and Hook's reply (printed); *LI*, 21 Oct. 1837; Stephens, *Hook*, I, 379.
5. Hook, *Three Reformations,* p. 72; Linstrum, p. 216; Stranks, p. 56.

acquired a knowledge of Gothic church design and architectural features by careful study. Chantrell's innate feeling for the style, perhaps reinforced by his layman's knowledge of the Anglican ethos, enabled him to incorporate towers, spires, turrets and crenellations in designs which delighted by their 'picturesque' quality. At the meeting the first resolution asserted the need for the alterations; the second was to approve the suitability of the plans on view; the remainder were concerned with raising and collecting a subscription, and appointing members and officers for a committee of management. All resolutions were unanimously accepted.[6]

Hook's introductory speech as chairman determined the mood of the meeting. He explained that because the pews in the present church were ill-arranged, there were seats for 1500, and floor space for 500 to stand. The alterations would provide 1200 extra seats, with 700 free for the poor, and 500 to rent. (It was to the poor, Hook reminded his hearers, that the Church was in the first place commanded to preach the Gospel.) Briefly likening the plight of Leeds Parish Church with that of the Temple in Jerusalem after the Babylonian exile, Hook pointedly directed the rich to their financial duty. When they compared the forlorn aspect of their House of God with the comfort and elegance of their own homes, he thought they would blush with shame, for although churches were built for people, they served to glorify God. District churches might be plain and cheap, but the Parish Church should be a handsome building, which said to those who saw it, 'See how churchmen love and honour their God . . . Come hither and worship . . .'. Passionately delivered, these words fired the enthusiasm of all present for the proposed reconstruction. Hook resumed his seat amidst loud and prolonged cheers.[7]

Of the sixteen gentlemen proposing and seconding the resolutions, most were in the Leeds upper middle classes, as defined by R. J. Morris, and the others mainly in the category next below.[8] The key theme was recognition of the need to provide more seats for those now flocking to St Peter's as 'the poor man's church'; they could not always be accommodated on Sunday evenings; some even started to arrive forty-five minutes before service time. This scheme would also meet the Vicar's known wish to extend further his ministry among the poor. The senior trustee, Henry Hall (1773–1859), declared that the present plan was the most worthy for the parishioners and for St Peter's itself. In over sixty years' attendance he had seen a variety of alterations, none benefiting either public or poor. Benjamin Gott made similar points, not only insisting that the poor must be accommodated, but

6. WYASL, LPC41/5, Cttee acct book, enc., Parishioners' meeting, 8 Nov. 1837 (printed); *LI*, 11 Nov. 1837; *LM*, 11 Nov. 1837; Linstrum, pp. 211–13, 373; Port, p. 83, Webster, *Chantrell*, pp. 17–24, 33–34.
7. *LI*, 11 Nov. 1837; Stephens, *Hook*, 1, 380–83.
8. *LPB, 1834*; *Morris*, pp. 165–66.

that the enlarged church must 'do honour to the architecture of the town'. With different emphases others made similar points. Thus the scheme received the parishioners' mandate, and after votes of thanks to the Vicar and trustees, the subscription list was opened for general signature. For Church-people the proceedings were extensively reported by the *Leeds Intelligencer* whilst the *Leeds Mercury* highlighted the most important consideration for Dissenters: a further example of Anglicans relying for funds on their own efforts.[9]

The consensus appearing at the parishioners' meeting for an edifice which would glorify God, witness for the Church, and bring honour to the town, became the driving force for the enterprise. No Anglican could be unaware of the remarkable record of Leeds Dissenters recently for building imposing and commodious chapels. Wesleyan Methodists had built four: Wesley (1816), Brunswick (1825), St Peter's (1834), Oxford Place (1835). Apart from Wesley each held 2000 or more people. The Independents had erected Queen Street (1825) and Belgrave (1836), with a total capacity of 3000, whilst the Baptists' South Parade (1826) had recently increased seating to 1400. These chapels impressed by their size or design. Similar architectural features occurred in West Riding towns such as Bradford, Halifax, Huddersfield, Pontefract and Wakefield. In those towns the leading Dissenting chapels were indeed the 'basilicas of West Yorkshire nonconformity'. Brunswick Chapel, Leeds, possessed a lavish and pleasing exterior of fine ashlar. The gleaming woodwork of the interior, the pulpit raised on fluted Doric columns, the monumental organ in its carved mahogany case, together produced an effect of sober magnificence. Chapels such as these, along with courthouses, libraries, exchanges and assembly rooms in West Riding towns, typified the spirit of emulation in public building so well depicted by Kevin Grady. In the reconstruction of St Peter's, Anglicans would do well if they could match the standard of Brunswick. Hook's scheme for altering St Peter's, the first major move in its rebuilding, was strongly supported by the natural leaders of the Anglican community. They eventually found themselves committed to erecting a completely new building, which became one of the most influential parish churches of the Anglican resurgence in the early Victorian era.[10]

The committee of management appointed at the meeting played a key role in the process of building and paying for the new Parish Church. Its members oversaw the progress of the work, administered the subscription, collected and applied the funds. The bankers Beckett, Blayds and Co. were the appointed treasurers. With a membership of about forty at any one time the committee could appoint further members as necessary.[11] The committee's

9. *LI*, 11 Nov. 1837; *LM*, 11 Nov. 1837; Grady, *Georgian Buildings*, p. 164.
10. *LI*, 11 Nov. 1837; Grady, *Georgian Buildings*, pp. 96–109, 164–66; Linstrum, pp. 200–07; 'Report 1839' p. 415.
11. WYASL, LPC41/5, Cttee acct book, enc., Parishioners' meeting, 8 Nov. 1837 (printed).

first meeting took place the day after its appointment. Adopting a methodical and systematic approach, it soon decided to meet weekly, for the better dispatch of business. Eventually the committee's work depended upon a core of about a dozen members, including the chairman. Its extensive membership meant, however, that commercial acumen, professional skills and business ability of a high order were accessible for particular problems.[12] The committee displayed ability to identify problems and take decisive action. Matters requiring detailed investigation or periodic supervision were confidently delegated to sub-committees, which were required to submit proposals for consideration before implementation could proceed. Sub-committees consequently dealt with discrete matters — such as the collection of instalments of subscriptions; the refurbishment and re-siting of the organ; the options for inside and outside features of the new building. From 1837 to 1842 over 230 meetings were recorded, with references to others taking place but not minuted. Although the Vicar's duties frequently took him elsewhere, he nevertheless chaired 139 meetings. Between them Henry Hall and Christopher Beckett, the two senior trustees, presided on sixty-six occasions, other regular attenders taking the remainder.[13]

For their duties the committee members were to need clear heads and stout hearts, for neither fundraising nor building operations proved straightforward. At the parishioners' meeting Hook had stressed the liturgical requirement for Holy Communion to be celebrated at the communion table in the sanctuary. The design on view at the meeting provided for the tower and organ to be removed from the centre to the north aisle, and for galleries at each side of a widened chancel. This achieved Hook's desire for a visible and accessible sanctuary.[14] The generous early response to the subscription apparently instigated a more ambitious implementation of Hook's aim. On 20 November, following a sub-committee recommendation, the committee approved Chantrell's amended plan for the tower, now to be positioned at the extremity of the north transept, instead of the north aisle. With the support of the Bishop of Ripon and the Archdeacon of Craven, the necessary faculty for this material change was duly issued by the Deputy Registrar of the Archbishop of York's Consistory Court on 7 December. Because of the urgency, the Archbishop waived the commission of view and inquiry normally held. Meanwhile, the committee had asked Chantrell to produce a 'second design' for altering the ends and the transepts of St Peter's. Amended plans for the east end were ready on 11 December. Ultimately a 'third design', approved on 13 January 1838, was used. It included a massive and ornamental tower rising from the ground at the extremity of the north transept; a chancel terminating in a polygonal east end, on the site of the former vestry; and a new vestry and

12. WYASL, LCP, 41/6, Cttee minute book, pp.15–16; Stephens, *Hook*, I, 383.
13. WYASL, LPC41/6, Cttee minute book, passim; LCP41/8, Rough minute book 2, passim.
14. *LI*, 11 Nov. 1837, 28 Aug. 1841; Stephens, *Hook*, I, 380.

separate robing rooms for clergy and choristers elsewhere. Estimates were approved but no details given.[15]

The third design, far more radical than the original scheme, virtually dispensed with the fourteenth-century fabric. In fact, preliminary explorations revealed a totally unsafe structure. Being overweighted, two of the four pillars supporting the central tower were cracked from top to bottom. Equally alarming, the foundations on which they rested consisted of loose stones and rubbish just below the surface. Pillars elsewhere had been extensively cut away to insert supports for galleries. If the intended gallery extension had commenced, the roof would have fallen in. Finding the old building rapidly crumbling away, committee members realized they were 'in the predicament of men building a new church, instead of repairing an old one'. Shoddy fourteenth-century construction and incautious alterations centuries later effectively sealed the old building's fate. Chantrell's third design was adopted in January 1838, but the hazards were not apparently publicized in detail until Hook made them known when appealing for further subscriptions in November 1839.[16]

After approval the third design was then publicly displayed. It attracted no special comment except for a hand-distributed circular issued by 'An Old Inhabitant', who also wrote to the *Leeds Mercury*. The author contended that the subscription would pay for a new building soon, and rescue the town from the disgrace of a 'patched up' Parish Church. His ideas were not Hook's. 'Old Inhabitant' wanted 'a regular, beautiful *Protestant* church', without the 'popish appendage' of Lady Chapel or baptistry; and strongly objected to 'the Vicar's crooked bantling' being 'palmed on the town'.

Chantrell replied in the *Leeds Intelligencer* on 10 March, under an identifiable pseudonym. St Peter's would be a new building, he declared, with the south wall alone retained, and the rest demolished. By removing the tower to the northern extremity, the whole length of the church would be thrown open from west to east, and the chancel made as wide as the nave. Chantrell carefully avoided mentioning the dangerous condition of the ancient fabric. If 'Old Inhabitant' achieved nothing else, he elicited the architect's rationale for the new church. By then St Peter's was closed for demolition, and went out on a high note. At the final service on 4 March 'not only were all the pews occupied, but the aisles were literally blocked'.[17]

'Old Inhabitant's' protest also highlighted the antithesis between 'Protestant' and 'Catholic' in the Church of England, especially the relative weight accorded by each to sermon and sacrament. Its author had become habituated

[15]. WYASL, LPC41/6, Cttee minute book, pp. 16–17, 19–20, 22–23, 271–74, Faculty copy, LPC50/1, Faculty original; *LI*, 28 Aug. 1841; *LM*, 28 Aug. 1841; Webster, *Chantrell*, pp. 131–32.

[16]. *LI*, 30 Nov. 1839; Stephens, *Hook*, I, 379; Webster, *Chantrell*, p. 134.

[17]. *LI*, 24 Feb., 10 Mar. 1838; *LM*, 3 Mar. 1838; Dalton, pp. 39–40; Webster, *Chantrell*, pp. 133–34.

to worshipping in a nave disjoined from its chancel and to receiving communion in its pews. Although in Leeds there existed some Dissenting chapels with fine interiors for preaching, there were then only two 'regular, beautiful Protestant churches' of the type he advocated. Holy Trinity (1727) and St Paul's (1793), with spires, classically proportioned exteriors, and room plan interiors after Wren, were both ideal for preaching but nevertheless preserved the unity of sanctuary and nave. Whether for sermon or sacrament there were other, better interior spaces for worship in Leeds than fourteenth-century St Peter's. 'Old Inhabitant' had, however, accurately perceived that the liturgical thrust of the new design was on the altar, at the rail of which communion in future would be given.[18] His objections fell on stony ground.

After St Paul's (1793) no new churches were built in Leeds until 1826. By then and subsequently the Gothic style was uniformly preferred. Equally there were no supporters for pew communions, which at the old Parish Church came about through particular circumstances. Other reasons for lack of adverse comment may have been admiration for Hook's contribution to the startling change in Anglican fortunes, and sheer delight in the prospect of a beautiful new Parish Church. By the autumn of 1839 the new building, apart from the tower, had taken shape and was greatly admired. More funds were obtained, and work continued until completion in the summer of 1841. A sense of history made the committee order a brass cross to be fixed in the floor of the new church at the central point of the old tower, with a brass point for each of its piers. The internal fittings were mainly complete by August. Consecration by the Bishop of Ripon was therefore fixed for 2 September 1841, to enable the aged Archbishop of York, formerly diocesan, to attend.[19]

The completed church was an imposing building, in a combination of fourteenth-century perpendicular and decorated styles. The massive centrally placed tower on the north front was undoubtedly its most memorable and individual feature. Internally the dark woodwork and the carved tabernacle-patterned gallery fronts added a note of sober richness. The brilliant colours of the painted windows, some of ancient glass, enhanced the church's interior effect, especially in sunlight. Paradoxically, however, as Linstrum observed, the huge galleries round three sides of the nave made St Peter's still resemble a Dissenting chapel in its seating. Indeed, the *Leeds Mercury* considered these galleries a great blemish in a Gothic church.[20] Gifts came from many quarters: a peal of bells; painted windows from richer individuals, and one from working-class parishioners collectively; a fine velvet altar cloth from Queen

[18.] *LI*, 17 Dec. 1836; *LM*, 3 Mar. 1838; Beresford, *East End, West End*, p. 157, fig. 6.3 (St Paul's); Grady, *Georgian Buildings*, p. 130, plate 24 (b) (Holy Trinity); Linstrum, p. 185.

[19.] WYASL, LPC41/6, Cttee minute book, pp. 113–14, LPC 41/8, Cttee rough minute book 2, 19 Apr., 17 May, 21 June, 3, 19 July 1841; *LI*, 30 Nov. 1839.

[20.] *LM*, 28 Aug. 1841; Linstrum, p. 215, fig. 168, p. 216; N. Pevsner, *Buildings of England: Yorkshire, the West Riding* (Harmondsworth, 1959), pp. 310–11.

Adelaide. For worship the new church provided a spacious uncrowded setting, unlike its predecessor, and splendid acoustics.[21] Anglican and Dissenting journals combined in praise. 'A noble monument of the taste . . . and the old-fashioned piety, and spirit of the Churchmen of that town', pronounced the *Church Intelligencer*; 'truly an honour to Leeds', said the *Leeds Intelligencer*; a 'splendid edifice', declared the *Leeds Mercury*.[22] Six years later the *Ecclesiologist* bestowed the final accolade: 'the first really great undertaking of the present age'.[23]

The Cost of a Handsome Church, 1837–44

Rebuilding St Peter's took nearly four years; freeing it from debt a further six. Far more work was required than initially expected. The committee added to its problems by ordering expensive extras, in the desire for an even more magnificent building. Bad trade, to which Hook referred more than once in letters, made people less forthcoming in subscriptions for rebuilding.[24] Shortage of orders, especially for woollen textiles, led to Relief Funds operating in Leeds township from December 1839 to April 1840, also from January to April 1842. Distress in the earlier period became extreme privation in the latter, when 'men of capital' were often in difficulties and the period became known as the Hungry Forties. The Relief Fund of 1842 terminated prematurely and the same year Chartist riots erupted in the town. After a shopkeepers' meeting in June drew attention to the resulting 'unparalleled distress' among working-class families, funds were somehow found for a soup kitchen, which ran from August 1842 to June 1843.[25]

An associated reason for local unemployment was the rapidity of technological change. In 1818 seventeen separate processes were identified in woollen cloth manufacture, from the open wool pack to packing the woven cloth ready for transport. Gott's factory in 1843, representing the best practice, showed the direction of change in Leeds. Twenty-one processes were now identified, along with increasing sub-division of labour, significantly accompanied by new, often powered, technology. John Marshall (1765–1845), pioneer of flax manufacturing in Leeds, regarded massive trade fluctuations as normal. After a peak of £37,383 in 1836, profits at Marshalls never again

---

[21.] WYASL, LPC41/5, Cttee acct book, enc., 'Rebuilding of Leeds Parish Church', Subscribers' meeting, 25 Oct. 1841 (printed), LPC41/6, Cttee minute book, pp. 90–91, 97, 99–101, LPC51/5, Bell Subscription; *LI*, 30 Oct. 1841.

[22.] *Church Intelligencer*, cited in *LI*, 11 Sept. 1841; *LI*, 4 Sept. 1841; *LM*, 31 July 1841.

[23.] *Ecclesiologist*, VII (1847), 46, cited in Linstrum, p. 217.

[24.] PH, fols 92–98, Hook to Pusey, 1 Dec. 1839, fols 103–16, Hook to Pusey, 9 June 1840; Stephens, *Hook*, I, 403–04, 408–09, II, 86–87.

[25.] *LI*, 28 Dec. 1839, 6 June 1840, 22 Jan., 30 Apr., 28 May, 2 July, 13, 20 Aug. 1842, 10 June 1843; *LM*, 28 Dec. 1939, 6 June 1840, 30 Apr., 2 July, 20 Aug. 1842, 10 June 1843.

approached this figure before 1851, whilst a very substantial loss occurred in 1843. In parallel, one Leeds flax firm in three foundered in the late 1830s, yet by the 1850s local flax manufacturers were employing 9500 workers. In the ten years required to pay for the Parish Church, notably higher poor relief expenditure occurred in 1837, 1841–43 and 1847–48. Such expenditure varied inversely with the local level of employment. As Morris says, the overall experience of fluctuations was 'a crucial part of middle-class consciousness'. The uneasy economic climate of these years perhaps made the middle classes not only more cautious in meeting the demands for funds from the Parish Church Committee, but possibly less willing, when substantial extra expenditure was incurred on ornamental details, as distinct from its structure.[26]

Erecting a new Parish Church entailed far heavier financial obligations than originally expected. Demolition and site preparation alone totalled £2461. When the new cost (£19,600) was announced in November 1839, a further subscription was required. Information about costs of churches built in England by the first Parliamentary Grant enabled relative costs to be compared. In Leeds the grant had already provided three imposing churches, Christ Church, St Mary's and St Mark's, at an average cost of £10,300. Each seated about 1250 people. Against these standards the estimate for St Peter's to accommodate 2450 must have seemed not unreasonable. Additionally, comparative costs were available for Parliamentary churches, with broadly equivalent accommodation, in populous urban places elsewhere: St Thomas's, Birmingham (2050, £14,263); St George's, Leicester (1800, £16,130); St George's, Sheffield (2030, £15,181); Holy Trinity, St Marylebone (2000, £24,709); All Souls, St Marylebone (1760, £19,612). By now Leeds was one of a new category of English provincial cities with populations of 100,000 or more, only exceeded by Manchester, Birmingham, and Liverpool. For the new Parish Church of the undoubted 'metropolis' of the West Riding; the revised cost information would not seem out of line.[27]

The splendid exterior in place by 1839 induced a general wish for the committee to order many embellishments: superior materials, expensive carving, structural additions. The result was magnificent at consecration in 1841, but the cost had reached £26,000, and the committee's debt £6000. Because of disputed quantity measurements between architect and contractors, final agreement was delayed until 1844, with the settled cost fixed at £29,770, and the contractors' case, it appears, largely conceded. Of the £5165 debt then outstanding, £3495 was owed to the masons; £370 to Chantrell, the balance of his 5 per cent fee; the remainder variously to seven contractors. Thus the final cost of rebuilt St Peter's was almost five times the cost of the alterations originally envisaged, but the parish now possessed an impressive

[26.] Connell and Ward, pp. 148–50; Morris, pp. 37, 64–67, 79–84, 91; Taylor, pp. 411–15.
[27.] *LI*, 30 Nov. 1839, 31 Aug. 1844; Morris p. 25; Port, pp. 132–39.

new church. The urge for magnificence and the spirit of emulation played their part. In 1839 one speaker provided a more graceful and equally valid explanation. It was the present generation acknowledging a communal debt to their ancestors by creating a worthy structure for future ages.[28]

Response to the Five Subscriptions, 1837–47

The parishioners' meeting with the Vicar on 8 November 1837 followed the procedures customary for charitable appeals in early Victorian Leeds described by Morris. The resolutions and committee members' names were published locally, as evidence of their authority, probity, and public standing. Names and amounts of all subscriptions or donations were then regularly published, acting as acknowledgments, and perhaps spurring others to contribute similarly, for such details were seen as indicators of social and financial status. Preliminary canvassing of potential large donors enabled £2400 to be announced during the parishioners' meeting, before the subscription for £6300 had even publicly opened. With over £6000 promised by 25 November the subscription's target was assured.[29]

Nine acknowledgment lists were published for the original subscription, the first containing most of the large contributions. Its total of £3709 came from 104 subscribers, mainly of £20 and upwards. Most were well-known in public activities, and from the upper strata of the middle classes. Even so, individual amounts were lower than in the Church Extension scheme of 1836. There were twenty major subscribers of £50 or more on both lists. In 1837 they subscribed less than half of their 1836 promises (£1345 against £2950); nineteen of those major subscriptions being from 50 per cent to 70 per cent less. In 1837 Hook himself started the list with £200. Perhaps from courtesy none of the wealthy laymen following put down more, though Benjamin Gott and Christopher Beckett equalled it. A valid explanation for some subscribers would be the bad trading conditions of 1837. Of local economic indicators selected by Morris, poor relief was up by one-quarter; Marshalls' profits were three-tenths of 1836; and Jowitts the wool staplers made a resounding loss (£6252). In 1837 the middle classes had clearly less to spare. Further, the instalment dates for the two schemes overlapped awkwardly in the first half of 1838.

28. WYASL, LPC41/5, Cttee acct book, enc., 'Rebuilding of Leeds Parish Church', Subscribers' meeting, 25 Oct. 1841 (printed), enc., MS Abstract of Accounts, audited 28 Aug. 1844, LPC41/8, Cttee rough minute book II, 2, 26 Sept., 21 Oct. 1841; *LI*, 30 Nov. 1839, 30 Oct. 1841.
29. WYASL, LPC41/5, Cttee acct book, enc., Parishioners' meeting, 8 Nov. 1837 (printed), enc., first subscription, lists 1, 2, 3; *LI,* 11, 18, 25 Nov. 1837; *LM*, 11 Nov. 1837; Morris, pp. 217–18.

Smaller amounts, usually appeared on later lists, for Hook often indicated sacrificial giving. One of 12*s* in a package asking the Vicar to 'except this trifel [*sic*]' was duly acknowledged, spelling unchanged. He never forgot the 'pence from the poor', totalling £300, collected weekly on 'begging-cards' by ladies often themselves of limited means. Individual workers at Tory-owned firms subscribed, probably voluntarily, since their numbers were small in relation to the totals employed: Cawoods (15, £3 4*s*. 6*d*.); Hives and Atkinson (74, £6); B. Russell, builder (27 £4 4*s*. 6*d*.). On the later lists many subscribers entered for one or two pounds. In practical terms these sums would never have built the Parish Church, yet Hook cited these donors as proportionately more generous than the rich. He also commended highly the subscribers of moderate means, who gave their five pounds cheerfully, yet felt the loss more than those subscribing hundreds. Out of £7365 promised for the first subscription, £7276 was received. Given the ills and accidents of life, the pledges were honourably fulfilled.[30]

With £7000 expended by autumn 1839, a second subscription of £9000 was required to complete the rebuilding. The revised cost was £19,600, but further funds of £3700 were expected from other sources. Trade was still poor. Although gentlemen crowded round the subscription table when the list opened on 27 November, only £5490 was eventually collected. By July 1840 matters were critical. Beckett and Co. placed £3000 at the committee's disposal against six promissory notes of £500, due in twelve months' time, from H. Hall, R. Bramley, W. Gott, J. R. Atkinson, J. M. Tennant (all trustees), and W. M. Maude. Work therefore continued. Keen competition for fifty-four new gallery pews, auctioned on 26 April 1841, realized £3649, including the auctioneer's fee (£91) presented to the building fund. Becketts' advance was accordingly repaid on 18 May, plus £78 2*s*. 5*d*. charges.[31]

At the consecration on 2 September 1841 it became known that St Peter's would be opening in debt, caused by the embellishments authorized in 1839. Subscribers were subsequently told on 25 October that these had been carried out to meet the general wish that St Peter's should rank among the most beautiful parish churches in England. With no dissentients the meeting voted a third subscription of £6000 to pay the outstanding accounts. Held open eleven months beyond the final instalment date, it closed in September 1843, at a disappointing £3433. Grants from the Incorporated and the Ripon

---

30. WYASL, LPC41/5, Cttee acct book, enc., Parishioners' meeting of 8 Nov. 1837, enc., first subscription list, list 1, enc., 'Rebuilding of Leeds Parish Church', Subscriber's meeting, 25 Oct. 1841 (printed), LPC41/6, Cttee minute book, pp. 5–10, first subscription lists 1–9; *LI*, 27 Feb. 1836, 31 Aug. 1844; Hook, *Duty and Progress*, p. 20; *LPB, 1834*; Morris, pp. 80–81.

31. WYASL, LPC25, Vicarage Book, MS list, 26 Apr. 1841 (54 purchasers), LPC41/5, Cttee acct book, fols 42, 50, enc., Subscribers' meeting of 25 Oct. 1841 (printed), enc., MS Abstract of Accounts, audited 28 Aug. 1844, LPC41/10, Cttee bank book (Becketts), 1839–45; *LI*, 30 Nov. 1839, 1 May 1841; *LM*, 1 May 1841.

Church Building Societies, along with excise duty refunds, provided a further £2275 by July 1844.[32] In August, however, long delayed finally agreed costings revealed debts of £5165. Once again a subscribers' meeting was held. On 28 August a severe Hook told those present that the rich among them had not pulled their weight in relation to their financial capacity. Unsurprisingly the tone of the meeting became subdued, but a fourth subscription was agreed. The first list showed £1586 promised, but the appeal did not thrive.

In 1845 the committee could not have met its obligations if a promissory note from an unnamed source had not enabled Beckett and Co. to advance £2200. "That a well-wisher would risk this amount stiffened the committee's resolve to clear the debts once and for all. Unlike its predecessors the fifth subscription circulated privately, and contained a proviso that if the sum of £5000 was not promised by 1 October 1845 all signatories were released individually from obligation. Hook headed the list once more. He had learned from experience: this time he put down (for him) the princely sum of £500. Three very wealthy laymen followed suit: C. Beckett; J. R. Atkinson; J. Gott. Altogether £5343 was promised, payable in quarterly instalments from 1 October 1845 to 1 April 1847. By safeguarding pledges, the 'release clause' elicited maximum response, but fortunate timing helped. Economic conditions in 1845 produced the best trade in Leeds since 1836: lowest poor relief, high profits for Marshalls and Jowitts. The subscription's quarterly receipts enabled debts to be gradually paid and funds set aside towards bank repayments. By 22 September 1847 the loan of £2300 (with fees) was discharged.[33] On 15 November Hook's payment of £80 cleared the remaining debt to Beckett's. He had initiated the project and seen it through to the end.

The Significance of Rebuilding Leeds Parish Church

In the nineteenth-century surge of Anglican church building, St Peter's, Leeds (1841), was one element among many of the Church's determination to improve its spiritual care of the people, especially in the increasingly populous districts of London, the Midlands and the North. It was part of a

---

32. WYASL, LPC41/5, Cttee acct book, enc., Report and resolutions of subscribers' meeting, 25 Oct. 1841, combined with subscription list, 29 Oct. 1841, enc., 'Rebuilding of Leeds Parish Church', 25 Oct. 1841 (printed), enc., MS Abstract of Accounts, audited 28 Aug. 1844, LPC41/10, Cttee bank book (Becketts), third Subscription, 1841–43; *LI*, 30 Oct. 1841; *LM*, 4 Sept., 30 Oct. 1841.

33. PH, fols 158–63, Hook to Pusey, 9 Aug. 1841; WYASL, LPC41/10, Cttee bank book (Beckets), 1845–51, 31 Dec. 1846, 22 Sept., 15 Nov. 1847, LPC41/11, Subscription Instalment Book, 1840–44, enc., Resolutions of meeting, 28 Aug. 1844, combined with subscription list (printed), LPC41/17, Circulars book, fifth subscription, MS list with actual signatures; *LI*, 31 Aug. 1844; Morris, pp. 80–81.

continuing process in which 479 new or rebuilt churches were consecrated during the quinquennium 1841–45. Even so, much depended on local initiatives by incumbents of varying churchmanship. During the 1830s the impulse in Leeds, for example, came from its High Church Vicar, much concerned with 'the beauty of holiness', but in Bradford and Huddersfield from Evangelical incumbents. At Leeds circumstances required an architect-designed new church. Bradford settled for a reconstruction, less impressive, of its south side. Huddersfield, different from either, decided upon what was literally a conservative re-creation, each part being taken down and rebuilt in turn, using the standing parts for guidance. All these projects occurred when medieval work was less well understood. Some decades later G. G. Scott 'restored' three of the West Riding's finest churches with greater awareness of possibilities. Nevertheless, St Peter's was memorable in its own right, its significance being heightened as the Parish Church of England's fifth city. Bishop G. W. Doane of New Jersey, the preacher at its consecration, regarded it as the model which best conveyed current thinking about church architecture and forms of service; and became their influential advocate in the United States. In Leeds itself the architect for the rebuilding of Mill Hill Unitarian Chapel (1848) adopted the proportions of St Peter's nave to chancel to his own smaller design. Within the Church of England Hook's new found use of chancels as places from which surpliced choirs could lead the singing gradually changed the conduct and ethos of parish worship into forms which lasted for more than a century. In 1847 it was not surprising that the *Ecclesiologist* praised the new St Peter's so highly.[34]

In the wider social and religious context, rebuilding Leeds Parish Church on the voluntary principle represented a realistic assessment that funds for church building would never again be voted by Parliament. Nevertheless, this spectacular Anglican application of their cherished principle delighted Leeds Dissenters, especially the Baineses of the influential *Leeds Mercury*. The entire cost of work and materials for St Peter's came from subscription funds, with an excise drawback, or remitted tax, of £575 paid on building materials, as the only 'state' element towards its cost. (This tax was payable by all on purchase, but remitted, subject to receipts, for work on Anglican churches alone.) At St Peter's consecration the *Leeds Mercury* expressed unalloyed pleasure at the achievement, charitably not voicing earlier strictures on the tax anomaly. For Churchpeople the completion of St Peter's acted as an

34. WYASL, RDBI, 'Archives of See of Ripon', p. 39, entry no. 27; Chadwick, I 213–14, 517–18; *Ecclesiologist*, VII (1847), 46, cited in Linstrum, p. 217; Gilbert, pp. 109–15, 130; Linstrum, pp.174–79, 214–17; Pevsner, pp. 122–23, 229–31, 271, 310–12, 418–20, 519–21; Stranks, p. 56.

encouragement to other parishes, and its imposing appearance and memorable services gained national renown.[35]

Between 1837 and 1847 the building committee learned at first hand the problems faced by Dissenters embarking on ambitious building projects — soaring costs and inadequate funds from subscriptions at critical stages. Only the first and last of the rebuilding subscriptions yielded the amounts requested; the second, third and fourth, being insufficient, made bank loans necessary on two occasions. Some expenses were unavoidable, such as the unsafe fabric making rebuilding inevitable. Other expenditure came through the euphoria induced in 1839 by the splendid appearance of the yet incomplete exterior. The embellishments and additions then ordered generated huge debts by 1841, whilst faulty cost estimates resulted in unanticipated further debts to contractors in 1844. The masons fared worst; the final measurements revealed £3495 owing, representing one-quarter of the ultimate entitlement. The private and unusual nature of the fifth subscription — to achieve £5000, or no individual liability — indicated a determination to end the repeated process. Including four contributions of £500 each, twenty-eight pledges represented £4405 of the £5343 obtained. The church as erected permitted only 1000 additional sittings, instead of 1200 intended, but the commitment of 700 extra for the poor was fully met, those for rent being reduced proportionately. The handsome church was indeed 'a standing sermon', where actions spoke louder than words. Better provision for the poor had prompted the alteration scheme. The reward was that from 1841 all these extra seats were consistently filled. In the rebuilding of St Peter's significance may be found at many levels of human behaviour.[36]

---

35. WYASL, LPC41/5, Cttee acct book, enc., MS Abstract of Accounts, audited 28 Aug. 1844; *LI*, 11 Nov. 1837; *LM*, 17 Dec. 1836, 11 Nov. 1837, 4 Sept., 1841; Wood, *Church Extension*, pp. 3, 6, 9.

36. WYASL, LPC41/5, Cttee acct book, enc., Committee Report to meeting, 25 Oct. 1841, enc., MS Abstract of Accounts, audited 28 Aug. 1844, LPC 41/17, Circulars book, fifth subscription, MS list of subscribers, RDS1/3 RDCBS Register, p. 22, RDS8/10, RDCBS, Third Report, 1842, p. 33; *LI*, 30 Nov. 1839, 30 Oct. 1841; Stephens, *Hook*, I, 382.

CHAPTER 7

Church Building and Parish Formation in Leeds, 1826–55

When W. R. W. Stephens claimed that in 1837 Hook found Leeds with one parish and fifteen churches, and left it with thirty-six churches and many parishes, his wording did less than justice to the efforts of many others, or to the influence of Peel's Act on church building and parish formation.[1] There were in fact three parishes and eighteen churches in Leeds at Hook's arrival.[2] To place the early Victorian contribution in perspective, the processes of church building and parish formation in Leeds are here discussed in a wider context: from 1826, when its first Parliamentary church was consecrated, to 1855, when the last church of Hook's incumbency was completed.[3]

The Need for More Churches in the Early Nineteenth Century

Between 1801 and 1811 the population of England and Wales increased by 14.3 per cent (8,892,536 to 10,164,256), whilst the number of churches (11,379 to 11,444) remained virtually static, because authorization to build churches for public (as opposed to private) worship involved great expense and sometimes an uncertain outcome. Yet needs were urgent. Population growth and increasing urbanization had resulted in crowded and populous urban parishes, especially in London, the Midlands, and Lancashire and Yorkshire.[4] In 1818, for an estimated total of 43,500 inhabitants of Leeds township, there were 4775 church seats available. Of this number the Parish Church and St John's between them provided about 1350 free seats for the poor, mainly at the Parish Church. Pew rents in the other churches in the township. Holy Trinity, St Paul's, and St James's, effectively excluded the poor.[5] The Dissenters' record in Leeds township was more impressive. By 1817 evangelical Dissenters possessed fourteen chapels containing 9200 seats. Unitarians, Arians, and Quakers in aggregate possessed a further 2310. With

1. Stephens, *Hook*, II, 392.
2. Wood, *Church Extension*, pp. 5–6, 15 (n.), 29.
3. Mayhall, pp. 299, 320, 671–72; Stephens, *Hook*, II, 361; Wood, *Church Extension*, pp. 5–6, 11–15, 29–30.
4. *Collier's Encyclopedia* (1967), IX, 183; Gilbert, pp. 28, 110–12; Port, pp. 5–6.
5. WYASL, RDS1/3, RDCBS, Register, p. 22; Morgan, p. 52; *Parochial System*, pp. 16, 22; 'Report 1839', pp. 415–16; Wood, *Church Extension*, p. 3.

more than twice the Anglican total of sittings. Dissenters may have equalled or exceeded Anglican provision for the poor.[6]

Churchpeople nationally recognized the need for new churches by launching the Church Building Society in February 1818, largely through the efforts of the 'Hackney Phalanx' of High Church clerics and laymen. In 1828 it became the Incorporated Church Building Society (ICBS), and as such made grants to new churches in Leeds.[7]

Need for statutory revision regarding church building and parish formation surfaced in 1810, when Lord Harrowby detailed in Parliament the antiquated procedures hampering Church extension. He suggested a Commission, but nothing ensued.[8] Five years later the Hackney Phalanx petitioned on the subject. In 1816, when writing to an influential peer, the Archbishop of Canterbury's chaplain contrasted Dissenting freedom with the building hurdles facing Anglicans.[9] Liverpool's Government responded in 1818 with an innovation. Its Church Building Act established a Church Building Commission (CBC), with powers to divide parishes, and one million pounds for building purposes.[10] The process of modernizing the medieval parish system began, accompanied by the gradual erosion of the authority of the 'mother church' incumbents.[11] In 1824 Parliament granted another £500,000 for Church extension; and from 1831 church building by subscription became more attractive when it extended rights of presentation.[12] Peel's Spiritual Care of Populous Parishes Act (1843) found an ingenious way of promoting Church extension without giving Dissenters cause for legitimate complaint. It used Church funds rather than the State's. The Ecclesiastical Commission was authorized to borrow from Queen Anne's Bounty to pay stipends to clergy, ahead of church erection, enabling them to gather congregations and raise building subscriptions. Many Leeds Churches benefited subsequently.[13]

Leeds Churches Erected at National Cost, 1826–32

Parishes exceeding four thousand inhabitants, with churchroom for less than one-fourth, qualified for a Parliamentary Grant, as did those where more than

---

[6.] *LM*, 4 Mar. 1837, 9 June 1938; 'Report 1839', 415–16; Grady, *Georgian Buildings*, p. 162–65.

[7.] G. F. A. Best, *Temporal Pillars: Queens Anne's Bounty, the Ecclesiastical Commissioners and the Church of England* (Cambridge, 1964), p. 196; Cornish, I, 77–79; G. Kitson Clarke, *Churchmen and the Condition of England 1832–1885* (1973), p. 47; Port, pp. 2–4, 7–14, 108–09; Varley, pp. 84–85; E. L. Woodward, *The Age of Reform, 1815–1870* (Oxford, 1938), p. 506.

[8.] Port, pp. 5–7.

[9.] Port, pp. 7–9, 12.

[10.] Best, p. 195; Cornish, I, pp. 79–81; Port, pp. 14–28; Varley, pp. 81–88.

[11.] BL, Gladstone Papers, MS 44, 213, fols 51–56, Hook to Gladstone, 22 Jan. 1844; Port, p. 191; Stephens, *Hook*, II, 225–28.

[12.] Port, pp. 93–94, 107–08.

[13.] Best, pp. 357–59, 547–48 (App. VII A).

TABLE 7.1

Leeds Churches Built by the First and Second Parliamentary Grants

Church	Parly Grant	Cost £	Aid £	Sittings Rented	Free Pews	Total Sittings
Christ Church (1826)	First	10,555	10,555	449	880	1329
St Mark's (1826)	First	9637	9637	400	800	1200
St Mary's (1827)	First	10,809	11,209	406	801	1207
St Stephen's (1829)	Second	3206	3206	500	500	1000
St Matthew's (1832)	Second	3735	3349	606	596	1202
	Total	37,942	37,776	2361	3577	5938

a thousand lived above four miles from a church.[14] With its main township in 1818 containing 43,500 inhabitants and churchroom for 4775, Leeds decidedly qualified for assistance. Of sixteen West Riding church sites subsequently identified by the Archbishop of York, three were in rapidly growing localities of Leeds township.[15] In this main township the first Parliamentary Grant paid for three churches erected in working-class areas on sites earlier selected: Christ Church (1826) in the south; St Mark's, Woodhouse (1826), in the north; and St Mary's, Quarry Hill (1827), in the east. All three churches were built at high cost when the CBC was still conspicuously extravagant. The second Parliamentary Grant later provided another two, built more economically in Headingley and Holbeck out-townships, reflecting the CBC's more cost-conscious approach. In Headingley township, St Stephen's, Kirkstall (1829) served an industrial village several miles from central Leeds; St Matthew's, Holbeck (1832) was built for a larger population and replaced a smaller chapel. Designed by architects in Yorkshire, all five Parliamentary churches were capacious, with one thousand to 1329 sittings.[16]

These five Leeds churches built at national cost formed part of a wider picture (Table 7.1).[17] Altogether the 'million' Parliamentary Grant provided the country with ninety-seven churches, of which the metropolis and the industrial areas received seventy-four: London (thirty-three); Lancashire (nineteen); West Riding of Yorkshire (sixteen); West Midlands (six). Within the West Riding their distribution was as follows: Leeds (three); Sheffield

[14.] Port, p. 24.
[15.] Beresford, *East End, West End*, p. 540, map, 1815; A. Elton and B. Harrison ed. *Leeds in Maps* (Leeds, 1989), pp. 10–14, maps, 1770, 1815, 1831; Morgan, p. 52; Port, pp. 138–39; Wood, *Church Extension*, pp. 5, 29.
[16.] Grady, *Georgian Buildings*, pp. 132, 165; Mayhall, pp. 299–300, 320, 338, 346–47; Port, pp. 24–25, 81–84, 86, 95–98, 138–39, 168–69, Plates Vc, Vd, VIIb; Webster, *Chantrell*, note 12, pp. 42–43, 46, 54–55, 62, 64, 66, 85, 89; Wood, *Church Extension*, p. 29.
[17.] Port, pp. 138–39, 168–69.

(three); individual woollen textile towns (eight); individual south Yorkshire towns (two).[18] The 'half-million' second Parliamentary Grant was spread much more thinly over 515 churches nationally. Although eighty-three in the West Riding were assisted by the CBC. only eighteen were provided at little or no local cost, including the two Leeds churches mentioned above. The other sixty-five of which each received a few hundred pounds towards their building funds, included nine of the subscription churches built in Leeds between 1843 and 1855.[19]

Built by Subscription, 1836–55

When Longley arrived at Ripon in 1836, grave disparities existed in church provision between the industrial archdeaconry of Craven, with 220 churches for 780,000 people, and the rural archdeaconry of Richmond, containing 110 churches for 120,000 inhabitants. For Anglicans, Parliamentary Reform meant that further churches at national cost were unlikely. Hence the Bishops of Lichfield, Chester, Winchester and Durham founded diocesan church building societies. At the invitation of prominent laymen, including five peers, Longley publicly launched the Ripon Diocesan Church Building Society (RDCBS) in 1838. Its objects were to encourage church and parsonage building by financial aid and technical information. From 1836 to 1855 sixteen Leeds churches were built by public subscription: two being started before the RDCBS was founded, or Hook arrived. The remaining fourteen commenced subsequently were all aided by the RDCBS, but only nine of these received assistance also from the second Parliamentary Grant.[20]

   In effect, from 1838 the RDCBS on behalf of the Bishop coordinated what had previously been a piecemeal church building effort by individual parishes. The Society's central and district organizations complemented each other. The Central Committee decided the size of individual grants in the light of funds available. The seventeen District Committees, grouped in parishes, made recommendations from detailed local knowledge. There was a judicious mingling of Central and District Committee membership. Sinclair of St George's, Leeds, was General Secretary for Craven and contact point for its eight District Committees. Hook and Christopher Beckett were Chairman and Treasurer respectively of the Leeds District Committee (RDCBSLD), and members of the Central Committee. Beckett's brother, William, succeeded to both positions in 1847. Just as District Committees were

---

[18.] Port, pp. 33–34, 132–39.
[19.] Port, pp. 95–98, 121–22, 140–73.
[20.] WYASL, LPC116, RDCBS, Leeds District, minute book, 5 Sept. 1838, RDB18, Longley's *Visitation Charge, 1838*, pp. 11, 13; *LI*, 23 Dec. 1837, 11 Aug., 1, 8 Sept. 1838; *LM*, 11 Aug., 8 Sept. 1838; Stephenson, p. 112; Varley, p. 120.

TABLE 7.2
Subscription Churches, unaided

Church	Cost £	Sittings Rented Pews	Free Pews	Total Sittings
Headingley Chapel (1838)	2582	435	130	565
St George's (1838)	11,000*	1046	609	1655

*Includes sums for gallery extensions at existing churches and towards additional clergy.

involved with initial consideration of applications for grants, so they were involved in their final stages. Grants were not disbursed until church consecration, and certificates of satisfactory completion had been received from the architect, along with separate confirmatory joint certificates from the incumbent, the District Chairman, and the District Secretary.[21]

Unaided Subscription Churches

Two subscription schemes in 1836 gave tangible evidence of reviving Church spirit in Leeds. For rebuilding Headingley Chapel £2582 was raised. Twenty wealthy subscribers provided £1691, including £200 from Lord Cardigan, whilst the comfortably-placed supplied the remainder. Sittings for the chapel, reopened in 1838, increased from 207 to 565, with 130 now free. Within two years there was reportedly little room to spare.[22] The upper strata of local society were also well represented on the subscription of £11,000 obtained for building St George's and church alterations elsewhere, as discussed in Chapter 2 (Table 7.2).[23]

Subscription Churches, Aided by RDCBS

St Thomas's, Stanningley (1841), resulted from the initiative of Thomas Furbank, incumbent of Bramley, who desired to provide a 'decent church' for the poor working population some distance from the township. In May

21. WYASL, LPC116, RDCBSLD, minute book, 29 Oct. 1838 (memo) 5, 19 Nov. 1838, 18 Oct. 1847, 14 Nov. 1852, 28 Nov. 1853; RDS1/3, RDCBS, Register of church endowment deeds and certificates of work completed, 1841–1878, RDS8/10, RDCBS, *Laws and Regulations.* . . (Leeds, 1839), pp. 1–22.
22. WYASL, RDS8/10, RDCBS, First Report, 1840, pp. 72, 91; *LI*, 1, 22 Apr. 1837, 27 Jan., 3, 10 Feb. 1838; *LM*, 27 Jan., 10 Feb. 1838.
23. *LI*, 27 Feb. 1836, 10 Nov. 1838; Grady, *Georgian Buildings*, p. 167; Fenteman, p. 59; Mayhall, pp. 440–41; Morris, pp. 307–08, 318; Wood, *Church Extension*, pp. 6, 9, 29.

TABLE 7.3

Subscription Churches without Parliamentary Grant, aided by RDCBS

Church	Cost £	Aid £	Sittings Rented Pews	Free Pews	Total Sittings
St Thomas's, Stanningley (1841)	1700*	500	283	162	445
St Luke's (1841)	1500*	200	160	302	462
St Peter's (1841)	29,770	1000	790	1660	2450
St John's, Moor Allerton (1853)	1780	200	**	**	250
St Matthias's, Burley (1854)	3200	375	222	288	510

*Approximate.
**No details, but free or small rent.

1838 he called a district meeting, and offered a site from his glebe.[24] Even with £200 from John Farrer, important locally, and £100 from Lord Cardigan, the resulting subscription of £1200 was insufficient (Table 7.3).[25] Building started in 1839, after a bazaar under the patronage of the Countesses of Harewood, Mexborough, and Warwick realized £564.[26] The RDCBS insisted on £480 of its £500 grant being earmarked towards repair and endowment funds. Rented sittings at 3s. yearly similarly testified to Stanningley's impoverishment.[27] St Luke's, North Street (1841), in the crowded St Peter's district, was established by Hook to serve a 'poor and uninstructed population' of seven thousand inhabitants. For this project his senior curate in 1839 collected subscriptions in Oxford.[28] In 1840, with £700 raised of £1500 required, Hook laid the foundation stone 'in faith', on a site given from his

---

[24.] LI, 19, 26 May, 22 Dec. 1838, 3 Apr. 1841.

[25.] WYASL, RDS1/3, RDCBS, Register, p. 18, Minister's Certificate, RDS8/10, RDCBS, First Report, 1840, p. 25, Fourth Report, 1843, p. 29 (St Thomas's, Stanningley); RDS1/3, Register, p. 23, Minister's Certificate, RDS8/10, First Report, 1840, p. 25, Third Report, 1842, p. 33 (St Luke's); LPC41/5, Cttee acct bk, enc., MS Abstract of Accounts, audited 28 Aug. 1844; RDS1/3, Register, p. 22, Minister's Certificate, RDS8/10, Third Report, 1842, p. 34 (St Peter's); LI, 10 Nov. 1849 (St John's, Moor Allerton); RDS1/3, Register, p. 238; LI, 10 Nov. 1849 (St Matthias's, Burley).

[26.] WYASL, RDS8/10, RDCBS, First Report, 1840, pp. 25, 91, Fourth Report, 1843, p. 29; LI, 7, 14 Sept., 9 Nov. 1839; LM, 7 Sept. 1839.

[27.] WYASL, LPC116, RDCBSLD, 18 Mar. 1939, RDS1/3, RDCBS, Register, pp. 18, Minister's Certificate, 115 (Endowment Consent), RDS8/10, First Report, 1840, p. 25, Second Report, 1841, p. 27, Fourth Report, 1843, p. 29, Fifth Report, 1844, p. 29; LI, 30 Mar., 4 May 1839.

[28.] PH, fols 70–78, Hook to Pusey, 3 Apr. 1839; LI, 8 May 1841; Beresford, East End, West End, pp. 268, 322, 439; Grady, Georgian Buildings, p. 167; Fenteman, p. 61; Mayhall, p. 469; Parochial System, p. 18.

glebe.[29] Contributions came from Hook's friends at Oxford (£100) and Bristol (£41 10s.), but mostly from subscriptions (£355) under £20, and also from special collections. Nevertheless St Luke's opened heavily in debt.[30] As little income was expected from 3s. 9d. yearly sittings, the £200 RDCBS grant was thankfully received.[31]

Hook's ambitious new Parish Church was also hampered by insufficient funds during construction and debts after consecration, but the new building provided 700 more free seats for the poor and 300 more rented sittings.[32] Chapel Allerton's Evangelical incumbent, John Urquhart, built St John's, Moor Allerton (1853), with contributions from nearby gentry. Progress was slow. The project was conceived in 1845, and completed eight years later.[33] St Matthias's ecclesiastical district, Burley, was created in 1849 when Evangelical laypeople secured a £150 clergy stipend from a local Anglican trust. William Sturgeon, Evangelical curate of St George's, was then appointed. His diligence obtained a completed church by 1854.[34]

Subscription Churches, Aided by RDCBS and from the Second Parliamentary Grant

The CBC grants for Leeds churches consecrated from 1845 were insufficient for church erection, hence local decisions favouring less grandiose designs prevailed.[35] In these churches, although markedly smaller than the early Parliamentary churches, all seats were free.[36] St Andrew's (1845) was erected in mean streets near St George's, in memory of Mrs Helen Sinclair, who during life had worked there among the poor. Relatives and friends subscribed handsomely towards its cost of £4400.[37] St Philip's (1847) was procured for Leeds as the third church in St George's original district. Sinclair obtained a site free of cost from John Gott along with promises of endowment from the

29. PH, fols 103–16, Hook to Pusey, 9 June 1840; WYASL, RDS8/10, RDCBS, First Report, 1840, p. 25; *LI*, 6 June 1840; *LM*, 6 June 1840.
30. WYASL, RDS8/10, RDCBS, First Report, 1840, p. 91; *LI*, 13 June, 31 Oct. 1840, 15 May, 9 Oct. 1841.
31. WYASL, LPC116, RDCBSLD, 18 Mar. 1839, RDS1/3, RDCBS, Register, p. 23, Minister's Certificate, RDS8/10, RDCBS, First Report, 1840, p. 25, Third Report, 1842, p. 33; *LI*, 30 Mar. 1839.
32. WYASL, LPC41/5, MS Abstract of Accounts, audited 28 Aug. 1844, LPC41/10,
33. Cttee bank book (Becketts), 1845–51, 31 Dec. 1846, 22 Sept., 15 Nov. 1847, LPC116, RDCBSLD, 2 Oct. 1841, RDS8/10, RDCBS, Third Report, 1842, p. 34.
34. WYASL, LPC116, RDCBSLD, 22 Oct. 1849; *LI*, 13 Oct., 10 Nov. 1849; Wood, *Church Extension*, p. 30.
35. WYASL, LPC116, RDCBSLD, 22 Oct. 1849, RDS1/3, RDCBS, Register, p. 238, Minister's Certificate; *LI*, 10 Nov. 1849, 12 Jan. 1850.
36. Port, pp. 55, 101–02.
37. WYASL, RDS1/3, RDCBS, Register, pp. 91, 129, 186, 192, 220, 221, 229, 240, 242; Port, pp. 168–69.

TABLE 7.4

Subscription Churches aided by RDCBS and Second Parliamentary Grant

Church	Cost £	Soc. £	Parl. £	Sittings Rented Pews	Free Pews	Total Sittings
St Andrews (1845)	4400	500	300	–	745	745
St Philips (1847)	3371	450	300	–	587	587
All Saints (1850)	3166	500	300	–	756	756
St Matthew's, Little London (1851)	2851	500	200	–	700	700
St Jude's, Hunslet (1853)	2671	500	300	–	600	600
St John's, New Wortley (1853)	3457	500	350	–	700	700
St Michael's, Buslingthorpe' (1854)	2170	500	300	–	600	600
St Stephen's, Burmantofts (1854)	2685	500	200	–	605	605
St Barnabas's, Little Holbeck (1855)	1660	500	250	–	564	564

Ecclesiastical Commission and £950 from three Anglican organizations. In January 1845 Sinclair launched an appeal with £2000 still required. High regard for Sinclair himself attracted a ready response. The Peel District, one created out of an existing parish, was gazetted in September and the foundation ceremony occurred two months later.[38] See Table 7.4.[39] All Saints (1850) was intended to be a magnificent church costing £10,000, but the donor, D. H. Haigh, abandoned the project on seceding to Rome in 1847, two months after Hook had laid the foundation stone.[40] As the site was already secured, Hook expedited the creation and endowment of a Peel District. The Crown appointed an Evangelical, William Randall, in January

38. WYASL, LPC116, RDCBSLD, 21 Aug. 1843, RDS1/3, RDCBS, Register, p. 91, RDS8/10, RDCBS, Fifth Report, 1844, pp. 22, 70–71, Sixth Report, 1846, p. 31; Port, pp. 168–69.
39. WYASL, LPC116, RDCBSLD, 5 Oct. 1844, RDS1/3, RDCBS, Register, p. 129, RDS8/10, RDCBS, Sixth Report, 1846, pp. 21, 31, 68, Seventh Report, 1847, p. 23; LI, 2 Nov. 1844, 11 Jan. 1845; Port, pp. 168–69.
40. WYASL, RDS1/3, RDCBS, Register, p. 91, RDS8/10, RDCBS, Sixth Report, 1846, p. 31 (St Andrew's); RDS1/3, p. 129, RDS8/10, Sixth Report, 1846, p. 31 (St Philip's); RDS1/3, p. 186, LI, 11 Nov. 1848, 10 Nov. 1849 (All Saints); RDS1/3, p. 192, LI, 11 Nov. 1848 (St Matthew's, Little London); RDS1/3, p. 220, LI, 15 Nov. 1851 (St Jude's, Hunslet); RDS1/3, p. 221, LI, 15 Nov. 1851 (St John's, New Wortley); RDS1/3, p. 229, LI, 23 Nov. 1850 (St Michael's, Buslingthorpe); RDS1/3, p. 240, LI, 15 Nov. 1851 (St Stephen's, Burmantofts); LPC116, RDCBSLD, 14 Nov. 1852, RDS1/3, p. 242 (St Barnabas's, Little Holbeck); Port, pp. 168–69 (all churches named in this note).

1848. Shortly afterwards the energetic Randall launched a building subscription.[41] Though plain, 'the universal wonder' was that the resulting church could have been built for so small a sum.[42]

The following churches reflected the growth and spread of Leeds in all directions. Little London became a Peel District in 1846, with a vigorous Evangelical incumbent, Richard Wolfe, who commenced services in the existing National School.[43] For his building fund Wolfe enterprisingly obtained a gift of £20 from the Queen Dowager, and her patronage for a bazaar in 1848, which grossed £800.[44] A. C. Ridings, Wolfe's successor, accepted C. W. Burleigh's design for a church costing £2800. A further bazaar in 1850 increased the building fund to £2400, enabling work to start. Subsequently consecrated as St Matthew's (1851), it was described by the *Ecclesiologist* as 'handsome and dignified'.[45] As Hunslet's built-up area spread ever nearer to Leeds, St Jude's (1853) was erected for the growing population.[46] Buslingthorpe, also expanding, received St Michael's (1854), with parts of Leeds and Woodhouse for its parish.[47] The other three churches came mainly from the parish of Leeds. St John's, New Wortley (1853)[48] and St Stephen's, Burmantofts (1854), were both designed by the Leeds architect Jeremiah Dobson.[49] St Barnabas's, Little Holbeck (1855), was smaller than originally intended, because of the district's poverty. The RDCBS therefore held unchanged the £500 grant awarded for the design first submitted.[50]

[41.] PH, fols 325–43, Hook to Pusey, 21 Mar. 1846, fols 391–97, Hook to Pusey, 20 Nov. 1846; *LI*, 17, 24, 31 Oct. 1846, 9 Jan. 1847; *LM*, 24, 31 Oct. 1846, 2 Jan. 1847.

[42.] *E(cclesiastical)C(omission) Ratified Schemes* (1848), VI, 55; *LI*, 7 Oct. 1848. *LM*, 4 Sept. 1847, 22 Jan. 1848.

[43.] WYASL, LPC116, RDCBSLD, 30 Oct. 1848, 22 Oct. 1849, RDS1/3, RDCBS, Register, p. 186; *LI*, 11 Nov. 1848, 10 Nov. 1849, 2, 9 Nov. 1850; *LM*, 9 Nov. 1850.

[44.] *EC Ratified Schemes* (1847), V, 91; *LI*, 15, 22 Aug., 3 Oct. 1846; *LM*, 22 Aug. 1846.

[45.] *LI*, 17 Oct. 1846, 4 Sept. 1847, 22, 29 Apr. 1848; *LM*, 29 Apr. 1848.

[46.] WYASL, LPC116, RDCBSLD, 30 Oct. 1848, RDS1/3, RDCBS, Register, p. 192; *Ecclesiologist,* cited in *LI*, 13 July 1850; *LI*, 8 July, 4, 11 Nov. 1848, 18 May, 6, 13 July 1850, 9, 16 Aug. 1851; *LM*, 13 July 1850, 9 Aug. 1851.

[47.] WYASL, LPC116, RDCBSLD, 12 Nov. 1851, 18 Oct. 1852, RDS1/3, RDCBS, Register, p. 220, *EC Ratified Schemes* (1852), VII, 376; *LI*, 6 Nov. 1847, 15 Nov. 1851.

[48.] WYASL, LPC116, RDCBSLD, 18 Oct. 1852, RDS1/3, RDCBS, Register, p. 229; *EC Ratified Schemes* (1852), VII, 222; *LI*, 19 Jan., 23 Nov. 1850.

[49.] WYASL, LPC116, RDCBSLD, 12 Nov. 1851, RDS1/3, RDCBS, Register, p. 221, *EC Ratified Schemes* (1852), VII, 376; *LI*, 15 Nov. 1851, Linstrum, p. 376; Port, p. 180.

[50.] WYASL, LPC116, RDCBSLD, 12 Sept., 5 Nov. 1851, RDS1/3, RDS1/3, RDCBS, Register, p. 240; *EC Ratified Schemes* (1852), VII, 376; *LI*, 15 Nov. 1851; Linstrum, p. 376; Port, p. 180.

Churches Built by Private Donors, 1845–52

In 1839 Hook approached Newman and Pusey about Oxford friends building a church in Leeds. Newman regretfully declined; Pusey contingently assented.[51] Four months later, Hook accepted an anonymous offer, via Pusey, to build a church.[52] Pusey's identity as donor was early conjectured, and posthumously confirmed.[53] In 1842 the foundation stone of 'Holy Cross' was laid on Cavalier Hill, a district of poverty and vice.[54] During construction Bishop Longley objected on doctrinal grounds to certain architectural features and even the church's name. Pusey renamed the church St Saviour's and conceded most points, but stood firm on retaining the inscription requesting prayers for the founder.[55]

Newman's secession in 1845 confirmed Hook's growing disquiet over 'Romanising' Tractarianism, and the repercussions delayed St Saviour's consecration slightly.[56] No public disorder or demonstration marked the consecration on 28 October 1845. When congratulating Pusey later on the arrangements, however, Hook still confessed to distress and shaken nerves,[57] because he dreaded reactions to Tractarian extremists injuring Church principles in Leeds.[58] One reaction indeed had already occurred. Leeds Evangelical clergy declined to attend the consecration, possibly prompting Hook to initiate a declaration of Anglican loyalty, signed by many clergy attending, including Pusey.[59] Contemporaries regarded St Saviour's, designed by J. M. Derick, as built in 'the purest Gothic style'. Pusey provided many

51. WYASL, LPC116, RDCBSLD, 18 Oct., 14 Nov. 1852, RDS1/3, RDCBS, Register, p. 242; *EC Ratified Schemes* (1852), VII, 376.
52. HA, S4, Newman to Hook, 12 Apr. 1839, Pusey to Hook, 29 Apr. 1839; PH, fols 70–78, Hook to Pusey, 3 Apr. 1839; Stephens, *Hook*, II, 12; Yates, *St Saviour's*, p. 3.
53. PH, fols 81–91, Hook to Pusey, 16 Aug. 1839; Savage and Tyne, pp. 2–3; Yates, *St Saviour's*, pp. 2–3.
54. *Bristol Mercury*, cited in *LI*, 21 Oct. 1843; *LI*, 4 Nov. 1843; Fenteman, p. 62.
55. PH, fols 192–95, Hook to Pusey, 25 Feb. 1842; *LI*, 12 Mar., 17 Sept. 1842; *LM*, 17 Sept. 1842; Savage and Tyne, pp. 3–5; Stephens, *Hook*, II, 190–92; Yates; *St Saviour's*, pp. 3–4.
56. *LM*, 25 Oct. 1845; W. H. B. Proby, *Annals of the 'Low Church' Party in England down to the Death of Archbishop Tait*, 2 vols (1888), I, 483–84; Savage and Tyne, pp. 7–8, 10; Stephens, *Hook*, II, 192; Yates, *Leeds High Church*, p. 28; Yates, *St Saviour's*, p. 4.
57. PH, fols 219–26, 20 Nov. 1843, fols 231–34, 29 May 1844, fols 279–81, 8 Sept. 1845, fols 282–85, 22 Sept. 1845, fols 293–97, 15 Oct. 1845 (all Hook to Pusey); *LI*, 18 Oct. 1845; *LM*, 18 Oct. 1845; Chadwick, I, 211; Stephens, *Hook*, II, 193; Yates, *St Saviour's*, p. 5.
58. PH, fols 219–26, Hook to Pusey, 20 Nov. 1843, fols 318–22, Hook to Pusey, 11 Nov. 1845; *LI*, 1 Nov. 1845; *LM*, 1 Nov. 1845; Yates, *St Saviour's*, p. 5.
59. PH, fols 163–73, 24 Sept. 1841, fols 174–76, 11 Oct. 1841, fols 182–91, 31 Jan. 1842, fols 212–13, 28 July 1843, 219–26, 20 Nov. 1843, fols 227–229, 25 Nov. 1843, fols 237–39, 15 Oct. 1844, fols 240–46, 23 Nov. 1844, fols 247–49, 23 Dec. 1844, fols 282–85, 22 Sept. 1845, fols 286–92, 6 Oct. 1845, fols 293–97, 15 Oct. 1845, fols 298–302, 17 Oct. 1845, fols 303–10, 20 Oct. 1845 (all Hook to Pusey).

details, and Pugin's influence was later detected.[60] At consecration the church presented 'a rather naked appearance', with pinnacles and spire missing, charitably ascribed to lack of funds. The interior reflected Tractarian tastes for medievalism: candles for illumination; nave and chancel both narrow; lockable chancel screen. The church cost £9500, including the glass which itself cost £1656. All 750 seats were free.[61]

The impulse for St Thomas's, Leylands, came from £2500 given anonymously in 1846, supplemented by £1500 raised elsewhere. Such support was needed for a church in this impoverished district, with an estimated cost of £4900. Two Parish Church curates gradually established a congregation and Sunday schools. At the foundation ceremony in 1849, M. J. Rhodes, by then known as the principal donor, declared that his contribution originated through earlier family association with the Leylands and his own respect for Hook's endeavours.[62] Containing 752 seats, all free, St Thomas's was consecrated in 1852, with only its nave completed. The cost exceeded the estimate. Hook himself raised £2000 for heating, lighting, repairs and endowment. William Butterfield, the architect, built the church of brick, with his characteristic polychrome-patterned walls. The design found little favour with the *Leeds Intelligencer*, nor any serious imitators in West Yorkshire.[63]

Holy Trinity, Meanwood (1849), was founded by Mary and Elizabeth Beckett to fulfil a cherished desire of their brother Christopher. Within eight months of his death in 1847 they obtained and endowed a Peel District, accepted the patronage, and appointed an incumbent.[64] The foundation stone was laid in 1848, on land given by the founders' late brother, Sir John Beckett Bt. Generous standards prevailed throughout, from the fine Meanwood stone used for the building, to the separate funds established for stipend, repairs, and maintenance of Christopher's parochial schools. When completed, the church contained 400 seats, all free. The disclosed cost was £4300, but was known to be much higher.[65]

The endeavours of Marshalls, flaxspinners, for their employees' welfare culminated in St John's, Little Holbeck (1850). In May 1847, with schools and

[60] PH, fols 313–17, Hook to Pusey, 31 Oct. 1845; *Church and State Gazette*, cited in *LM*, 13 Dec. 1845; *LM*, 25 Oct., 1 Nov. 1845; Pollen, pp. 39–40; Stephens, *Hook*, II, 192–93.
[61] *Bristol Mercury*, cited in *LI*, 21 Oct. 1843; Savage and Tyne, p. 4, illustration facing p. 24; Linstrum, pp. 219–20.
[62] *LI*, 1 Nov. 1845; *LM*, 1 Nov. 1845; Fenteman, p. 62; Savage and Tyne, p. 8.
[63] WYASL, LPC116, RDCBSLD, 7 Oct. 1846; *LI*, 17, 24 Oct. 1846, 6 Oct. 1849; *LM*, 29 Sept. 1849.
[64] WYASL, LPC116, RDCBSLD, 7 Oct. 1846, 1, 22 Oct. 1849, 28 Oct. 1850, RDS1/3, RDCBS, Register, p. 202; *LI*, 17 Oct. 1846, 6 Oct., 10 Nov. 1849, 23 Nov. 1850, 1 Nov. 1851, 31 Jan., 7 Feb. 1852; *LM*, 29 Sept. 1849, 3 May 1851; Fenteman, p. 63; Linstrum, p. 227.
[65] *EC Ratified Schemes* (1848), VI, 36; *LI*, 27 Mar., 4 Sept., 6, 13 Nov. 1847; *LM*, 4 Sept., 20 Nov. 1847; Taylor, pp. 418–22.

a clergyman already provided, their payment of £3000 for an endowment, and £4000 towards church construction enabled a Peel District to be created. At the foundation ceremony the following November, Bishop Longley publicly commended J. G. and H. C. Marshall for their responsible use of wealth.[66] The London architect George Gilbert Scott designed the church in the plain lancet style preferred by the founders. The chaste and dignified exterior complemented the spacious effect of the interior, where slender clustered columns supported a stone-vaulted roof. Oaken pews provided 600 seats, all free. A minister's house, glebe and repair fund completed Marshalls' gift.[67]

Legislation and Church Building, 1818–55

From 1818 legislation gradually adapted the Church to nineteenth-century conditions. Although the Church Building Act (1818) provided the CBC with funds for building churches, their record was disappointing. Only 219 churches were built by 1837, and sixty more authorized. The greatest benefit of this Act was in simplifying the procedures for parish division, which greatly stimulated Anglican voluntary church building. Peel's Act (1843), by paying stipends to clergy for churches yet unbuilt, was even more effective. Between 1821 and 1861, when these statutes were largely used, the total of churches nationally increased by 3173 to 14,731, fewer than 300 having been provided by the CBC, constituting an essentially voluntary church-building effort unparalleled since the Reformation.[68]

Church building in Leeds typified the national pattern. Twenty-five churches, including three replacements, were consecrated between 1826 and 1855, all reflecting the spiritual needs of rapidly growing districts. At insignificant local cost, two parliamentary grants paid for five churches erected between 1826 and 1832. Dissenters and Catholics in the Reform Parliaments removed the possibility of further State bounty. Leeds Churchpeople turned reluctantly but ever more enthusiastically to self-help. From 1836 to 1855 twenty new churches were built. The sixteen public subscription churches exemplified the revived Anglican confidence and heightened awareness of the need to make the Gospel accessible to the poor. For subscription churches consecrated between 1845 and 1855 an important precipitating factor was the pre-existence of a stipend, usually but not invariably from the Church's central funds available through Peel's Act. Founders of the four donated churches similarly sited their churches in poor districts.[69]

66. *LI*, 27 May 1848, 13 Oct. 1849; *LM*, 13 Oct. 1849; Pevsner, p. 327.
67. *EC Ratified Schemes* (1847), V, 412; *LI*, 14 June 1845, 24 Oct. 1846, 6, 13 Nov. 1847; *LM*, 13 Nov. 1847; W. B. Stephens, 'Elementary Education and Literacy' in *Modern Leeds*, pp. 235–36.
68. *LI*, 2, 9 Nov. 1850; *LM*, 9 Nov. 1850; Fenteman, p. 64; Linstrum, pp. 226–27.
69. Gilbert, p. 28; Port, pp. xi, 113, 140–73.

Legislation for Parish Division from 1818 to Hook's Leeds Vicarage Act, 1844

Until the nineteenth century the formation of new parishes involved complicated legal procedures or private statutes, and was rare before 1818, when the Church Building Act provided general legislation, and appointed Church Building Commissioners to divide parishes through Orders-in-Council. Up to 1844 they created 450 ecclesiastical districts, consolidated chapelries and new parishes, and a further 450 until disbanded in 1856. However, brisk demand for Peel Districts from 1843 onwards meant that the Ecclesiastical Commissioners thereafter rapidly acquired the major role in parish division.[70]

Before Hook's arrival the notion surfaced that pastoral oversight of Leeds was beyond one clergyman's personal capacity. Early in his incumbency Hook assigned districts to incumbents of auxiliary churches. More extensive parochial reorganization was anonymously advocated in 1842. By the end of 1843 Hook had reached his own solution. He disliked Peel's Act because it rendered incumbents of mother churches helpless against erosion of their rights, but decided to work with it. He also intended to set an example by surrendering vicarial rights on churches remaining outside general legislation. For these churches he would obtain parishes by means of a private Act of Parliament.[71] Hook's proposals appeared in January 1844. Pastoral districts would be attached to the churches affected, and parochial status awarded as soon as they possessed both an entirely free nave and a parsonage. Vicarial rights would then be surrendered and patronage transferred to the Bishop.[72] For his parishioners' sake Hook was very willing to accept a contemplated one-third reduction of his £1200 income.[73] After prior discussion and agreement from the Bishop, the Ecclesiastical Commissioners, and the Leeds clergy, Hook's published proposals secured widespread Anglican approval.[74]

Local reactions were mixed. Where the *Leeds Intelligencer* perceived altruism, the *Leeds Mercury* discerned unworthy ambition. 'Dissent in Danger' again placarded the streets.[75] Some Vicarage trustees, especially Christopher Beckett, opposed vehemently. His attitude moderated only as Evangelical

[70.] WYASL, RDB1, Archive of the See of Ripon, pp. 39–43; *LI*, 16 Nov. 1850 (Report of RDCBS meeting, Richmond); Wood, *Church Extension*, pp. 29–30.
[71.] Port, pp. 5, 25, 35–37, 111, 119, 191.
[72.] BL, Gladstone Papers, MS 44, 213, fols 51–56, Hook to Gladstone, 22 Jan. 1844; *LI*, 4 Feb. 1837, 19 Feb. 1842; *Parochial System*, pp. 15–32; Stephens, *Hook*, II, 165, 168, 225–26; Wood, *Church Extension*, pp. 9–11.
[73.] W. F. Hook, *Letter to the Parishioners of Leeds* (Leeds, 1844); *LI*, 20, 27 Jan. 1844; *LM*, 27 Jan. 1844; Stephens, *Hook*, II, 164–77; Stranks, pp. 64–65; Wood, *Church Extension*, pp. 9–15.
[74.] Stephens, *Hook*, II, 165; Stranks, p. 64.
[75.] *LI*, 20 Jan. 1844; Stephens, *Hook*, II, 168–69, 174–75; Stranks, p. 65.

opposition cooled.[76] Dissenters left the field on hearing that Hook's measure would exclude Church rates on new parishes.[77] Towards Parliamentary costs Hook received £50 from Lord Eldon, £200 from John Hardy M. P. but nothing apparently from prominent Leeds Anglicans. The Becketts' opposition precluded Hook from raising funds in Leeds. In June 1844, however, Leeds clergy raised sufficient for Hook to meet otherwise ruinous £1400 Parliamentary costs.[78] Unexpectedly, William Beckett offered to introduce Hook's bill in Parliament. Gladstone, at Hook's request, gave powerful and spiritually informed support in the debate.[79] After a smooth Parliamentary passage the bill received Royal Assent in August.[80] Parliament, however, prevented four of the chapelry presentations from being surrendered.[81] Hook's Act was not unique, but became the best known Anglican example of public-spirited generosity devoid of self-seeking.[82]

The Process of Parish Division in Leeds, 1826–55

For parish division the Church Building Act of 1818 operated until 1843, when joined by Peel's Act, and in 1844 by Hook's Leeds Vicarage Act. Parish formation dates are shown in parentheses:

Church Building Act, 1818 (2)

St Mark's, Woodhouse (1826)   St Stephen's, Kirkstall (1829)[83]

Spiritual Care of Populous Parishes (Peel's) Act, 1843 (12)

St Andrew's (1845)   Holy Trinity, Meanwood (1849)
St Philip's (1847)   All Saints (1850)

---

76. BL, Gladstone Papers, MS 44, 213, fols 57–62, Hook to Gladstone, 25 Jan. 1844; *LI*, 20, 27 Jan., 27 Apr. 1844; *LM*, 27 Jan., 3 Feb., 6 Apr. 1844; Stephens, *Hook*, II, 176–77; Stranks, p. 65.
77. BL, Gladstone Papers, MS 44, 213, fols 65–66, Hook to Gladstone, 29 Jan. 1844; HA, K6/33, Hook to Mother, 17 Mar. 1844; Stephens, *Hook*, II, 175.
78. *LM*, 22 June 1844.
79. PH, fols 231–34, Hook to Pusey, 29 May 1844; HA, K6/34, Hook to Mother, 20 June 1844; *LI*, 17 Feb., 6 Apr., 25 May, 22 June 1844; *LM*, 6 Apr. 22 June 1844; Stephens, *Hook*, II, 174–76.
80. BL, Gladstone Papers, MS 44, 213, fols 69–70, Hook to Gladstone, 17 June 1844.
81. *LI*, 13, 20, 27 July, 3, 10, 17 Aug. 1844; Stephens, *Hook*, II, 176; Wood, *Church Extension*, pp. 13–15.
82. BL, Gladstone Papers, MS 44, 213, fols 69–70, Hook to Gladstone, 17 June 1844; *LI*, 22 June 1844; Wood, *Church Extension*, pp. 13–15.
83. *LI*, 6 Apr. 1844; Ward, p. 224.

St John's, Little Holbeck (1850)   St Michael's, Buslingthorpe (1854)
St Matthew's, Little London (1851)   St Stephen's, Burmantofts (1854)
St Jude's, Hunslet (1853)   St Matthias's, Burley (1854)
St John's, New Wortley (1853)   St Barnabas's, Little Holbeck (1855)[84]

Leeds Vicarage Act, 1844 (4)

St John's, Leeds (1845)   Hunslet (1847)
St Saviour's, Leeds (1846)   Farnley (1851)[85]

Co-operating incumbents like Hook were vital for implementing Peel's Act.[86] Many new English parishes were created by 1854 including: Bradford (five); Halifax (four); Sheffield (eight); Manchester (seven); Wolverhampton (fourteen).[87] J. H. Bromby of Hull, however, was notably obstructive.[88] New parishes meant new patrons, a necessity Hook accepted gracefully. In extreme contrast, H. M. Wagner, Puseyite Vicar of Brighton, retained his patronage by designating fourteen churches built between 1825 and 1867 as chapels-of-ease.[89] From 1836, as Leeds Anglicanism revived, mainly under Hook, clergy and parishioners mostly built their own district churches. Apart from St Saviour's, it proved more convenient to use Peel's Act as the means of obtaining parish status.[90]

---

84. Port, p. 25; Wood, *Church Extension*, p. 6.
85. *EC Ratified Schemes* (1845), II, 528 (St Andrew's); (1846), III, 357 (St Philip's); (1848), VI, 36 (Holy Trinity, Meanwood); (1848), VI, 55 (All Saints); (1847), V, 412 (St John's, Little Holbeck); (1847), V, 91 (St Matthew's, Little London); (1852), VII, 376 (St Jude's, Hunslet); (1852), VII, 376 (St John's, New Wortley); (1852), VII, 222 (St Michael's, Buslingthorpe); (1852), VII, 376 (St Stephen's, Burmantofts); (1852), VII, 222 (St Matthias's, Burley); (1852), VII, 376 (St Barnabas, Little Holbeck).
86. *EC Ratified Schemes* (1846), III, 415 (St John's); (1847), V, 117 (St Saviour's); (1848), VI, 45 (St Mary's, Hunslet); (1852), VII, 459 (St Michael's, Farnley).
87. Walton, pp. 216–17.
88. *EC Ratified Schemes, General Index to End 1854* (1855), p. 33 (Bradford); p. 101 (Halifax); p. 217 (Sheffield); p. 159 (Manchester); p. 259 (Wolverhampton). Endowment of parishes in Wolverhampton was made possible by Wolverhampton Church Act (1848), which diverted the possessions of the suppressed Deanery of the Royal Peculiar of Wolverhampton to the Ecclesiastical Commissioners. See J. D. P. Walters, 'The Impact of Anglican Evangelicalism on the Religious Life of Wolverhampton and its Locality in the period 1830–1870' (unpublished MPhil thesis, Council for National Academic Awards, 1984), pp. 39–42.
89. L. M. Brown, 'Modern Hull', in *Victoria County History: County of York, East Riding, I, The City of Kingston upon Hull*, ed. K. J. Allison (1969), 215–77.
90. Hennock, 'Anglo-Catholics', pp. 175–88, map facing p. 188.
91. Stephens, *Hook*, I, 371–72, II, 163–66, 392; Stranks, pp. 64–66; Wood, *Church Extension*, pp. 6–15.

CHAPTER 8

The Path to Mutual Respect: Evangelical and High Church in Leeds, 1836–51

Contemporaries rightly ascribed the beginning of the Anglican resurgence in early-Victorian Leeds to the local scheme for Church extension successfully launched in February 1836. Detailed newspaper reports of the inaugural meeting give the distinct impression of Churchpeople aware of the need to recover ground lost to Dissenters during the previous fifty years. We need to remember that Richard Fawcett, Vicar of Leeds since 1815, inherited a cure where his predecessor Peter Haddon (1788–1815) had done little to provide extra church accommodation for a local population which had at least doubled during his tenure. Fawcett was a moderate Evangelical, notable more for his willingness to co-operate with evangelical Dissenters than for powerful delivery of the evangelical message. He possessed neither the personality nor the desire to impose his views on others. Indeed, among Fawcett's subordinate clergy some were more fervently Evangelical than their Vicar, others less so, if at all. The most fiery Evangelical clergyman was undoubtedly Miles Jackson, resident curate-in-charge of St Paul's since 1814, and future pamphleteer in 1838 against the Oxford Tracts. The clergy present at the extension scheme meeting were mainly Evangelical. Amongst the laymen present or recorded as elected to the Building Committee of thirty-seven, many subsequently became Hook's supporters. With church principles and Tractarianism still unproclaimed in Leeds, the broad distinction among Churchpeople was between Evangelical and non-Evangelical. In this connection, whatever Fawcett's deficiencies in parish strategy, his personality was sufficiently irenic to induce a spirit of collaboration for the good of the Church. Hence in 1836 a Church extension scheme Evangelically inspired and led, secured the willing and harmonious cooperation of all shades of local Anglican opinion.[1]

Emerging High Church Preferences, January–March 1837

After Fawcett's rather unexpected death in January 1837, the vicarage trustees pursued their search for the best clergyman for Leeds at two levels. Publicly

---

[1.] *LI*, 13, 20, 27 Feb., 30 Mar., 4 June, 10, 17, 24 Dec. 1836, 28 Jan. 1837; *LM*, 27 Feb., 17, 24 Dec. 1836, 28 Jan., 4 Feb., 25 Mar. 1837; M. Jackson, *Oxford Tracts Unmasked* (1838).

they invited applications countrywide, gave candidates' names to the press, and met weekly to scrutinize the applications and testimonials received. Privately and confidentially they also approached candidates of their own choice. Negotiations on their behalf were conducted by the senior trustee, Henry Hall. From the outset the trustees seem to have excluded Evangelicals from consideration, not perhaps for lack of eminent Evangelicals in important cures, but rather from a desire for a more distinctly Anglican message than Fawcett, had been able, or cared, to deliver. Moving with speed, the trustees initially approached the energetic Samuel Wilberforce, already a distinguished High Churchman. Very attracted, he gave the proposal serious thought, but regretfully declined. Whether there was anyone else in mind is a moot point, but Henry Hall's son, Robert, also a trustee, recalled favourable reports of Hook. He satisfied himself of their veracity, and became Hook's enthusiastic advocate. Less than a month after Fawcett's death, Hook was asked whether he would serve if elected. Afterwards, the *Leeds Mercury* roundly asserted that Hook's election resulted from the machinations of the old Corporation's High Tories, the 'high and dry' Establishmentarians of an earlier day.[2]

An Evangelical memorial to the trustees against Hook's appointment had repercussions probably unexpected by its promoters. It crystallized attitudes amongst influential Churchpeople beyond the narrow circle of the trustee body, and resulted in a 'very respectably signed' counter-memorial, which in effect supported Hook's candidature. The signatories were leading parishioners likely to welcome Hook's arrival, and to respond to his personality and teaching, whatever their personal beliefs previously. The Evangelicals' memorial in fact elicited a previously unsuspected degree of support in Leeds for the 'new' style of High Churchmanship represented by Church principles.[3]

Leeds Clergy, 1837

After Hook arrived in Leeds the doctrine of Justification by Faith alone, so prized by Evangelicals, and enshrined in the Anglican Articles of Religion, never became a contentious issue, for Hook held it as firmly as the most convinced Evangelical. The strains in Leeds occurred over the different understandings of the nature of the Church and the authority of Scripture. Hook and High Churchmen maintained that the Scriptures were to be interpreted in the light of the tradition of the undivided Primitive Church. For Hook the Church of England was Catholic, with ministry transmitted in unbroken succession from Christ himself through the apostolic succession. For Evangelicals their Church's order was important, but they nevertheless

---

[2] *LI*, 11 Feb. 1837; *LM,* 4 Feb., 25 Mar. 1837; see Chapter 3.
[3] See Chapter 3.

considered that Scripture was its own supreme doctrinal authority, to which the Church itself must adhere, without looking to 'tradition' for interpretation.[4]

Because it was Hook's fixed policy to respect the autonomy and beliefs of his subordinate incumbents, irrespective of his own views, it is highly likely that the Leeds clergy were so informed, when he met them before the election. If so, it would account for their pleasure at the prospect of Hook's success, and the reality of their support after his arrival. Those incumbents who were decidedly Evangelical in 1837, William Williamson (Headingley), Joseph Wardle (Beeston), John Holroyd (Christ Church), and Edward Cookson (St Mary's, Quarry Hill), remained so. Only in rare instances, and on matters which touched Evangelicals' deepest convictions, did these perpetual curates withhold their support from Hook's actions. That said, it was still possible to demonstrate Evangelical affinity by actively participating in the regular meetings of various societies dear to Evangelicals. Among these were the Church Missionary Society and the London Society for Promoting Christianity among the Jews, both Anglican, and the undenominational Bible Society. From 1838, however, William Sinclair became Evangelicalism's most able advocate in Leeds. He confined himself to principles, avoided personalities, and won golden opinions amongst townspeople.[5] However, it was not the case with every Evangelical clergyman in Leeds. The Revd Miles Jackson, curate-in-charge of St Paul's, refused to join with his fellow clergy in their acceptance of Hook. He went to extraordinary lengths in fulminations from the pulpit, railing against Hook's holding the doctrine of baptismal regeneration, and describing his parish priest as 'a papist' and 'one of the Oxford Tract men'. By January 1838 these attacks were being reported in the *Leeds Mercury*. A month later Jackson apparently lost all control by denouncing Hook as 'the man of sin'. Although privately troubled, Hook maintained a dignified silence. Nevertheless when Jackson (under the pseudonym of 'Clericus') attacked Hook in a letter to the *Leeds Intelligencer*, Hook felt it would do harm if left unanswered. At Hook's request, Pusey supplied a learned refutation, which in turn led to a further outburst.[6] By July 1838, although Jackson must have realized that he was 'preaching his congregation away', he could not let his animosity rest, and severely criticized Hook's doctrines in his secretary's report to the Leeds CMS Association. He was publicly checked by the association president, Henry Hall, who ruled that his remarks were out of

---

[4.] Acts 20. 27 (AV); *LI*, 22 Apr. 1837, 20 Apr. 1844, 29 Mar. 1845; *LM*, 22 Apr. 1837.

[5.] BL, Gladstone Papers, MS 44, 213, fols 5–8, Hook to Gladstone, 26 Mar. 1838; PH, fols 103–16, Hook to Pusey, 18 Feb. 1840; *LI*, 10, 17 Nov. 1838; *LM*, 10, 17 Nov. 1838; Steele, p. 188; Taylor, pp. 454–55.

[6.] PH, fols 48–51, '2 in Advent 1837', fols 60–61, 3 Mar. 1838, fols 62–69, 24 Mar. 1838 (all Hook to Pusey); WYASL, LPC25, Vicarage Book, MS note on press cutting of meeting of 15 Mar. 1837, apparently from *LI*, 18 Mar. 1837; *LI*, 30 June 1838; *LM*, 13 Jan. 1838, 2 Nov. 1839.

line and must be expunged. When Jackson expostulated, the clergy present refused to support him. Diminishing influence combined with this public humiliation probably unsettled Jackson. He resigned the following year.[7]

Growing Crises, 1837–41

In the Bishop of Ripon the Evangelical clergy of Leeds had a powerful ally. Though a High Churchman, Longley was less exclusive than Hook. Viewing Church affairs from a wider perspective, Longley was always ready to support those who proclaimed the Gospel and circulated the Holy Scriptures. Nationally he was the Patron of the Anglican London Society for Promoting Christianity among the Jews (LSPCJ) and a Vice-President of the undenominational BFBS. As diocesan he accepted the office of Patron of the Leeds and District CMS Association a month after Hook's arrival, and later became Patron of the Leeds BFBS, jointly with the Earl of Harewood. Longley's actions were seen by the societies concerned as signs of episcopal approval. Whatever his private feelings, on this occasion Hook did not take public issue with his diocesan, as at Coventry in 1830.[8] Even so, Hook continued the uncompromising stand against Evangelical societies foreshadowed in his inaugural sermon at Leeds. On that occasion he adjured the congregation that charity, gentleness and courtesy were required in dealings with people of different views. Eventually, however, he disregarded his own advice. In 1839 he told a crowded meeting of the SPG's Leeds Association, one of his favoured organizations, that there were societies conducted by Churchmen to which he would not concede the name of Church societies, because of their doctrinal shortcomings. Hook was referring, as everyone in the hall and the later newspaper readers well knew, to the great Evangelical societies, the CMS, LSPCJ and the recently founded Church Pastoral Aid Society (CPAS). If Hook hoped to discourage Evangelicals from membership of the local associations of these societies, his arrogance was likely to have the opposite effect.[9]

Leeds Evangelical associations varied in their reactions. The LSPCJ made no comment, probably the best course, but the CMS felt Hook's slights keenly, with the increased attendance at the May 1837 meeting indicating a closing of ranks. Unlike the LSPCJ, the CMS members regularly defended their status as a Church society. Sinclair in 1840 dismissed Hook's assertions

7. PH, fols 48–51, Hook to Pusey, '2 in Advent 1837', CMS Archives, *Yearly Proceedings*, IV (1813–15), pp. 722–25, XV (1839–40), alphabetical entry for Leeds; *LI*, 28 July 1838; *LM*, 28 July 1838, 2 Nov. 1839.
8. BLO, L(ondon) S(ociety for) P(romoting) C(hristianity among the) J(ews). *Jews' Society Reports* (sic) (1837), p. 28; *LM*, 21 Oct. 1837; F. K. Brown, *Fathers of Victorians: the Age of Wilberforce* (Cambridge, 1961) p. 353; Hylson-Smith, p. 98.
9. *LI*, 22 Apr. 1837, 19 Oct. 1839; *LM*, 22 Apr. 1837.

that the CMS lacked strict Church principles as 'idle and silly cavils'—strong words for him. Sometimes Hook was unsure of his facts. Following Sinclair's comment, Hook told an SPCK meeting that the SPG was 'the *real* Missionary Society of the Church of England', hence the CMS had no reason to be in Leeds. If not mischievous, Hook's remarks were misconceived, since the CMS Association had been continuously active in Leeds since 1813, twenty-one years before the Leeds SPG Association was founded.[10]

Critical remarks against the BFBS by Hook in 1839 prompted its Anglican members in Leeds to take issue with him at their anniversary in 1840. Dr Holmes from the chair stoutly defended the validity of Anglican and Dissenting joint endeavours for Bible distribution. In a quasi-placatory gesture to Hook, he said that he wished to speak and think well of those who felt it their duty to oppose the Bible Society, but after much reflection he considered their arguments groundless and futile. Those who described a union of Churchmen and Dissenters as 'a degrading amalgamation' should consult the Archbishops of Canterbury and York, both of whom were the Society's Patrons. Holmes's remarks were loudly applauded. Being subjected to humorous ridicule in his own parish was probably a new experience for Hook. In one respect Holmes succeeded: Hook troubled the local BFBS no more. Unconvinced by the Archbishops' example, Hook, in 1841, issued a pamphlet describing undenominational religious activities as 'an unholy and unhallowed mixture of the orthodox with the heretics'.[11]

The adversial nature of Leeds Church politics was further exacerbated in Hook's dispute with the CPAS. This had been founded in 1836 to provide pastoral assistance, clerical or lay, to overburdened incumbents serving populous parishes or scattered communities. When awarding grants, however, it soon became clear that these were reserved for localities where the incumbent and his intended curate were Evangelical in belief and practice. Affronted High Churchmen consequently founded the Additional Curates Society (ACS) in 1837, for clerical assistance only, but imposed no doctrinal requirements beyond the proposed curate's acceptability to the diocesan concerned. Hook and Dr Longley subscribed generously, with Leeds soon benefiting from ACS supported curates.[12] The ACS, however, did not establish a network of local associations to stimulate interest and funding, unlike the CPAS, whose Leeds association was formed in July 1839, probably through Sinclair's initiative. According to the chairman, the gentlemen

[10.] CMS, *Proceedings*, IV, 89, 457; Hole, *Early History CMS*, pp. 255, 262, 287–88; R(hodes) H(ouse) L(ibrary), *SPG Report* (1836), p. 21; *LI*, 3 June 1837, 28 July 1838, 8 June 1839, 30 May, 6 June 1840.

[11.] *LI*, 24 Oct. 1840; *LM*, 24 Oct. 1840; W. F. Hook, *Scriptural Principles as Applicable to Religious Societies* (1841), p. 4.

[12.] *LI*, 13 May 1837, 7 Apr. 1838, 1 Dec. 1839, 25 Apr., 17 Oct. 1840, 6 Feb. 1841; Chadwick, I, 449–50; P. B. Coombs, 'A History of the Church Pastoral Aid Society 1836–1861' (unpublished MA thesis, University of Bristol, 1960), pp. 30–37; Cornish, pp. 83–84.

present were already known to each other from attending meetings of the Leeds associations of the BFBS, CMS, and LSPCJ. His announcement that the Bishop, already a Vice-Patron of the Parent Society, was happy to become the Leeds Association's President was greeted with 'heartfelt' pleasure. It was a decidedly Evangelical occasion. No identifiable High Churchmen were present.[13]

Three months later, in October 1839, whether by chance or design. Hook at a local SPG meeting used the occasion to voice objections to the CPAS policy of reserving its funds for recipients who followed 'Calvinistic tradition'. Further, he deprecated the management committee's practice of seeking information about candidates already in possession of testimonials acceptable to the bishops concerned. In the West Riding Hook was almost a lone voice, for most incumbents were Evangelicals. In 1839 the CPAS allocated one-fifth of its assistance to Yorkshire, where it was maintaining thirty-eight curates and seven laymen to keep Evangelicalism there strong and well.[14]

Late in 1840, perhaps to parallel CPAS efforts for Yorkshire Evangelicals, Hook decided to organize a grand demonstration of public support for the ACS. In prior publicity he made it clear that a wealthy parish like Leeds should be contributing more for its clergy. A crowded meeting took place on 1 February 1841 in the town's largest hall, with many influential laymen and nearly fifty clergymen on the platform. Hook was called to the chair. Speakers dwelt too much on the foundation and organization of the CPAS, and on its alleged disrespect for the episcopacy. Too little was said about the work of the ACS in the country, and especially in Leeds, where it was then maintaining six curates. Probably the most contentious remarks came from Hook. He accused the CPAS of disobedience to the Archbishop of Canterbury and the Bishop of London, for having refused their conditional offer to accept CPAS membership, provided the society abandoned its funding of lay assistants. For that disobedience, Hook declared, 'the spiritually-minded could not see Christ in the Church Pastoral Aid Society'. The master of rhetoric had perhaps not realized the wounding impact on the CPAS of this form of words, or its repercussions on himself. What is certain, however, is that Stephens omitted all account of this ACS meeting from Hook's biography, whereas on this occasion also, as in all his dealings with Evangelical societies, Hook had struck the first blow.[15]

CPAS reaction was immediate. Sinclair, the association secretary, made a reasoned defence in the local press, pointing out that the SPG (a society known to enjoy Hook's approval) followed the same procedures as the CPAS,

[13.] *LI*, 20 July, 19 Oct. 1839, 27 Mar. 1841; *LM*, 13, 20 July, 19 Oct. 1839, 27 Mar. 1841; *LPB 1834*; Coombs, pp. 44–46, 48.
[14.] *LI*, 17 Aug., 19 Oct. 1839; *LM*, 19 Oct. 1839; Cornish, I, p. 84; Yates, 'Religious Life', p. 254.
[15.] *LI*, 2, 23 Jan., 6 Feb. 1841; *LM*, 6 Feb. 1841; Stephens, *Hook*, II, 67–68.

when selecting missionaries. By then Sinclair had already published, for more permanent record, a pamphlet entitled *Reasons for Supporting the Pastoral-Aid Society*. John Atkinson, a leading Evangelical lawyer, was extremely pointed. How, he asked in the *Leeds Intelligencer*, could anyone disobey an offer, how could a clergyman who had rebuked his own diocesan, as Hook at Coventry, make such a charge?

The institutional rejoinder to Hook came on 23 March 1841 at the CPAS Association's annual meeting. Hook's accusations were considered so serious that the Revd W. Pullen, CPAS Secretary, attended as the principal speaker. In the Bishop's unavoidable absence he had arranged for Dr Holmes to preside. There was a large attendance, with thirty clergyman in support on the platform. Without naming Hook, Holmes chided him in the same tone of humorous ridicule adopted at the BFBS. He trusted, if he should see a society having the patronage and concurrence of his diocesan, he would have the good sense and the modesty to abstain from any public attack. The strongest denunciations, obviously a previously agreed tactic, came from clergy outside Leeds. Speaking last the Revd T. Kennion, Harrogate, declared he would never sanction CPAS funds being given to a man 'who preached Popery in a Protestant pulpit . . .', an accusation manifestly unfair to Hook, but cheered vociferously. The packed and enthusiastic meeting warned Hook that Evangelicalism in Leeds was again a force to be reckoned with.[16]

The final act of events set in train by the ACS meeting took place at the Leeds SPCK district meeting on 31 March 1841, with the Bishop presiding. Earlier, a letter had appeared in the *Leeds Intelligencer* asking parishioners to rally to Hook's support. As he rose to speak, a lengthy outburst of cheering, clapping and stamping occurred, probably from the working-class Operative Conservatives. Intending to portray the SPCK as a unifying influence for Anglicans, whatever their churchmanship, Hook later described himself as overset by this enthusiastic reception. Diverted from his purpose and carried away by his own rhetoric, he asserted that, as there were now two parties in the Church, he would nail his colours to the High Church mast. The Bishop rose, and with difficulty among the hubbub restrained Hook from continuing in this vein. Checked in full flow, Hook was deflated, and could do no more than formally propose a resolution expressing appreciation of the SPCK's contribution to Church life. There was general dismay at the turn of events. The Bishop accepted a spontaneous resolution of thanks for Hook's endeavours. Henry Skelton, cloth manufacturer, declared that exertions such as Hook's for the SPCK and for Leeds had not been equalled in any other parish in England. If amidst his trials he proved mortal and fallible, who had not? The resolution was passed with acclamation. Hook apologized for

16. *LI*, 6, 13 Feb., 27 Mar. 1841; *LM*, 6, 13 Feb., 27 Mar. 1841; Coombs, p. 88, cites a pamphlet by Revd W. Sinclair, *Reasons for Supporting the Pastoral Aid Society*, dated 4 Feb. 1841.

unintentionally disturbing the harmony of the proceedings. If he had felt able to continue, he said, his object had been to promote peace.[17]

Growing Mutual Respect: High Church and Evangelicals, 1841–51

The Bishop's prompt intervention over Hook's flight of oratory suggests that he would have acted similarly had he presided at the recent ACS meeting. The whole unfortunate train of events would thus have been stopped in its tracks. However that may be, Longley's prompt action brought all concerned to their senses. After the meeting the dejected Hook offered to resign. He knew he spoke more strongly than he intended, and saw more good in his friends, and less in his adversaries, than justifiable. The Bishop, however, induced a better frame of mind. In a long letter to the Bishop, which was published, Hook said that he had wished to stress the importance of the SPCK maintaining its neutrality towards all shades of Anglican opinion. He also would have made a plea for Churchmen to discuss contentious issues as brothers, and not as 'foes engaging in a deadly feud'. In spite of this, Hook privately accused himself of wicked conduct, bringing disgrace on the Catholic cause. In May he saw the Bishop, to ask his forgiveness, and quieten his own conscience. The *Leeds Mercury* put the issue in its starkest terms, declaring Hook a divisive influence since his arrival, by introducing scarcely known doctrines, and attacking men and societies who differed. Hook nevertheless persevered in his new course. By 1843 Hook was advocating mutual forbearance on 'things indifferent'—practices and opinions within the Church where no regulations existed, yet aroused strong feelings and contention.[18]

The attitudes of the societies and their supporting clergy also changed. The Leeds SPCK avoided controversy by discontinuing anniversary meetings and substituting annual sermons.[19] The Leeds SPG followed suit, until the need for funds reinstated quarterly and annual meetings from 1846. At the Leeds celebrations of the SPG's sesquicentenary during 1851 the Evangelical Sinclair

17. *LI*, 27 Mar., 3 Apr. 1841, *LM*, 3 Apr. 1841; Stephens, *Hook*, II, 67–73.
18. BLO, Wilberforce Papers, c. 66 fols 67–68, Hook to Robert Wilberforce, 2 Jan. 1841; PH, fols 48–51, '2 in Advent 1837', fols 81–91, 16 Aug. 1839, fols 154–57, 30 Apr. 1841 (all Hook to Pusey); *LI*, 10 Apr. 1841, 9 July 1842; *LM*, 3, 17 Apr. 1841, 9 July 1842; W. F. Hook, *A Letter to the Right Reverend the Lord Bishop of Ripon on the State of Parties in the Church of England* (1841), pp. 14–15; W. F. Hook, *Mutual Forbearance Recommended in Things Indifferent* (1843), pp. 25–26, 29–32, 34; Stephens, *Hook*, II, 71–72, 74–77.
19. *LI*, 9 July 1842, 30 Dec. 1843, 6 Jan. 1844, 22 Mar. 1845, 14 Nov. 1846, 13 May, 4 Nov. 1848; *LM*, 9 July, 1842, 6 Jan. 1844, 29 Mar. 1845, 31 Oct. 1846.

was one of the speakers.[20] By then, the adversarial spirit had long vanished. As early as 1842, Dr Holmes declared that the SPCK, SPG, CMS and LSPCJ deserved the zealous support of all Christian people. Similarly in 1843 Sinclair affirmed that CPAS and CMS members entertained no unkind feelings for fellow Churchmen who opposed their societies; from him personally would come no harsh or injurious word. Evangelical clergy began to express a more exalted doctrine of the Church than they were sometimes credited with. Holmes told CPAS members that they belonged to 'a true branch of the universal Church of Christ'. For Sinclair the Church of England was a Reformed Church which had found 'the middle course' as 'the divinely appointed instrument' for propagating Christian truth.[21]

Coincidentally or otherwise, within months of Hook's humiliation in 1841 the CMS and the LSPCJ amended their constitutions to give the episcopate an ex officio role, thus removing Hook's chief ground of complaint. He accepted membership of the CMS, though not of the Leeds Association, but never joined the LSPCJ. Hook's uncompromising attitude towards the undenominational BFBS remained unaltered, though he continued to abstain from derogatory comment.[22] The climax of disputation between High Church and Evangelical at Leeds in 1841 made those concerned realize that such public and rancorous disagreements were discreditable to the Church and must not be allowed to continue. From 1847, after the first shock of Tractarian secessions from St Saviour's the rapprochement became ever closer.[23]

---

[20] WYASL, RDB18, *Bishop of Ripon's Visitation Charge, 1844*, pp. 25–27; *LI*, 14 Sept. 1844, 12 July 1845, 10 Jan., 18 Apr., 17 Oct. 1846, 20 Feb., 23 Oct. 1847, 3 June, 4 Nov. 1848, 13, 20 Nov. 1849, 2 Nov. 1850, 18 Jan., 6 Dec. 1851; *LM*, 18 Apr. 1846, 4 Nov. 1848, 2 Nov. 1850, 18 Jan. 1851.

[21] *LI*, 5 Mar. 1842, 25 Mar. 1843, 20 Apr. 1844; *LM*, 25 Mar. 1843.

[22] BLO, *LSPJC Report* (1842), pp. 37–38; CMS, *Proceedings*, XVI (1841–42), XVII (1842–43), XVIII (1843–44), Lists of Annual Subscribers; *LI*, 21 Aug., 18 Dec. 1841; *LM*, 7, 28 Aug., 24 Dec. 1841; E. Stock, *The History of the Church Missionary Society*, 3 vols (1899–1916), I, 389–95.

[23] PH, fols 479–90, Hook to Pusey, 3 Aug. 1847.

CHAPTER 9

Conflicting Loyalties: St Saviour's Church

The Need for Reassessment

From its consecration in October 1845 to 1851, St Saviour's was served by advanced Tractarian clergy who sometimes found their ecclesiastical exemplars in medieval England or nineteenth-century Rome. Conversions to the latter sporadically occurred, especially in 1851 after an episcopal inquiry. Before the end of 1847 sufficient secessions and variations from Anglican practice had occurred to extinguish the long-standing friendship between Hook and the church's patron, E. B. Pusey.

Primary sources for these events are numerous including the *Statement of St Saviour's Clergy*, J. H. Pollen's more personal *Narrative of Five years at St Saviour's, Leeds* and Bishop Longleys' *Visitation Charges* of 1844, 1847, and 1850 and his *Letter to the Parishioners of St Saviour's* in 1851. Most of the authors of secondary sources such as Grantham, Yates, and Savage and Tyne rely particularly on the accounts of St Saviour's clergy and Pollen. However, the additional information was available in Longley's publications, local newspapers and Hook's letters to Pusey (as compared to the edited extracts in Liddon's biography). This was sufficient in quantity to suggest that a re-examination of the topic was required.[1]

Tractarianism came into existence as a movement in the Church of England in 1833 following Keble's protest against the reform Government's perceived Erastianism. Its name came from the ensuing *Tracts for the Times*, a series which continued until 1841. Through its publications and its protagonists, Tractarianism forcibly asserted doctrines considered insufficiently known, especially the Catholicity, Apostolic faith and order of the Church of England. Hook and like-minded High Churchmen had been promulgating these doctrines as 'Church principles' for many years before 1833, and agreed with the general sentiments of the *Tracts*, though not always with the detail or stridency of tone. Thus it was through the long-standing friendship between Hook and E. B. Pusey, the Tractarian leader, that St Saviour's, the first

---

[1] Chadwick, I, 70–71; R. W. Church, *The Oxford Movement: Twelve Years* (1891), pp. 109–25, 146; Cornish, I, 222, 229–32; G. W. Herring, 'Tractarianism to Ritualism: A Study of Some Aspects of Tractarianism outside Oxford, from the Time of Newman's Conversion in 1845, until the First Ritual Commission in 1867' (unpublished DPhil thesis, University of Oxford, 1984), p. 18; Hylson-Smith, p. 113; Moorman, pp. 338–40; P. B. Nockles, 'Continuity and Change in Anglican High Churchmanship in Britain, 1792–1850' (unpublished DPhil thesis, University of Oxford, 1982), pp. viii–x, xxvi, xiii–xiii, ix; Yates, *St Saviour's*, p. 27.

Tractarian church in the North of England, came to be built in Leeds. The decision to build was made in 1839, but the church was not completed until 1845. By that time great changes had occurred within the movement. From 1839 onwards extreme Tractarians like Frederick Oakeley and W. G. Ward queried the English Church's ecclesial validity. In 1845 they left for Rome, as did Newman. Pusey, however, stayed within the Church of England. The Tractarian ferment at Oxford was over, but Pusey's example enabled less extreme Tractarian views to survive in English parishes.[2]

W. F. Hook and the Oxford Tractarians, 1836–45

According to J. R. H. Moorman, the very first *Tract* was an appeal to party spirit and a call to strife. From 1833 doctrines and practices articulated by Tractarian writers engendered controversy. Favourable on some issues, Hook nevertheless measured each by Church principles, supporting or opposing as appropriate. Sometimes indeed he considered that the Oxford divines lacked perspective: by inflating minor issues they actually retarded Church principles.[3] In 1836, for example, Hook assisted Newman and Pusey's vain attempt to induce Oxford University to inhibit R. D. Hampden, the supposedly unorthodox, but recently appointed Regius Professor of Divinity.[4] Rejoicing in the Reformation, Hook was at one with Samuel Wilberforce in 1838 in regarding as impolitic the refusal of Newman, Keble and Pusey to subscribe to the Oxford Martyrs' Memorial.[5] Even so, the evangelical *Christian Observer* and the *Record* in 1839 lumped Hook in with these three, along with Isaac Williams and Manning, as traitors to the Church of England.[6] Hook was one of the few High Churchmen to support Newman in 1841 over *Tract 90*'s 'Catholic' interpretation of certain Anglican Articles of Religion. When consulted by Newman, Hook advised him to re-publish with

[2.] HA, NB22, fols 13–16, Pusey to H. Hall, 2 Mar. 1837; WYASL, LCP25, Vicarage Book, Pusey to Hall, 2 Mar. 1837; Chadwick, I, 199–201, 211; Church, pp. 112, 129, 221–23, 241–42; Cornish, I, 239, 243, 293; Herring, pp. 24–28, 35, 43, 45–46; Moorman, p. 342; G. Rowell, *The Vision Glorious: Themes and Personalities in the Catholic Revival in Anglicanism* (Oxford, 1983), p. 74; Stephens, *Hook*, I, 151–60.
[3.] BLO, Wilberforce Papers, d. 38, fols 129–30, S. Wilberforce to Hook, 29 Jan. 1838, d. 38, fols 133–34, S. Wilberforce to Hook, 5 Feb. 1838; MS Eng. Lett. d. 368, fols 35–36, Hook to J. W. Croker, 3 Apr. 1839; *British Critic*, 50, p. 402, cited in *LI*, 6 Apr. 1939; Church, p. 126; Hylson-Smith, p. 115; Moorman, p. 343; Nockles, pp. ix–x, 441, 449–52, 455–57, 470; Stephens, *Hook*, I, 160.
[4.] HA, K6/14, Hook to Mother, 23 Mar. 1836; Chadwick, I, 114–20; Church, pp. 167–70; Cornish, I, 259–60; Rowell, pp. 77–78.
[5.] BLO, Wilberforce Papers, d. 38, fols 138–39, S. Wilberforce to Hook, 7 Dec. 1838, fols 140–42, S. Wilberforce to Hook, 26 Dec. 1838; Chadwick, I, 176–77; Church, pp. 219–21; Cornish, I, 263–64.
[6.] Chadwick, I, 177.

explanatory material, but then to end the series with a final *Tract*. Hook also encouraged Newman not to despond over 'a little bit of a scrape'. Subsequently, Hook thought differently. He told Gladstone in December 1841 that he had sacrificed his character, as a sound Churchman, by supporting Newman over *Tract 90*. Of all the numerous Tractarian controversies in which Hook involved himself, this was the longest held against him.[7]

In spring 1839, deeming himself 'to all intents and purposes an Oxford Tract man', Hook invited Oxford friends to build a church in Leeds. Some months later, an anonymous offer came through Pusey. In accepting the offer, Hook wished its Tractarian connections to be made public, suggesting that if Pusey were to preach in Leeds, his gentle manner would remove prejudice. Of the same mind in September 1840, Hook told Pusey that his presence at the stone-laying would achieve the same end. Hook's attitude changed during 1841, however, when he realized that some of his own flock had become alienated by his support of Newman. By January 1842, thoroughly alarmed about local reactions, Hook had told Pusey that if he were to attend the foundation ceremony, every stone would be regarded as laid 'with a popish intent'. Overt Tractarian connections, Hook considered, would alienate parishioners further.[8] When informing the Ripon Diocesan Church Building Society shortly afterwards of the gift of a church, Hook described the donor as 'a nameless friend', with no mention of Pusey as the donor's agent. The foundation stone of 'Holy Cross' was laid by Hook himself, with no prior announcement, on 14 September 1842, the feast of the Holy Cross. The *Leeds Mercury* professed mystification at unseemly secrecy about the ceremony and the donor's identity. According to a report appearing in Leeds in October 1843, Pusey was a donor jointly with other Tractarians, and also as having chosen the stained glass. If so, declared the *Mercury*, it would cast a light 'beautifully accordant with the dim doctrines of Anglo-Catholic divines'. As certain Tractarians became ever more pro-Roman,

7. BL, Gladstone Papers, MS 44, 213, fols 23–26, 15 Dec. 1841, fols 31–32, 17 Dec. 1841, fols 33–34, 21 Dec. 1841, (all Hook to Gladstone), fols 27–30, Gladstone to Hook, 16 Dec. 1841, fols 37–38, Gladstone to Hook, 23 Jan. 1842; *LM*, 27 Mar. 1841; Nockles, pp. 455–57, 472, 474 (citing from Hook's letter to Newman of 17 Mar. 1841 in Oratory MS Correspondence that in 'times of peace' Hook would have had 'a little quarrel' with Newman 'for some things in Tract 90'), 475; Stephens, *Hook*, II, 65–67, 94–103, 107–11, 185–90.

8. HA, K6/23, Hook to Mother, 6 Mar. 1839; PH, fols 81–91, 16 Aug. 1839, fols 132–34, 24 Sept. 1840, fols 182–91, 31 Jan. 1842, (all Hook to Pusey); *LM*, 24 Apr. 1841; Herring, p. 28; G. I. T. Machin, *Politics and the Churches in Great Britain 1832 to 1868* (Oxford, 1977), pp. 82–83; R. D. Middleton, *Newman at Oxford: His Religious Development* (Oxford, 1950), pp. 174–89; Stephens, *Hook*, II, 63–67, 75–76.

Hook awaited the completion and consecration of the new Tractarian church with foreboding.[9]

The Founder and the Patronage

Pusey represented himself as the founder's agent until St Saviour's consecration on 28 October 1845, when the petition to consecrate described him as founder and leading patron. That evening, however, in his sermon, Pusey referred to the founder as if it were someone other than himself, a distinction noted by Hook and others. In August 1847 Hook privately attempted to persuade Pusey to surrender the patronage to the Bishop, alleging that it had been obtained by 'equivocation', but Pusey in his lifetime repudiated neither patronage nor anonymity. 'Pure humbug', Hook told Robert Wilberforce in 1852, about the continuing mystery over St Saviour's founder, but did not elaborate further.[10]

Pusey's first proposal, in 1841, for an incumbent in this slum district, displayed a less-than-sure touch. He had in mind a married cleric of scholarly bent and delicate constitution. Not so, replied Hook; we need energy and enthusiasm; we need Church principles, but no Tractarian extremists. Three years later, with completion in sight, Hook gave Pusey permission to approach George Hills, Hook's curate working in what would become St Saviour's district. Hills exactly fitted Hook's specification, but was not interested. Spontaneously, without telling Hook, Hills suggested Richard Ward, formerly Hook's curate. At one time he had been highly regarded by Hook, but later he thought Ward rash and tactless. Aware of Hook's earlier view, Pusey apparently approached Ward, without informing Hook. Ward consulted Edward Jackson, his confidential friend (and also Hook's). Jackson told Ward he was 'most unfit' for the position, but said nothing to Hook. Still doubtful, Ward allowed himself to be over-persuaded by Pusey. Ward's appointment was announced in January 1845, but his arrival seemed uncertain until August.[11] The sequence of events detailed above is based on letters from

9. PH, fols 192–95, Hook to Pusey, 25 Feb. 1842; WYASL, RDS8/10, RDCBS, Third Report, 1842, p. 65; *Bristol Mercury*, cited in *LI*, 21 Oct. 1843; *LI*, 5 Mar., 17 Sept. 1842, 7 Jan., 29 July 1843, 21 Dec. 1844; *LM*, 17 Sept. 1842, 28 Oct. 1843; Grantham, pp. 7–8; H. P. Liddon, *Life of Edward Bouverie Pusey*, 4 vols (1894–1898), II, 473–74; Savage and Tyne, pp. 5–6, 8, 49–50; Stephens, *Hook*, II, 190–92.
10. BLO, Wilberforce Papers, c. 66, fols 162–63, Hook to Wilberforce, 13 Oct. 1852; PH, fols 470–90, Hook to Pusey, 3 Aug. 1847; *LI*, 1 Nov. 1845; Grantham, pp. 9–10; Liddon, II, 497; Savage and Tyne, pp. 10, 49–50; Stephenson, p. 200.
11. PH, fols 54–58, 15 Jan. 1838, fols 62–69, 24 Apr. 1838, fols 70–78, 3 Apr. 1839, fols 140–46, 13 Jan. 1841, fols 147–53, 23 Feb. 1841, fols 231–34, 29 May 1844, fols 430–35, 24 Dec. 1846, fols 455–63, 6 Feb. 1847 (all Hook to Pusey); WYASL, LPC112/1, List of Leeds Parish Church Staff, 1836–1900; *LI*, 6, 13 June 1840; Sykes, pp. 11–12, 15–16, 45; Yates, *St Saviour's*, p. 6.

Hook to Pusey at various times between 1838 and 1847, and available to Liddon for Pusey's biography. They suggest, rather, a series of gaps in communication which left Hook faced with a *fait accompli*, and will not bear Liddon's contention that Ward enjoyed Hook's confidence when appointed, or derived satisfaction from the appointment.[12]

Tractarian Worship and Churchmanship in Leeds

For a better appreciation of events at St Saviour's from 1845 to 1851 a brief discussion of Tractarian worship is necessary. Central to Tractarian theology was an awed sense of the mystery of Divine self-revelation — the Incarnation issuing in the Divine indwelling. For Tractarian clergy, richness of Eucharistic worship best conveyed the reality of Divine grace. Oakeley's Margaret Chapel in London was a pattern of Tractarian high ceremonial. 'Mystery and movement, colour and ceremonial' were judged more powerful adjuncts to worship than restraint and well-polished sermon, especially among the urban poor. However, the 'worth' of the worship must be reinforced through the holiness, devotion, and pastoral care of the priests concerned. These ideas were not new to Leeds. In 1848 the Tractarian incumbent of St James's, George Ayliffe Poole, had published a series of articles describing how ritual and ceremony could convey religious truth. Hook, however, thought some 'ornaments', such as lace fringes and stoles with crosses were marks of 'folly', likely to do Church principles great injury. Moderate Tractarians, if moving circumspectly, in practice experienced little difficulty. The more extreme, such as W. J. E. Bennett at St Paul's, Pimlico, and Bryan King, at St George's-in-the-East, occasioned riots.[13]

From 1845 strongly Tractarian clergy with these ideals of worship and ministry brought a new element to Church life in Leeds. They found two distinct groupings to Leeds clergy around Hook and Sinclair, both natural leaders. Hook's group, the more numerous, included the curates attached to the Parish Church, and the incumbents of the four influential central churches. All were High Church, except for the moderate at St John's, who nevertheless supported Hook. The High Church sphere of influence covered the populous east and central districts of the main township. The Evangelical zone, also densely peopled, consisted of a crescent-shaped area in the north and west, where the churches possessed Evangelical incumbents. After Hook in 1839 accepted Pusey's offer of a church, its siting in the High Church area was almost inevitable. Hook provided land in the Parish Church district at

---

12. PH, fols 269–70, Hook to Pusey, 11 Aug. 1845; Liddon, II, 481–82, III, 113; Stephens, *Hook*, II, 194–95.
13. PH, fols 92–98, Hook to Pusey, 1 Dec. 1839; *LI*, 22, 29 Feb., 7 Mar. 1840; Chadwick, I, 212, 301–03, 497–501, 508; Rowell, pp. 11, 14–17, 116–17, 130–31, 133.

Hill House Bank, often known as St Peter's Bank, where a new National School since 1840 was used for a congregation gathered by Hook's hardworking curates.[14] Hill House district became St Saviour's responsibility in 1845. Advanced Tractarian clergy sent by Pusey became a distinct 'third element' within Leeds Anglicanism. Regretting the Reformation, they took as a pattern the medieval Church and contemporary Rome. Avoiding local clergy, they associated with Tractarians elsewhere. Parochially separate from 1846, as neighbours, they exceeded Hook's worst fears.[15]

The Consecration of St Saviour's: a Tractarian Statement

St Saviour's consecration, postponed following Newman's secession, took place on 28 October 1845. The lengthy solemnities included choral Mattins and Holy Communion, elaborate and dignified in accordance with Tractarian ideals for 'richness' in worship. The handsome nave seated 450 laypeople, 200 stood in the aisles, 260 surpliced clergy occupied the chancel and transepts. Bishop Longley, mindful of recent Tractarian secessions, delivered a cautionary sermon. Emphasizing the blessings bestowed on the English Church — the open Bible, the ordained ministry, the Holy Spirit — he warned of the dangers ensuing, if, like the Israelites of old, these divine blessings were unjustly abused.[16] For the evening choral service a newspaper account exists, by 'Presbyter', possibly Anglican, probably Dissenting, certainly hostile. The author claimed that the mainly chanted service made it impossible for the crowded congregation to participate in the 'old-fashioned, plain, and *Protestant* way'. Pusey's sermon on Penitence was judged an 'over-rated laudation of Mary Magdalene', 'Popish' in interpretation and heavily reliant on quotations from the Fathers. The unsympathetic wording nevertheless points to the depths of Pusey's patristic knowledge and also the 'richness' of the worship being attempted. Probably glad that no public disorder had marred the day, Hook professed entire satisfaction with the arrangements. The concerted absence of twelve Leeds Evangelical clergy struck the only discordant note.[17]

[14.] PH, fols 80–91, 16 Aug. 1839, fols 154–57, 30 Apr. 1841, fols 163–73, 24 Sept. 1841, fols 174–76, 11 Oct. 1841 (all Hook to Pusey); LI, 4 Jan., 11, 25 Apr. 1840, 31 July, 23 Oct. 1841, 22 Apr. 1843, 28 Dec. 1844, 2 Aug. 1845; LM, 21 Sept. 1839; Beresford, *East End, West End*, pp. 359, 373; Chadwick, I, 168; Taylor, pp. 480–81.

[15.] BLO, MS Eng. Lett., c. 663, fols 202–03, Hook to Manning, 4 Oct. 1848; Beresford, *East End, West End*, pp. 173–75; O. Chadwick, Editor's Introduction, in *The Mind of the Oxford Movement* (1960), pp. 11–64, esp. pp. 52–53; Chadwick, *Victorian Church*, I, 212–14; Cornish, I, 273–75; Pollen, pp. 163–64, 166–67.

[16.] LI, 1 Nov. 1845; Liddon, II, 495; Pollen, p. 38; Savage and Tyne, pp. 10–11; Stephenson, p. 206.

[17.] PH, fols 318–22, Hook to Pusey, 11 Nov. 1845; LM, 1 Nov. 1845; Savage and Tyne, p. 12.

At the consecration the attendance of 260 clergymen gave Hook the opportunity to instigate an address to Bishop Longley affirming loyalty to the Church of England. Headed by Hook, Pusey, and Churton, it attracted 159 signatures, including sixty from Ripon diocese. Longley's reply highlighted the doctrinal truth and purity of the English Church, and cautioned against reviving discontinued devotions, or yearnings for the (studiously unnamed) Papacy. Once charitably disposed to certain Tractarian usages, apart from their tendency to disparage the Reformation, Longley had become more wary through pre-consecration dealings with Pusey over the church's name, inscriptions, glass, communion plate, and altar-linen. The ethos of worship evident at the consecration would not allay his misgivings. The cautionary aspects of his reply uncannily predicted St Saviour's future course.[18]

The Incumbency of Richard Ward, 1845–47

Until St Saviour's received parish status in August 1846, Ward as its incumbent was ecclestically subordinate to Hook. Initially Ward experienced difficulty in obtaining 'advanced' Tractarian curates. John Slatter, Ward's curate until June 1846, was previously at St Peter's, where his work and example impressed Hook.[19] The deacon J. G. Cazenove succeeded Slatter, having earlier enquired from Hook whether he could join St Saviour's without compromising his Anglicanism. Shortly after Ward became Vicar, he issued a printed manual for communicants, whose teaching about the consecrated elements of Holy Communion Cazenove found troubling. He declined to distribute the Manual. With the agreement of Ward and the Bishop, Hook accepted Cazenove, considering himself to have 'saved' Cazenove from a 'Colony of Romanizers'. Slatter and Cazenove were 'good Anglicans' whose influence Hook considered beneficial for Ward. A third was Edward Jackson, now ordained, and serving at St Peter's, but resident with the community at St Saviours.[20]

Under Ward the community followed a rigorous pattern of daily worship. From seven in the morning to ten at night, canonical hours were kept (Prime, Mattins, Sext, Nones, Vespers, Evensong, Compline), along with Holy

---

18. PH, fols 313–17, Hook to Pusey, 31 Oct. 1845; *LI*, 3 Jan. 1846; *LM*, 10 Jan. 1846; Grantham, pp. 8–9; Liddon, II, 484–85, 492; Pollen, pp. 39–40; Savage and Tyne, pp. 7–8, 11–12; Stephens, *Hook*, II, 192–93; Stephenson, pp. 198–99; Yates, *St Saviour's*, p. 4.
19. BL, Gladstone Papers, MS 44, 213, fols 51–56, Hook to Gladstone, 22 Jan. 1844; PH, fols 231–34, 29 May 1844, fols 258–61, 22 Feb. 1845, fols 264–66, 6 Apr. 1845, fols 267–68, 21 May 1845, fols 269–70, 11 Aug. 1845 (all Hook to Pusey); *EC Ratified Schemes* (1847), V, 117; Pollen, pp. 16–17 (Slatter's letter), 43–44 (Cazenove's letter); Savage and Tyne, p. 14.
20. PH, fols 353–61, 7 Nov. 1846, fols 419–23, 21 Dec. 1846, fols 430–35, 24 Dec. 1846, fols 455–63, 6 Feb. 1847 (all Hook to Pusey); Grantham, p. 12; Liddon, III, 113; Pollen, pp. 43–44, 47–48, 53 (all Cazenove's letter); Savage and Tyne, p. 13; Stephens, *Hook*, II, 195.

Communion and morning, afternoon, and evening services on Sundays. Time required in church, along with meals in community, meant less contact with parishioners. Apart from the sick, many poor people complained that they were less well looked after than by Hook's two curates formerly. Rumours spread about practices forbidden by the Bishop. There were signs that Ward was flagging under the strict, self-imposed regime.[21] In response to Ward's request, reinforcements arrived in September 1846. George Case, newly ordained, came first, followed by R. G. Macmullen, Fellow of Corpus Christi, Oxford, a tough and determined cleric, with a brief from Pusey to reorganize and reinvigorate. According to Cazenove, Macmullen infused new life into everything.[22] Nevertheless, he was too 'advanced' for Leeds. His sermon on the intercession of saints attracted unfavourable comment, relayed by Hook to Pusey, who requested Macmullen to send the sermon to the Bishop. Episcopal censure and refusal of a licence to officiate increased Macmullen's existing disenchantment with the English Church.[23]

Disturbed by these events and either aware of, or anticipating, impending secessions, Hook 'repudiated' St Saviour's on 15 December 1846, by referring in a public lecture to 'Romanisers' introducing medieval doctrines. Egged on by Macmullen, Ward expostulated violently. On 30 December Hook curtly informed Pusey that Macmullen and two community laymen, Haigh and Wilkinson, had seceded. According to the *Leeds Intelligencer* they had been in touch with Oscott Roman Catholic College for some weeks.[24] Addresses by Evangelical clergy and laity to the Bishop severely criticised Hook and Church principles. Initially despondent, Hook was heartened by support from the *Leeds Intelligencer*, and by being designated 'a champion of the Church' in a vote of thanks from five hundred Church Sunday School teachers.[25]

Pusey had discounted Hook's repeated warnings about likely secessions, but afterwards sent Marriott to investigate. Marriott told Hook (who

[21] PH, fols 325–43, Hook to Pusey, 21 Mar. 1846, fols 455–63, Hook to Pusey, 6 Feb. 1847; Grantham, p. 12; Liddon, III, 113; C. T. Longley, *A Letter to the Parishioners of St Saviour's, Leeds, by the Right Rev. the Lord Bishop of Ripon: With an Appendix of Documents* (1851), pp. 21–22; Pollen, pp. 43–44 (Cazenove's letter); Savage and Tyne, p. 13; Yates, *Leeds High Church*, pp. 74–75; Yates, *St Saviour's*, pp. 6–7.

[22] Liddon, III, 113; R. D. Newman, *Pusey and Bloxam: An Oxford Friendship* (1947), p. 164; Pollen, pp. 46–48 (Cazenove's letter); Yates, *St Saviour's*, p. 7.

[23] PH, fols 406–16, 19 Dec. 1846, fols 430–35, 24 Dec. 1846, fols 455–63, 6 Feb. 1847 (all Hook to Pusey); *LI*, 9 Jan. 1847; Grantham, p. 13; Liddon, III, 114; Longley, *Bishop's Letter*, p. 22; Pollen, pp. 51–53 (Cazenove's letter); Savage and Tyne, pp. 14–15; Stephens, *Hook*, II, 196; Yates, *St Saviour's*, pp. 7–8.

[24] PH, fols 366–81, 15 Nov. 1846, fols 391–97, 20 Nov. 1846, fols 406–16, 19 Dec. 1846, fols 424–29, 22 Dec. 1846, fols 436–39, 30 Dec. 1846 (all Hook to Pusey); *LI*, 9 Jan. 1847; *LM*, 2, 9 Jan. 1847; Hook, *Three Reformations*, pp. 14, 26, 52, 58–60, 69.

[25] BL, Gladstone Papers, MS 44, 213, fols 91–92, Hook to Gladstone, 15 Jan. 1847, fols 95–96, Hook to Gladstone, 20 Feb. 1847; PH, fols 464–69, Hook to Pusey, 24 Feb. 1847; *LI*, 9, 16 Jan., 20 Feb. 1847; *LM*, 9, 16 Jan., 6, 20 Feb. 1847.

informed Pusey) that the unrest at St Saviour's was attributable to Macmullen, whom Marriott already knew as a Romanist. Meanwhile Pusey had accused Hook of persecuting 'the innocent Macmullen out of the Church of England'. Pusey later acknowledged himself mistaken in Macmullen, and as having done much mischief in sending him to Leeds. Bishop Longley attributed Macmullen's departure to resentment at censure and inhibition. Liddon's view that Hook was responsible has slender warrant.[26] Marriott's conclusion that a 'more patient and less variable man' was required for St Saviour's reflected adversely on Pusey's judgement. Ward agreed to resign. His curate, Case, followed suit. Over 300 parishioners sent an address to Bishop Longley on 18 January 1847, affirming Ward's entirely Anglican teaching. The Bishop accepted their view, but added that Ward had accepted influence from others, and disobeyed the Bishop's specific injunctions. Parishioners had escaped many dangers, he continued. As their spiritual father he would protect them from beliefs and practices rejected by the English Church. Shortly afterwards Ward and Case left Leeds.

Replying on 2 February to the Evangelical clergy, Longley stressed his determination to uphold Reformation principles. A 'very dangerous experiment upon the Church of England' had occurred at St Saviour's, he argued. Macmullen, intruding without Episcopal consent, had tampered with people's faith and allegiance, making Longley mistrustful about patrons' judgement. Hook's spirits were further lifted when the Bishop, replying later to the Evangelical laity, insisted that no other Leeds pulpit had proselytized for Rome.[27]

The Incumbency of Thomas Minster, 1848–50

Ward's successor from May 1847 was A. F. Forbes, who resigned some months later, following his consecration as Bishop of Brechin. J. H. Pollen, Merton College, Oxford, officiated temporarily until Thomas Minster arrived from Farnley Tyas in April 1848. Minster proved 'advanced', re-established community life and canonical hours, and introduced daily choral services. Those receptive to their message found the services for the third anniversary in 1848 'sublimely uplifting'. In contrast, the *Leeds Intelligencer* rebuked St Saviour's clergy for unduly exalting the priesthood and mounting

---

26. PH, fols 353–61, 7 Nov. 1846, fols 391–97, 20 Nov. 1846, fols 419–23, 21 Dec. 1846, fols 430–35, 24 Dec. 1846, fols 443–45, 'Early in 1847' (all Hook to Pusey); Liddon, III, 128–31; Longley, *Bishop's Letter*, p. 22.

27. PH, fols 470–73, Hook to Pusey, 15 Mar. 1847; *LI*, 30 Jan., 6, 20 Feb. 1847; *LM*, 30 Jan., 6, 20 Feb. 1847; Liddon, III, 130; Longley, *Bishop's Letter*, p. 22; Pollen, p. 56; Savage and Tyne, p. 16; Stephens, *Hook*, II, 201–04.

a 'religious pageant'. Unlike London in comparable circumstances, no riots ensued.[28]

More disturbing to Bishop Longley were the reports, shortly after Minster arrived, of a clandestine system of confession at St Saviour's. The Tractarian 'system' of running a parish emphasized celebrating the Eucharist, visiting the sick, and educating the young. Confession, it professed, was desirable at certain stages in life: confirmation; return to the sacraments; serious illness; point of death. J. M. Neale and G. R. Prynne both advocated confession for children. After 1845 the first groups to practise regular confession were Tractarian clergy among themselves. G. W. Herring emphasized that the approach adopted for confessing laity depended on age and station. If requested, Tractarian clergy would hear confessions irrespective of the wishes of husband or parent, sometimes arousing violent objections.[29] In October 1848 certain individuals (including Hook, according to Liddon) informed the Bishop that most of the fifty St Saviour's candidates presented for confirmation had previously been to confession. If Hook was one of those involved, it was within his responsibility as Rural Dean and Bishop's Officer. Certainly Hook objected to St Saviour's teaching that confession was a means of grace, rather than of comfort. His sermon on 29 October 1848, later printed as *Auricular Confession*, described the Anglican requirement for confession as voluntary and exceptional, Scriptural and Primitive — unlike the Roman practice of obligatory and regular. Keble interpreted Hook's words as attacking private confession and authoritative absolution.[30]

With specific evidence, Longley confronted Minster, who admitted 'periodically confessing' parishioners, using the private authoritative absolution, provided by the Prayer Book, for the Visitation of the Sick. In January 1849 Longley required abandonment of this system, and restricted private confession to the sick, or, on request, for consciences unquiet otherwise. Minster promised unreserved obedience. By August, however, the Revd R. F. Blaker publicly denounced a 'clique of unfledged birds' — Romanizing St Saviour's clergy — for introducing a deceitful system to Leeds. As Leeds at that juncture was in the grip of a cholera epidemic, during which *all* local clergy and ministers were labouring heroically to succour the victims, public

---

28. WYASL, St Saviour's 7/1, Letter of Revd James Davies of Abenhall, Glos. to his Mother about dedication festival, 7 Nov. 1848, pp. 1–26 (photocopy); *LI*, 6 Nov. 1847, 11 Nov. 1848; Grantham, pp. 16–17, 19; Liddon, III, 133, 355–56; Pollen, pp. 74–76; Savage and Tyne, pp. 17–19; Yates, *St Saviour's*, p. 10, see also note 48.

29. Herring, pp. 186–87, 194–95, 197, 200–01, 204, 212, 219; Longley, *Bishop's Letter*, p. 22; Moorman, pp. 353, 364–65.

30. WYASL, LPC 112/1, Parish Church Record, entry for Confirmations, 3 Oct. 1848, RDB1, 'Archives of the See of Ripon', Bishop's letter to Rural Deans on requirements of the office, Mar. 1848 (lithographed facsimile), RDB18, *Bishop's Visitation Charge*, 1847, Note III, List of Rural Deans; *LI*, 17 July 1847, 10 June (Archdeacon's Charge), 7 Oct., 9, 30 Dec. 1848; *LM*, 7 Oct. 1848; Liddon, III, 356–58; Pollen, pp. 77–80, 88–91; Stephens, *Hook*, II, 218–20.

attention was focused on matters of life and death. Blaker's strictures sparked no controversy.[31]

In April 1850, Minster and his curates, Crawley, Beckett and Rooke, despatched a solemn protest to their diocesan and the two Archbishops against the Judicial Committee of Privy Council's decision that insufficient grounds existed for the Bishop of Exeter's continued refusal, for doctrinal reasons, to institute C. G. Gorham to the cure of Brampford Speke. St Saviour's clergy were also conspicuously absent from the subsequent meeting of Leeds Deanery clergy, convened to record thanks to the Bishop for his Pastoral Letter on the decision's implications. At his September Visitation Longley stated he was watching those with Romanizing tendencies closely, having already formally warned against wilful revival of medieval practices.[32]

Later that year, the Pope's creation in September of an English territorial hierarchy flushed out Roman sympathizers in Leeds and elsewhere. Eleven or twelve Tractarian clergy met privately at St Saviour's autumn anniversary, and formally resolved that, given its pre-Reformation history, the final authority for the Church of England in matters of Catholic faith, lay with the Papal See. This declaration was signed by those present. F. Hathaway of Shadwell, near Leeds, sent a copy to Professor W. H. Mill at Cambridge University, requesting his concurrence. Mill refused. He severely rebuked Hathaway, and sent the correspondence to Hook, whom he knew as the senior Leeds clergyman. Early in November a Leeds Deanery meeting affirmed their support for Reformation principles, and their determination to maintain 'the integrity of the Church of England in its Protestant as well as its Catholic character'. Forty-seven clergy, of all shades of Churchmanship, signed. Hathaway and the St Saviour's clergy were the notable absentees. They did, however, attend an archdeaconry protest meeting on 27 November, when Hathaway insistently attempted to tone down a motion critical of the 'arrogancy' of 'the Bishop of Rome', into a 'solemn protest against the papal bull'. At some point Hook, who had just received the communication from Mill, publicly queried Hathaway's Anglican status by then reading Hathaway's letter. Archdeacon Musgrave, as Chairman, conceded the propriety of Hook's question, but ruled that Hathaway was entitled to speak. Beckett and Rooke of St Saviour's voted with Hathaway; over 250 voted against. For all concerned it was a severe test of conscience, belief, and action.[33]

31. *LM*, 11 Aug. 1849; Liddon, III, 358–59; Longley, *Bishop's Letter*, pp. 22–26; Morgan, p. 64; Pollen, pp. 127–38, 225–50; Savage and Tyne, pp. 22–24; Stephens, *Hook*, II, 223, 261–62.
32. WYASL, RDB18, *Bishop's Visitation Charge*, 1850, pp. 8, 32–34; *LI*, 4 May, 1, 22 June, 27 July, 14 Sept. 1850; Chadwick, *Victorian Church*, I, 250–64; Cornish, I, 321–30; Pollen, pp. 155–58; Stoughton, II, 177–80.
33. *LI*, 2, 9, 23, 30 Nov., 7 Dec. 1850; *LM*, 19 Oct., 9, 23, 30 Nov. 1850; Chadwick, *Victorian Church*, I, 286–301; Cornish, I, 340–52; Grantham, pp. 14, 23; Longley, *Bishop's Letter*, p. 29; Pollen, pp. 165–67, 176, 201–03.

Leeds Rural Deanery Chapter and St Saviour's, 1850

The revelations about St Saviour's clergy at the archdeaconry protest meeting seem to have decided four Evangelical Leeds clergy to bring matters into the open. Those involving themselves were: Fawcett (St Mark's); Crosthwaite (St Andrew's); Randall (All Saints); Holmes (Leeds Grammar School). At the monthly Ruridecanal Chapter Meeting on 2 December they voiced their disquiet about proceedings at St Saviour's. The Chapter thereupon arranged to publish urgent notices of a special meeting on 9 December: 'To consider and adopt such measures as appear to be necessary in reference to the doctrines and practices now prevalent at St Saviour's Church'.[34]

Contemporary accounts of subsequent events appeared in the *Leeds Intelligencer,* the *Leeds Mercury,* and the versions of St Saviour's clergy, Bishop Longley and J. H. Pollen.[35] At the special Chapter meeting, the Revd George Urquhart, Meanwood, immediately moved that the members had no powers to consider the matter. There was possibly some degree of 'support' for the proposal, but it failed to find a seconder, so Hook continued with the meeting. St Saviour's clergy later represented this as an unprecedented abuse of a Rural Dean's authority. Pollen indeed insinuated that Hook's behaviour was an ignoble exercise in self-preservation. The more likely explanation is that it represented ordinary meeting procedure. As spokesman for the accusers, Fawcett then laid the charges in similar terms to the notice of the meeting, with the Chapter deciding to request the Bishop to institute further inquiries. According to the Bishop, the Chapter's decision was by 'a large majority', but the accuser Randall referred to it later as 'unanimous'.[36]

The Bishop of Ripon's Investigation and its Consequences, 1850–51

The Bishop received the Chapter's request on 10 or 11 December, and decided to proceed under the Church Pluralities Act, 1838 (1 and 2 Victoria, c. 106. sec. 98), which empowered diocesans to give curates the opportunity to refute charges. If the diocesan was then satisfied that the charges were still well-founded, he could revoke their licences summarily, and without further process. The fairest course, the Bishop decided, was to give the accused the opportunity of confronting and cross-examining the accusers. Each side would then have opportunity to demonstrate the strength of their case. Because of unalterable engagements for several weeks from mid-December,

[34] *LM,* 11 Jan. 1851; Pollen, pp. 179–80; *The Statement of the Clergy of St Saviour's, Leeds, in reference to the Recent Proceedings against them* (Leeds, 1851), p. 15.
[35] *LI,* 11 Jan. 1851; *LM,* 11 Jan. 1851; *St Saviour's Clergy Statement,* pp. 15–16; Longley, p. 29; Pollen, pp. 179–80.
[36] *LM,* 11, 25 Jan. 1851; *St Saviour's Clergy Statement,* pp. 15–16; Liddon, III, 361; Pollen, p. 180; Savage and Tyne, p. 26.

the Bishop fixed a very early day (13 December) to relieve the accused from the stress of delay. Hence the accused later complained of the shortness of notice, which arrived only the day preceding. The accuser Randall subsequently pointed out that St Saviour's clergy were notified of the specific charges at the Ruridecanal meeting of 9 December, with Fawcett having given Beckett of St Saviour's similar details on 2 December. Randall observed that if the accused had not in fact had effective previous notice of the charges, it was strange that in one day they could find about forty witnesses prepared to testify.

For the hearing the Bishop brought his deputy-registrar, the Leeds solicitor E. J. Teale, as his legal assessor, to ensure that due legal process was observed. He did not, however, appoint or sit with any clerical assessors. Besides the accused curates, there were six other Leeds clergy present: the four accusers, Fawcett, Crosthwaite, Randall, and Holmes; Hook as Rural Dean and Vicar in whose vestry the inquiry was being held; and Edward Jackson as that parish's Clerk-in-Orders. St Saviour's clergy fastened on the notion that six was apparently the number for a commission of inquiry, and that, if not a commission, then the six clergy known as their 'most active and keen' adversaries were there to function as a 'contrivance' serving the same purpose. In fact the four accusers at the ordinary and special Ruridecanal Chapter meetings fulfilled the same role before the Bishop. Neither Hook nor Jackson were there as accusers. During the ten hours the Bishop was sitting, Hook never spoke at all, and Jackson only to query an assertion by Minster which to Jackson's own knowledge was dishonest and disingenuous. The Bishop insisted that no clergy were present as his assessors. His findings were based on his own evaluation of the facts presented.[37]

On 13 and 14 December 1850, therefore, before the Bishop of Ripon, accusers and accused confronted each other, bringing witnesses to support their respective cases. Charges were made — solely against the curates of St Saviour's — 'of preaching Romish doctrines, and of encouraging Romish observances and practices'. On 23 December the Bishop notified the curates Beckett and Rooke that evidence had been produced at the investigation, which they did not contradict and could not shake. It claimed that they had both been involved in a system of private confession and authoritative absolution, without the sanction of the Church, and in direct opposition to his own express written injunction. Each curate was also informed briefly of the precise circumstances on which these findings were based.[38]

37. *LI*, 21 Dec. 1850; *LM*, 28 Dec. 1850; *St Saviour's Clergy Statement*, pp. 3, 16; Longley, *Bishop's Letter*, pp. 13–14, 30–31; Pollen, p. 180; Savage and Tyne, p. 26.
38. *LI*, 21 Dec. 1850; *LM*, 28 Dec. 1850; *St Saviour's Clergy Statement*, pp. 3–6, 16, App., pp. 1–6; Grantham, p. 24; Longley, pp. 13–14, 30, 36–37; Pollen, p. 180; Savage and Tyne, p. 26; Stephens, *Hook*, II, 290; Yates, *Leeds High Church*, pp. 29–30; Yates, *St Saviour's*, p. 12.

Later the Bishop illustrated the system of confession at St Saviour's by citing the full evidence of 'Mrs M.A.' She was a candidate for confirmation in 1849, instructed by Rooke, then a deacon, and Beckett, already a priest. Whilst a deacon, Rooke required her to go to Beckett for private confession. Beckett received her, knowing she had not come spontaneously, and asked questions about her sexual conduct before and after marriage. This caused shame and distress. Beckett also alarmed her by putting his hands on her head when pronouncing absolution. Afterwards 'M.A.' told her husband she had been to confession. He was displeased, and she could never bring herself to tell him the questions Beckett asked. She made her communion shortly after confirmation in October 1849. When Rooke was subsequently ordained priest, he repeatedly urged her to come to him for confession. Through dislike of confession 'M.A.' had not been to communion since the first occasion. The Bishop gave these facts in his *Letter to Parishioners of St Saviour's* (1851). He also noted that during two hours as a witness 'M.A.'s testimony could not be shaken or invalidated, or her integrity impugned. His finding was that Rooke had directed 'M.A.' to go to Beckett for confession and absolution, and that Beckett, aware of her unwillingness, had received her, and subjected her to indelicate questioning. Further, that Rooke had also, when a priest, pressed 'M.A.' to confess to himself, though knowing of her husband's disapproval, and left 'M.A.' with the impression that she could not come to communion otherwise.[39]

Because Rooke had been, at his own urgent request, at St Saviour's informally for experience, but not officially licensed, the Bishop's sentence was immediate inhibition. Beckett, however, being licensed, was permitted by statute to appeal against revocation of his licence to officiate, and remained at St Saviour's until the appeal should be finally determined. At some stage the Revd H. Coombs came to assist him. St Saviour's parishioners in January 1851 addressed their Vicar, Thomas Minster, expressing confidence in their clergy, especially about confession. Minster in reply referred to the 'interposed authority' of the diocesan, adding that it might become his duty to lead his parishioners elsewhere. The wording was a notable example of a Tractarian distinguishing the office of the Bishop from its holder. It confirmed Dr Longley in his view that St Saviour's clergy had been following practices 'unknown since the Reformation'. Crawley's licence was revoked on 6 February, and Minster resigned on 10 February. There was one unexpected consequence. Richard Ward alleged to the Bishop that Hook in 1845 held

[39] *LI*, 28 Dec. 1850; *St Saviour's Clergy Statement*, App., pp. 1, 4; Longley, pp. 31–37; Yates, *Leeds High Church*, p. 29; Yates, *St Saviour's*, pp. 12–13.

the same views on confession as those now condemned. Hook was, however, able to satisfy the Bishop to the contrary.[40]

By March 1851 rumours abounded of impending secessions. On visiting Leeds, Pusey discovered that two former St Saviour's clergy would be returning to Leeds as Roman priests. On 28 March, Ward and Crawley became Roman Catholics; on 3 April, Minster, Rooke, and Coombs; and Case, Hathaway, and Pollen at other times. Starting with Macmullen in 1847, nine out of fifteen priests connected with St Saviour's joined the Roman Church. After the initial outrage the general feeling in Leeds was one of relief. Beckett did not secede, and left St Saviour's in June, when his appeal was not upheld, and his licence was at last revoked.[41] Pusey appointed J. W. Knott as Vicar in July 1851. Knott and his successors proved enduringly loyal to the Church of England.[42]

The Nature of the Conflict at St Saviour's, 1845–51

From its consecration in 1845 until early in 1851, there was a battle, mainly in private but at times spectacularly public, between the Bishop of Ripon and St Saviour's clergy for the souls of its parishioners. At issue was a very big question: did the Reformation settlement of the English Church, as evinced in the liturgy, ordinals, and formularies of the Book of Common Prayer (1662), contain the fullness of the Catholic faith? Bishop Longley was in no doubt. He regarded the Reformation as having restored 'the primitive Catholic verities'. At his visitations he repeatedly warned the assembled clergy of the spiritual dangers of nurturing medieval doctrines and devotional practices long discontinued. Before St Saviour's was completed, therefore, the Bishop was suspicious about the building's proposed medieval features and fittings, and also about Pusey's desire there for a small college of celibates. Nor after consecration did Pusey's choice of clergy to serve St Saviour's inspire Longley with confidence. Probably the Bishop was not fully aware of Pusey's difficulties in getting clergy to serve a situation exemplified by the number of priests who converted to Rome. Community life and canonical hours meant that St Saviour's clergy mixed very little with other Leeds clerics,

[40.] LI, 11, 18, 25 Jan. 1851; LM, 11 Jan., 1 Feb. 1851; St Saviour's Clergy Statement, App., pp. 4–12; Grantham, p. 25; Herring, p. 259; Liddon, III, 362–63; Longley, pp. 36, 42–50; Pollen, pp. 183–93; Savage and Tyne, p. 27; Stephens, Hook, II, 345–47; Yates, St Saviour's, p. 15.
[41.] LI, 22 Mar., 5 Apr., 28 June 1851; LM, 15, 22 Mar., 5 Apr. 1851; Grantham, pp. 26–27, 33–34; Liddon, III, 364–65; Longley, p. 19; Savage and Tyne, pp. 27–28; Stephens, Hook, II, 291; Yates, Leeds High Church, p. 30; Yates, St Saviour's, pp. 15, 29, 32.
[42.] BLO, Wilberforce Papers, c. 66, fols 162–63, Hook to R. Wilberforce, 13 Oct. 1852, fols 164–67, Hook to R. Wilberforce, 3 Nov. 1852; LM, 19 July 1851; Grantham, pp. 27–32; Liddon, III, 366; Savage and Tyne, pp. 29–56; Yates, Leeds High Church, p. 31; Yates, St Saviour's, pp. 17–27.

except on formal occassions. There was an impression that they preferred to associate with Tractarians from elsewhere.[43]

In the first confrontation at St Saviour's shortly after parish status was attained, the Bishop acted firmly and speedily, because he had the text of Macmullen's sermon on the intercession of saints from which to base his censure. After the resulting secession of Macmullen and the two community laymen, Dr Longley personally prevailed on Ward to resign his post as Vicar. By the end of January, Ward and his curate Case had left. Thomas Minster, Vicar from April 1848, had by January 1849 been formally required by the Bishop to abandon the system of regular private confession. Minster had agreed, yet the rumours of its existence still persisted. If so, did this mean that Minster placed the system of regular confession and private absolution above his promise to the Bishop, or were his curates out of control? Paradoxically, the Papal decision in September 1850 to create a Roman Catholic English hierarchy enabled St Saviour's clergy to resolve the dilemma for themselves. It can be no coincidence that they and their Tractarian associates, assembled for the church's fifth anniversary, met in private and affirmed the Papal See's supremacy in matters of faith. This was the point at which they should have informed their respective diocesans and tendered their resignations. Instead, they informed Professor Mill, and set in train Hook's disclosure at the archdeaconry meeting, which impelled their accusers to collect evidence and bring charges.[44] Some very determined personalities on both sides were involved in these events. Longley's own actions stemmed from his high concept of episcopacy. He was determined to protect 'his poor unlettered people' from what he saw as uncatholic doctrine. He was too even-tempered and well-balanced, however, for the secessions at St Saviour's in 1851 to make him change his existing policies in relation to his clergy. Moderate Tractarians were acceptable in the See of Ripon; those among Hook's clergy, for example, experienced no difficulty.[45]

43. BL, Gladstone Papers, MS 44, 213, fols 51–56, 22 Jan. 1844, fols 57–62, 25 Jan. 1844, fols 67–68, 9 Feb. 1844 (all Hook to Gladstone); WYASL, RDB18, *Bishop's Visitation Charges* (1844), pp. 27–29, (1847), pp. 33–39, (1850), pp. 31–35; *LI*, 14 Sept. 1844, 11 Sept. 1847, 14 Sept. 1850; P. A. Adams, 'Converts to the Roman Catholic Church in England' (unpublished BLitt thesis, University of Oxford, 1977), p. 87; Herring, p. 67; Longley, pp. 5, 21–22; Pollen, pp. 60–61; Stephenson, pp. 197–98; Yates, *Leeds High Church*, p. 25; Yates, *St Saviour's*, pp. 4–5.
44. PH, fols 182–91, 31 Jan. 1842, fols 325–43, 21 Mar. 1846, fols 353–61, 7 Nov. 1846, fols 362–65, 13 Nov. 1846, fols 366–81, 15 Nov. 1846, fols 382–90, 18 Nov. 1846, fols 391–97, 20 Nov. 1846 (all Hook to Pusey); *LI*, 30 Nov. 1850, 12 Apr. 1851; Longley, p. 29.
45. *LI*, 30 Jan. 1847, 5, 12, 19 Apr. 1851; *LM*, 5, 12, 19 Apr. 1851. Chadwick, *Victorian Church*, I, 507; Church, p. 394; D. N. Jacques, 'The Clergy of the Diocese of Ripom 1836–1888, with particular reference to the Influence of the Oxford Movement (unpublished MPhil thesis, University of Leeds, 1988), pp. 36–37; Longley, pp. 2–11; Stephenson; pp. 198–99.

CHAPTER 10

Hook and Political Dissenters in Leeds, 1837–51

During the 1820s the British Government ceased to regard Anglican religious affiliation as the touchstone for political loyalty. Equal rights to civil and municipal office followed — for Dissenters in 1828, and Roman Catholics in 1829. Nevertheless, Dissenters still experienced many social disadvantages. The Church's baptismal certificate remained the most readily acceptable proof of age or identity. Except for Quakers and Jews no marriages were legal apart from those at the relevant parish church. Although the parish graveyard was available to all denominations, the choice for Dissenters was between the Anglican service or burial in silence. Other powerful irritants existed: liability to pay tithes and Church rates; exclusion from university study at Oxford or graduation at Cambridge, limiting admission to certain professions. Many other civil disabilities for Dissenters were still in place in the 1830s. They were repealed piecemeal subsequently with the last as late as 1898[1]. Empowered by the new parliamentary and municipal franchises, political Dissenters actively sought redress. Mainly Liberals, they often controlled boroughs and influenced legislation. Tithe commutation and civil registration of births, marriages and deaths resulted in 1836.[2]

The Nature of Dissent in Early Victorian Leeds

From the mid-1830s it became clear that Dissenters in Leeds outnumbered Churchpeople by about two to one. Hook rather grimly privately observed that Methodists constituted the 'Established Religion' in the town. Mainly Wesleyans, they accounted in total for seven-tenths of Leeds Protestant Dissenters by 1851, representing 42 per cent of the worshipping population. Methodists were usually non-political and towards Hook their attitude was of decorous respect. Indeed, one prominent circuit minister regarded Hook so highly that in 1837 he placed two daughters under Hook's tuition to increase their understanding of primitive Catholicism. In Leeds Hook never became a target of Methodist criticism for High Church views. Other evangelical Dissenters, Independents and Baptists possessed important congregations,

---

[1.] Chadwick, *Victorian Church*, I, 80–81, 90; Gilbert, p. 163; Varley, p. 163; W. R. Ward, *Religion and Society in England, 1790–1850* (1972), pp. 133–34.
[2.] *LI*, 17 June 1837; *LM*, 4 Mar., 1 July 1837; Chadwick, *Victorian Church*, I, 61, 142–46; Cornish, I, 117–22; Gilbert, p. 163; Ward, pp. 112–13.

whilst Old Dissent Unitarians and Quakers wielded civic influence beyond their numbers.[3] It was from the non-Methodist denominations that Leeds political Dissenters drew leadership and strength of numbers. As elsewhere they had benefited from franchise extensions. They worked through the vestry, churchwardens' elections and the Town Council, where their Liberal predominance enabled them to translate policies into action. Extremely articulate, political Dissenters were so convinced of the validity of their religious beliefs that they considered it a duty to expose what they saw as Hook's erroneous beliefs. If this simultaneously damaged Establishment influence, they counted it a bonus. Edward Baines, Jr (1800–1890), editor of the Liberal *Leeds Mercury*, gave political Dissenters free run of its columns.[4]

Hook as a High Church Target for Leeds Political Dissenters

After Hook's arrival, Baines as an evangelical Independent grew increasingly restive about Hook's claims for Anglican preeminence among religious bodies for apostolic ministry and pure Catholic doctrine. In December 1837 Hook's refusal to work with the undenominational Town Mission released Baines's pent-up irritation about Hook's exclusive High Churchmanship. A *Leeds Mercury* editorial declared that the Vicar of Leeds was 'no arrogant, fiery or self-indulgent priest', but courteous and kind, a conscientious and indefatigable pastor. Yet no man was so bigotedly devoted to his own Church, or apparently so incapable of comprehending how the Church of Christ could mean anything but the Church of England. Hook later claimed that the Book of Common Prayer was the only work which preserved the primitive tradition of Christianity; Baines dismissed Hook's assertions as wild, shameful and monstrous nonsense — 'a choice *morceau* of the theology of the Puseyites'.[5] In similar vein Baines insinuated that Hook was a covert Romanist. When, for instance, Hook supported Newman over *Tract 90*, Baines branded him as 'wholly Romish'. Later, as Anglican secessions to Rome increased, Baines depicted Hook as a likely candidate.[6] The *Leeds Mercury's* attitude towards the doctrines of Catholicity and Apostolicity was interesting. When proclaimed by Hook, it trumpeted objections. Towards the Roman Catholic Church, exhibiting an even more exclusive religious

3. BLO, Wilberforce Papers, d. 17/2, fols 340–41, Hook to Wilberforce, 20 Dec. 1838; Coleman, p. 41; Hennock, *Fit Persons,* p. 357, App. III; Stephens, *Hook* I, 401, 406, 412; Ward, p. 258.
4. Binfield, p. 62; J. R. Lowerson, 'The Political Career of Edward Baines (1800–1890)' (unpublished MA thesis, University of Leeds, 1965), p. 30; Read, *Press and People*, pp. 128–29, 205–06; Taylor, pp. 435–42.
5. *LM*, 18, 25 Mar., 22 Apr., 23 Dec. 1837, 11 Aug. 1838, 23 Feb., 2 Mar., 29 June 1839.
6. *LM*, 24 Apr. 1841, 9, 23 Nov. 1844.

attitude, its references were respectful, as due to those with common disabilities and shared political loyalties.[7]

Sometimes Baines would inflate personal issues by publishing information insufficiently checked. In September 1838 the *Leeds Mercury* announced that Hook had been dismissed as Queen's Chaplain for asserting before Queen Victoria that the Church's existence did not depend on its Established status. Baines contended that Hook richly deserved dismissal, 'for addressing such historico-theological nonsense to the Royal ear'. On learning shortly afterwards that no dismissal has occurred, Baines declared without apology that he had been misled by *The Times's* report. (The sermon as delivered, published as *Hear the Church*, rapidly achieved wide circulation.) In 1839 Baines stopped his press to report that Hook had served notice to expel Sinclair from St George's pulpit. Sinclair responded that the issue concerned a technicality of vicarial jurisdiction, which quashed adverse implications against Hook, forcing the *Leeds Mercury* to express 'great regret' for printing the story.[8] In 1843 Baines overreached himself. His newspaper had generated tremendous Dissenting opposition nationally against clauses in Sir James Graham's draft Factory Bill which would have secured Anglican predominance in proposed factory district schools. Baines alleged complicity between Hook and the factory inspector R. J. Saunders, who had undertaken the preliminary enquiries. This accusation Hook strongly denied. Pressed for proof, Baines cited a private letter from Hook to Saunders, 'found in a London Street' and indirectly coming to Baines. Saunders thereupon accused Baines of participating in a dishonourable transaction, by irregularly retaining a private letter and using it as justification for a baseless allegation. Baines could never fully exonerate himself from this attempt to tarnish Hook's reputation.[9]

Other political Dissenters with a grievance against Hook or the Church knew that almost certainly the *Leeds Mercury* and often the *Leeds Intelligencer*, would print particulars. A few examples will suffice. Of Hook's critics, the most vehement was the Revd J. E. Giles, sharp and cutting, the uncompromising evangelical minister of South Parade Baptist Chapel. Giles was enraged by Hook's lofty attitude towards Dissenting ministers, in denying their ministerial function and categorizing them as 'teachers'. When Giles's widowed father-in-law remarried in 1838, the announcement in the *Leeds Mercury* struck its own counterblow. There was no mention of the legal ceremony conducted by Hook at Leeds Parish Church, the sole reference being to the 'religious ceremony' by the 'Rev. J. E. Giles' at the Baptist

[7]. *LM*, 7 July, 29 Sept., 6, 13, 20, 27 Oct., 3 Nov. 1838, 25 June 1842, 12 Oct. 1844, 18 Oct. 1845, 19, 26 Oct., 2 Nov. 1850.
[8]. *LI*, 2, 9 Mar. 1839; *LM*, 1, 8 Sept. 1838, 23 Feb., 2 Mar. 1839.
[9]. *LI*, 7, 14, 21, 28 Oct., 11 Nov. 1943; *LM.* 4, 18, 25 Mar. 7, 21, Oct., 4 Nov. 1843; Chadwick, *Victorian Church*, 1, 340–42; Cornish, 1, 206–09; Lowerson, p. 142; Ward, pp. 247–48, 279.

Chapel.[10] In 1841 Hook's unchanged attitude showed him in a poor light. He received from the Revd. R. W. Hamilton, Belgrave Independent Chapel, an invitation from local Dissenting ministers for clergy to join their workhouse service rota. In conveying the clergy's decision to decline, Hook replied to Hamilton in the third person, 'to avoid even the appearance of conceding a principle'. The *Leeds Mercury* commented on Hook's avoidance of the title of 'Reverend'. Hamilton replied irenically that he would not wish a style of address at the expense of principle. Hamilton's colleagues decided to 'unmurmuringly endure' Hook's imputations.[11] Misrepresentation by the *Leeds Mercury* in 1843 greatly alarmed Hook. A speech by a politically prominent Leeds Unitarian, Hamer Stansfeld, referred to an anonymous Puseyite tract which described marriages by Dissenting ministers as 'blasphemous', not binding, and 'legalised adultery'. The *Leeds Mercury*, however, attributed these comments to one of Hook's Leeds *Tracts*. Much disturbed, Hook tackled Stansfeld in open correspondence. Stansfeld admitted that he had missed the unauthorized substitution in proof, and allowed it to stand after publication. Preserving anonymity, the original publisher from Boston, Lincolnshire, discounted both attributions. Hook advised Stansfeld to be wary of the *Leeds Mercury's* assertions about the Church, as the journal's character was so well known. Baines expostulated, but Hook left Baines to exculpate himself.[12]

In 1845 Giles left Leeds hurriedly for personal reasons. Political Dissenters' criticism of Hook for High Churchmanship ceased, except in 1847 by the *Leeds Mercury*, following the secessions at St Saviour's. Hook's subsequent *rapprochement* with Evangelical Leeds clergy also influenced Baines, who by 1850, without irony, described Hook as 'among the brightest ornaments of the Church'.[13]

Political Dissenters, the Leeds Vestry, Churchwardens, and Church Rates, 1822–36

According to the *Manchester Guardian*, Dissenters' resentment about exactions in support of the Church headed their list of grievances in 1834. Opposition to Church rates was keenest in the expanding industrial North and Midlands, where Dissenting zeal and organizational flexibility had largely prevailed against a rigid parochial system, clerical inertia, and episcopal complacency. In Yorkshire, opposition was early and determined, with Sheffield, Leeds, Bradford, and Dewsbury raising the issue from 1818. They were the

---

[10.] *LI*, 9 Apr. 1836, 2 June 1838; *LM*, 2 Apr. 1836.
[11.] *LI*, 27 Mar. 1841; *LM*, 3 Apr. 1841; Taylor, pp. 431–35.
[12.] *LI*, 22, 29 Apr., 6, 13 May 1843; *LM*, 6, 13 May 1843; Taylor, pp. 602–03.
[13.] *LM*, 13 Sept. 1845, 2, 9 Jan. 1847, 23 Feb. 1850; D. Fraser, *Urban Politics in Victorian England* (Leicester, 1976), pp. 18, see also note 29, 269, 286, re note 29.

forerunners of the more widespread agitation that grew from 1830 onwards.[14] The attainment of civil rights in 1828 increased urban Dissenters' resentment at compulsory rate levies made by vestries towards the running costs of parish churches. Between 1832 and 1837 several Parliamentary attempts at remedy came to nothing.[15] Political Dissenters in Leeds, however, opted early for local action. Edward Baines, the elder, editor of the *Leeds Mercury*, the influential Liberal journal, realized that control of the Leeds vestry, which authorised Church rates, was vital. With Edward his son, Baines from 1819 campaigned for two objectives: creation of a climate of opinion against Church rates amongst ratepayers voting at vestry meetings; election of churchwardens prepared to subject all rate proposals to rigorous scrutiny.[16] Derek Fraser has discussed how churchwardens of St Peter's then possessed other functions in the community than those directly concerning the Parish Church. In this chapter, however, the discussion relates solely to their impact on Church life.[17]

Baines's first success was to secure disclosure of detailed churchwardens' accounts in 1822, when the vestry refused to authorize further grants until itemized accounts were published. A turning point in the composition of the churchwarden body occurred in 1826, when the Anglican Liberal wool-stapler, J. A. Buttrey, was elected. The following year he led a group composed equally of Liberals and Tories. From 1828 onwards Liberals constituted the majority until supplanted in 1842 by Chartists. Buttrey delivered his masterstroke in August 1833. After years of regularly levying a rate, he announced that the unexpended balanced of £437 from the previous year was sufficient for anticipated expenses. The following year a half penny rate was imposed to provide the sacraments but from 1835 no Church rate was ever again levied in Leeds.[18]

Leeds Tories, as Anglicans, did not cede control of the vestry to Liberals, mainly Dissenters, without a struggle. Year by year they attempted to carry their list of candidates. Edward Baines, Jr, without desiring office himself, acted as election manager for the Liberals. Feelings ran high in the years after the Reform Act. In 1833 George Hirst, a Tory Merchant, had to abandon his attempt to put the Anglican list. Next year, after more than three hours of virtual riot, the vicar, Richard Fawcett, left the chair, and the vestry illegally elected seven Liberals to serve with the vicar's warden. In the 1830s such scenes in the manufacturing districts were not uncommon, at a time when

[14.] Chadwick, *Victorian Church*, I, 86; Cornish, I, 158–59; Gilbert, pp. 118–20; Morris, pp. 123, 230; Ward, pp. 133–34, 191–92.
[15.] Chadwick, *Victorian Church*, I, 87–89; Cornish, I, 158–63; Woodward, p. 511.
[16.] Fraser, 'Churchwardens', p. 3; Read, *Press and People*, p. 115; Taylor, pp. 435, 439; Ward, p. 178.
[17.] Fraser, 'Churchwardens', pp. 1–22.
[18.] *LM*, 31 Dec. 1836, 12 Jan. 1839; Fraser, 'Churchwardens', pp. 3–6; Fraser, 'Politics and Society', pp. 273–74, 285; Read, *Press and People*, p. 115; Yates, 'Religious Life', pp. 252–53.

Dissenters nationally were making a concerted effort to secure statutory abolition of the rate. Local Reformers were often successful in permanently preventing compulsory Church rates being levied: Birmingham (1831); Manchester (1835); Bradford (1848); Rochdale (1849).[19]

Nationally there were 632 contests between 1833 and 1851: 484 successful in resisting rates, 148 unsuccessful. Owen Chadwick pointed out that unnumbered localities simply refrained from inviting a foregone defeat. With two special exceptions, discussed below, Hook was of the same mind. It was not, however, until the Compulsory Church Rates Abolition Act of 1868 that the whole contentious issue was finally laid to rest.[20]

Hook and the Leeds Churchwardens, 1837–51

In 1837 Hook came to a town where no Church rate had been levied since 1835. Indeed in December 1836, late in Fawcett's incumbency, a public meeting was held (part of a national campaign by four hundred Dissenting bodies) which resolved to petition the Government to abolish Church rates. Two well-known Churchmen, heard respectfully but with much laughter, made the case unsuccessfully for the rate, especially in relation to religious services for the poor.[21]

Current anti-rate feeling did not prevent the churchwardens from seeking a rate in August 1837. They planned Hook's discomfiture, hoping to expose him to insults from an unruly crowd, and provoke him into remarks damaging to his reputation. On 17 August thousands gathered in the Coloured Cloth Hall yard. Public meeting procedures were followed. Edward Johnson, chief warden, postulated expenses totalling £355 11s. 6d. An associate moved a half penny rate. The Vicar's warden John Garland (Anglican) seconded. Speaking first, the Revd J. E. Giles, Baptist minister, dextrously combined personal abuse of Hook with a reasoned case against ratepayers being compelled to meet Establishment running costs. Hook surprisingly declined to counter Giles's arguments, 'because he knew the crowd would not listen'. Instead, he thanked Mr Giles for enabling him to demonstrate a 'very high church

[19.] Chadwick, *Victorian Church*, I, 47, 86, 147; P. F. Chance, 'Religion and Politics in Birmingham, 1830–1850' (unpublished BPhil thesis, Open University, 1982), p. 16; C. M. Elliott, 'Social and Economic History of the Principal Protestant Denominations in Leeds, 1760–1844' (unpublished DPhil thesis, University of Oxford, 1962), pp. 192–94; Fraser, 'Churchwardens', pp. 5–13; Jowitt, p. 42; Lowerson, p. 152; Read, *Press and People*, pp. 78–79, 128; M. A. Smith, 'Religion in Industrial Society: The Case of Oldham and Saddleworth, 1780–1865' (unpublished DPhil thesis, University of Oxford, 1988), pp. 5, 99–101; Ward, pp. 178–89, 191–92.

[20.] Chadwick, *Victorian Church*, I, 152; Gilbert, pp. 118–20, 163; Woodward, p. 511.

[21.] *LI*, 17, 24 Dec. 1836, 14 Jan., 25 Feb., 1, 8, 15, 22, 29 Apr., 6, 27 May, 3 June 1837; *LM*, 24 Dec. 1836, 28 Jan., 4 Feb., 11, 18, 25 Mar., 1, 22 Apr., 27 May 1837; Chadwick, *Victorian Church*, I, 146–47; Cornish, I, p. 163.

'principle' — he forgave him. Hook then turned to Giles and bowed. A storm of cheering ensued. *Pace* W. R. W. Stephens the rate was not passed. It was not even put to the vote, an amendment to adjourn having been successfully obtained before the substantive motion could be taken.[22]

Hook emerged from the meeting with more credit than his churchwardens had planned, though this jocular gesture had increased Giles's existing personal animosity. Already doubtful about the efficacy of Church rates, Hook never again sanctioned an approach to the vestry for St Peter's running costs, preferring to rely on voluntary donations. Even so, he felt it necessary to impress upon the incoming churchwardens that they incurred financial obligations by accepting office. In September 1837, at Hook's request, Archdeacon Musgrave visited Leeds for this purpose. Showing them the result of several years' parsimony, service-books and prayer-books in tatters, and surplices in rags, Musgrave formally required replacement, confirming that necessities for public services were the only requirements for churchwardens' concern. Edward Johnson thereupon asked if wardens were bound to replace unconsumed consecrated wine poured on the floor after Holy Communion. Hook explained that any unconsumed consecrated wine — the 'blood of Christ' — was normally consumed by poor communicants when present, otherwise by fire or consecrated ground. Musgrave advised, and Hook concurred, that less wine should be consecrated initially, to enable requirements to be gauged more exactly.[23]

Hook's letter of 5 April 1838 in the *British Magazine* gave a fuller explanation. It referred to the Holy Communion rubric that unused consecrated wine must be consumed in church. By custom at St Peter's, poor communicants were invited to do this. If clergy were to have substituted on that occasion, when no poor communicants were present, Hook realized that Dissenter churchwardens would ensure maximum unfavourable publicity. With fire unavailable, Hook made a piscina, probably where the chancel's side-wall formed a crevice with the adjoining flagstone, enabling the excess wine to drain into consecrated ground. In 1842, however, Giles told a national meeting that Hook would not allow excess consecrated wine to 'be polluted by the lips of the poor', since Hook's new church contained a sink, down which Hook had even stuffed consecrated bread.[24] Giles was ostensibly illustrating 'superstitious practices' of Anglican clergy, but had not checked his facts. In the *British Magazine* Hook deplored Giles's 'reckless falsehoods', particularly the distorted construction placed on Hook's attitude to the poor, which Hook interpreted as a deliberate attempt to alienate their affections

[22] BLO, MS Eng. Lett., d. 368, fols 37–39, Hook to J. W. Croker, 9 Nov. 1839; WYASL, LPC39/1, Vestry Book, 17 Aug. 1837, LPC49/1, Sequestration Papers, Churchwardens' minute. book 10 Aug. 1837; *LI*, 19 Aug., 30 Sept., 1837; *LM*, 19, 26 Aug., 9 Sept. 1837; Stephens, *Hook*, II, 375–77.
[23] *LI*, 30 Sept., 7 Oct. 1837; *LM*, 30 Sept., 21 Oct., 4, 18 Nov. 1837; Stephens, *Hook*, I, 374.
[24] *British Magazine*, Hook's letter, cited in *LI*, 7 July 1838; *LI*, 11 June 1842; *LM*, 18 June 1842.

from the Church. Giles replied, citing 'a churchwarden' as informant. A Baptist ex-churchwarden declared churchwardens heard about 'stuffed' bread from someone clearing the pipe. Chantrell, the church's architect, revealed that he had designed and installed the piscina without Hook's knowledge and that it would take a ramrod to stuff bread down the pipe. The obstruction, wrote J. M. Tennant, of the Building Committee, was lime or plaster inspected by him after removal. It was unstained by wine, indicating a piscina unused since Church consecration. Hook came better out of the interchange than Giles.[25]

The obstructive attitude of Baines's Dissenting Churchwardens towards Hook reflected their resentment of the Establishment and dislike of his High Churchmanship. Their readiness to involve Hook's deepest religious convictions in controversy he found personally more distressing. In 1841 a ludicrously short election bred Liberal over-confidence. A three-sided contest occurred in 1842 between Liberals, Conservatives and Chartists. Initially it was difficult for Hook to decide who was successful. The second show of hands produced a large majority for the Chartists. Tactical voting had occurred. D. Fraser considered that Liberals and Chartists had combined as an anti-Church gesture. Equally possible, of course, was that Tories, especially Operative Conservatives, had joined with Chartists to oust the Liberals.[26] Though committed to preventing Church rates, the Chartist churchwardens were co-operative in other respects. Hook viewed the departure of Dissenting churchwardens with relief, and in 1843 described the Chartists as the only churchwardens since his arrival in Leeds who he could regard as honourable, straightforward, and gentlemanly. Their predecessors were indignant, but in 1844 Hook repeated his assessment, stating that Chartists had ascertained and fulfilled their legal obligations, unlike churchwardens earlier, who had been obstructive. During five years in office Chartists and Hook regarded each other with mutual esteem.[27]

From 1847 Vestry elections returned Anglican Conservatives as churchwardens each year. Election proceedings were usually short, the *Leeds Mercury* commenting in 1849 that they lacked the excitement of former years. Chartists continued to put candidates forward up to 1850, but were never again successful. A disputed election in 1850 caused a local stir. One account

[25] WYASL, LPC39/1, Vestry Book, 23 Apr. 1840, 15 Apr. 1841, 31 Mar. 1842; *British Magazine*, June 1842, cited in *LI*, 11 June 1842; *LI*, 18, 25 June 1842; *LM*, 18, 25 June 1842.

[26] WYASL, LPC39/1, Vestry Book, 30 Mar. 1837, 4 Apr. 1839, 23 Apr. 1840, 15 Apr. 1841, 31 Mar. 1842; *LI*, 1 Apr. 1837, 21 Apr. 1838, 6 Apr. 1839, 25 Apr. 1840, 17 Apr. 1841, 2 Apr. 1842; *LM*, 1 Apr. 1837, 21 Apr. 1838, 6 Apr. 1839, 25 Apr. 1840, 17 Apr. 1841, 2 Apr. 1842; Fraser, 'Churchwardens', p. 18 and 58 (note); Stephens, *Hook*, II, 118–21.

[27] WYASL, LPC39/1, Vestry Book, 31 Mar. 1842, 20 Apr. 1843, 11 Apr. 1844; *LI*, 2, 9 Apr. 18 June 1842, 22, 29 Apr. 1843, 13 Apr. 1844, 22 Mar. 1845, 18 Apr. 1846, 10, 17 Apr. 1847; *LM*, 2, 16, 23, 30 Apr. 1842, 22, 29 Apr. 1843, 13 Apr. 1844, 29 Mar. 1845, 18 Apr. 1846, 10, 17 Apr. 1847; Fraser, 'Churchwardens', pp. 18–19; Rusby, pp. 281–84.

conveyed that Hook took the vote with unseemly speed, once the Anglican list had been seconded; the other that the Chartists were not ready with their list when nominations were being taken. Hence, when John Shaw, the Chartist agent, requested his list to be put, Hook refused, because voting had taken place. He suggested that the Chartists should elect their own list after he left the chair. The Archdeacon's court in April could then decide between the two lists. The Chartists did as Hook suggested, but allowed their claim to lapse by failing to attend the Archdeacon's court to test their claim.[28]

Although it was ten years into Hook's time at Leeds before the vestry elected Anglican churchwardens, his attitude and personality prevented the difficulties experienced in the 1830s by Richard Fawcett, his predecessor. Similar difficulties at Manchester led the wardens there to make payment of the rate voluntary. Within Leeds borough, however, semi-rural Headingley's vestry continued to levy a Church rate, with the chapelry incumbent, William Williamson, successfully proceeding against Quakers for non-payment in 1843 and 1844. Fortunately for Hook, as parish priest, Williamson's actions did not result in lengthy litigation, as at Braintree (1837–1853), or imprisonment of conscientious and determined defaulters such as Thorogood at Chelmsford or Baines at Leicester.[29]

Dissenters in Leeds had successfully stirred up feeling against Church rates in Fawcett's time. With Hook they encountered a Church leader able to sense the mood of a great industrial town. No later than 1841 he informed the Dissenting churchwardens that he would provide for worship at St Peter's by voluntary subscription without recourse to Church rate. In 1846 he reaffirmed this stance, and the congregation's readiness to continue raising annually the £600 or £700 necessary for the church and its services. This attitude avoided the fate of Rochdale Parish Church, which fell into debt and dilapidation, because the Vicar, J. E. N. Molesworth was too rigid to consider a voluntary rate or preach for subscriptions. By contrast Hook's conversion to voluntaryism enabled the rebuilding and upkeep of Leeds Parish Church, combined with an admirable standard of divine worship. Thus Edward Baines's perception in 1819 that control of the vestry was the key factor in levying or refusing a rate eventually led to a permanent cessation of compulsory Church rate in Leeds more than thirty years before its statutory abolition. In Leeds the

[28] *LI*, 29 Apr. 1848, 14 Apr. 1849, 6 Apr., 4 May 1850; *LM*, 14 Apr. 1849, 6 Apr., 4 May 1850, 26 Apr. 1851; Fraser, 'Churchwardens', p. 21, cf. note 21.

[29] WYASL, LPC41/19, Churchwardens' Treasurer, Acct Book, 1847–52, inc. minutes of Churchwardens' meetings, 1847–51, LPC41/20, Treasurer's Cash Book, ordinary expenses of Parish Church, 1847–54, inc. minutes of Churchwardens' meetings, 1847–52, LPC41/22, Subscription Book, ordinary expenses, 1847–52, LPC 41/24, Subscription Book, ordinary expenses due at [Archdeacon's] Visitation, 1851; Brotherton Library Special Collections, Society of Friends, Carlton Hill Archives, L17, Brighouse Monthly Meeting, Sufferings Record, 1829–56, pp. 40–41, date of seizure, 25 Feb. 1843 (reference kindly supplied by Mr R. S. Mortimer); *LI*, 18 May 1844; Chadwick, *Victorian Church*, I, 149–50, 155–58; Cornish, I, 163–68; Stephens, *Hook*, I, 219; Ward, pp. 178–82.

initial exasperated Anglican acceptance of defeat over the rate in Fawcett's time was transformed by Hook into a generous and enthusiastic Anglican response for the voluntary support of their Parish Church.[30]

Church, Town Council, and Burial Grounds, Leeds 1836–50

One of the largest towns among the 178 English boroughs whose old corporations disappeared at the end of 1835 was Leeds. Nonconformist Liberals held sway there until 1895; in Birmingham and Leicester their dominance lasted even longer. For Leeds Anglicans it meant that the long-standing co-operation between the Church and the municipal authority could no longer be taken for granted. However, as an initial gesture of goodwill, not repeated, the inaugural council in 1836 elected several Anglican Tories as aldermen.[31] The municipal changes also affected the Parish Church. Previously the Anglican close corporation had attended officially on particular occasions. With the council this no longer applied. Attendance became an individual matter. Some Dissenters refrained, as elsewhere. Of thirteen Mayors between 1836 and 1849, the four Anglicans continued the custom. Three evangelical Dissenters and one Unitarian also attended, the latter explicitly to demonstrate goodwill, whilst one Roman Catholic and four Unitarians quietly stayed away.[32] More important than civic attendance, however, was the reality of municipal power. By 1836 Liberal Dissenters also controlled the Workhouse Board, the vestry, the churchwardens and the magistrates' bench. Through the vicar's freehold, the Church still controlled the parochial graveyards, which were becoming increasingly overcrowded. Here Dissenters' 'grievance' remained, for their funerals had to be conducted by Anglican rite, or held in silence. It was a situation not remedied nationally until 1880.[33]

By 1841 overcrowding malpractices became public. Gravediggers were arraigned for clandestinely removing coffins after the funeral, to partly-filled graves elsewhere. These surreptitious acts were carried out unknown to the relatives of the deceased. Informed of the difficulties, the churchwardens told the master gravedigger that they had not funds to purchase additional land.

---

[30] LI, 18 Apr. 1846; LM, 24 Dec. 1841, 18 Apr. 1846; Fraser, 'Churchwardens', pp. 5, 14; Ward, pp. 188–89.

[31] Chadwick, Victorian Church, I, 111; Forster, pp. 12–15; Fraser, 'Politics and Society', pp. 279, 283; Hennock, Fit Persons, pp. 13, 17, 29; Mayhall, pp. 433–36; Taylor, pp. 30–31; T. Woodhouse, p. 363; Woodward, pp. 460, 462–63.

[32] LI, 17 Dec. 1836, 30 Nov. 1839, 20, 27 June 1840, 13, 20 Nov. 1841, 14, 21, 28 Nov., 12 Dec. 1846, 2 Dec. 1848, 17 Nov. 1849; LM, 17 Dec. 1836, 16, 30 June 1838, 27 June 1840, 6, 13, 20 Nov. 1841, 7 Jan. 1843, 2 Dec. 1848; Fraser, 'Politics and Society', p. 284; Mayhall, pp. 440, 449, 458, 463, 468, 478, 487, 498, 512, 523, 551, 570, 580; Taylor, p. 31.

[33] Fraser, 'Politics and Society', pp. 279–80; Gilbert, p. 163; Hennock, Fit Persons, p. 180; Mayhall, p. 437.

One publication immediately blamed the churchwardens as 'Whig-Radicals' nominated by Edward Baines, Jr. When the churchwardens became legally compelled to seek a rate from the vestry, 'A Lover of Consistency', probably J. E. Giles, wrote strongly against authorizing public funds to extend 'the parson's freehold'. The churchwardens' proposal on 17 December 1841 for a rate of 11d. in the pound was decisively rejected. Over 10,000 voted against.[34] Having engineered the impasse, the Dissenter churchwardens approached their council allies. Hook could legally have secured a mandatory rate, but preferred to await the result of council deliberations about a municipal cemetery, provision for which they would take powers through promoting private legislation. As the Bill was being drafted, Church and council proved mutually co-operative. Hook ceded vicarial rights to a new parochial graveyard. With Bishop Longley he assented to clauses in the draft Bill for all denominations to have the right to be buried by their own minister. The resulting Leeds Burial Ground Act (1842) was the first to empower a town council to operate municipal cemeteries. Its example was soon followed by councils of all descriptions.[35]

By this course, Hook ceded to the council income from all interments, memorials and inscriptions formerly accruing through his graveyard freehold. In partial recompense, the council's act awarded joint compensation of one shilling to Hook and the Clerk-in-Orders solely for interments in the designated Anglican section. The council accordingly purchased land at Burmantofts for Beckett Street Cemetery and at Hunslet similarly. Even before Bishop Longley consecrated the Anglican portions in September 1844, council members were cavilling at paying the awarded compensation out of equivalent fees for consecrated and unconsecrated ground.[36] Councillor Joseph Cliff's later proposal for a one shilling additional charge for Anglican interments began years of controversy. Having conceded much to secure equity of burial rites for Dissenters, Hook protested against the discriminatory impost contemplated. On 25 November 1844 the Liberal Dissenting majority nevertheless approved the additions, the Act being silent on fees. The influential Liberal Alderman J. H. Shaw, Anglican, declared that the additional charge would raise a quarrel which would not disappear until it was withdrawn. Supporting Hook, the prominent Chartist Joshua Hobson

[34.] BL, Gladstone Papers, MS 44,213, fols 31–32, Hook to Gladstone, 17 Dec. 1841; WYASL, LPC39/1, Vestry Book, 15 Apr. 1841; *LI*, 16 Jan., 20 Nov., 18 Dec. 1841; *LM*, 16, 30 Jan, 27 Nov., 18 Dec., 1841; *Leeds Wednesday Journal*, 20 Jan. 1841, cited in *LI*, 23 Jan. 1841.

[35.] *LI*, 8 Jan., 19 Feb., 11 June, 2, 9, 16, 30 July 1842, 7 Jan. 1843, 2 Oct. 1847; *LM*, 8, 15, 22 Jan., 9 Apr. 4, 11, 18 June, 16 July 1842; S. Barnard, *To Prove I'm Not Forgot: Living and Dying in a Victorian City* (Manchester, 1990), pp. 197–98.

[36.] *LI*, 9, 16, 30 July 1842, 9, 30 Sept., 21 Oct. 1843, 31 Aug., 7, 14, 21 Sept. 1844; *LM*, 11 June, 16 July, 17 Dec. 1842, 30 Sept. 1843, 13 Jan. 7, 14 Sept., 5 Oct. 1844; Barnard, pp. 6–8, 197; Mayhall, p. 481.

averred that Hook had shown the reverse of the grasping spirit now alleged.[37] For Beckett Street the cheapest interment became: Dissenters 8*s.*: Anglicans 9*s.* Public discontent forced reconsideration, especially since the comparable Anglican graveyard fee was uniformly 3*s.* In February 1845 the leading Liberal, Alderman Tottie, Unitarian, urged equal scales to reciprocate the Established Church's concessions, which had made the Burial Ground Act possible. The Council decided to reduce charges but maintain discrimination. For the cheapest graves Dissenters were to pay 2*s.* 6*d.*, Anglicans 3*s.* 6*d.*[38]

Even the Council's very competitive revised charges failed to attract. The old parish graveyard apparently inspired ties not easily broken. (Between 1845 and 1847 one Anglican clergyman alone personally conducted 995 funerals there.) In contrast, Beckett Street cemetery's first year from 14 August 1845 recorded 120 burials (Dissenters 85, Anglicans 35). When the council reviewed these figures in 1846, Councillor Lister, Conservative and Dissenter, likened the low usage to 'a species of religious persecution' and an unfair charge. For the Liberal Dissenting majority his words fell on stony ground. The mood was against accommodation with the Church. In 1847 the Liberal and Methodist Councillor Joseph Richardson's attempt to inflame public opinion by presenting graveyard malpractices of 1841 as still extant was conclusively rebutted. Richardson's disclosure that each interment at Leeds cost the Council £5 8*s.* 6*d.*, and at Hunslet £36 8*s.* 5*d.*, was more likely to influence changes of mind if not of heart.[39] Such dismaying figures induced the Council on 1 October 1847 to address Hook's subsequent proposals seriously. The main problem, he suggested, was the Council's additional one shilling tax on Anglican municipal cemetery burials, it was so unlike their co-operative attitude before the Act was passed. The council's subsequent 'violation of conscience', Hook continued, would be resisted until remedied. He would then happily petition the Bishop for churchyard closures. If need be, however, churchyards would remain open and more land purchased. Alderman Lupton remarked that the vicar's arguments were cogent and his self-sacrificing spirit well attested. After discussion the additional shilling for Anglican interments was withdrawn. Hook then petitioned the Bishop as promised.[40]

With fees reluctantly equalised, controversy respecting the cemetery now focused on the Anglican chaplain's stipend. It had been fixed in 1844 by the council at £80 yearly, in parity with the Nonconformist chaplain's. The Anglican chaplain's post was currently vacant, but the Church could only appoint at the Council's request. Following negotiation, the Council made

[37.] *LI*, 9, 16, 30 Nov., 1844; *LM*, 2, 30 Nov. 1844.
[38.] *LI*, 18 Dec. 1841, 7, 14 Sept. 1844, 1 Mar. 1845; *LM*, 5 Jan. 1850.
[39.] *LI*, 23, 30 Nov. 1844, 15 Aug. 1846, 14, 21 Aug., 30 Oct. 1847; *LM*, 14 Aug., 11 Sept. 1847; Barnard, pp. 1–2; Fraser, 'Churchwardens', p. 20.
[40.] *LI*, 2, 30 Oct. 1847; *LM*, 30 Oct. 1847.

their consent conditional upon the Bishop's approving a much reduced stipend of 40s. yearly, supplemented by £78 yearly from Hook. With a thousand Anglican burials expected annually, the Bishop would 'not permit himself to be disgusted', and agreed. Hook's contributions, acknowledged quarterly, kept this unusual arrangement to the fore. Perhaps, however, it induced the council in November 1849 to ask Hook, if in return for fixing the Anglican chaplain's stipend at £80 yearly, he and Edward Jackson, Clerk-in-Orders, would commute their statutory compensation per Anglican burial of 8d. and 4d. respectively. Hook was conciliatory. Against legal advice and actuarial opinion Hook agreed to accept the nicely judged but hardly tempting offer of £30 yearly whilst vicar. He prevailed upon Jackson to accept similarly, on the joint understanding that cemetery fees were to remain equal. Effective on 1 January 1850, all matters in dispute were then regarded as satisfactorily settled.[41]

For Church and Dissent in early Victorian Leeds the Establishment was the irremovable common factor in their religious life. From the 1820s Dissenters began to be aware that their numerical advantage gave them political influence. By packing vestry meetings to elect churchwardens, they appointed sufficient Reformers, mostly Dissenters, to first reduce, then prevent Church rates. Richard Fawcett as vicar found their proceedings an unwelcome novelty. By 1837, when Hook arrived, the pattern was set. More resilient that Fawcett, Hook turned the stalemate over Church rates to advantage. His personality and hard work enthused his congregation to provide not only for a new Parish Church, but also for its upkeep and the maintenance of a first-rate choir.[42]

Because Hook's adoption of voluntaryism delivered St Peter's from financial stringency, political Dissenters' interest in churchwardens' posts declined. After their defeat by Chartists in 1842 they were never again serious contenders. However, on the town council they were still powerful. Although Hook and Bishop Longley had willingly surrendered legal rights (and Hook considerable income) to enable Dissenters to have their own ministers and services in the municipal cemetery, the council proved intent upon charging Anglicans higher interment fees. When forced by Hook's unflinching opposition, and compelling economic considerations, to equalize fees, they swiftly retaliated by fixing the annual stipend for the incoming Anglican cemetery chaplain at one-fortieth of that of his Nonconformist opposite number. It needs to be said that Hook's disputes with the council were about obtaining equal treatment for Anglicans regarding fees and chaplaincy, and

[41]. *LI*, 9 July 1842, 7 Sept. 1844, 30 Oct., 13 Nov. 1847, 11, 18 Nov. 1848, 5 Jan. 1850; *LM*, 16 July 1842, 7 Sept. 1844, 30 Oct., 20 Nov. 1847, 11, 18 Nov. 1848, 5 Jan. 1850; Barnard, pp. 1–2; Fraser, 'Churchwardens', p. 21; Mayhall, pp. 481–82.
[42]. BLO, MS Eng. Lett. d. 368, fols 37–39, Hook to J. W. Croker, 9 Nov. 1839; Fraser, 'Churchwardens', pp. 3–13.

ANGLICAN RESURGENCE UNDER W. F. HOOK

not the unseemly wrangles for money as might be gathered from the accounts of Fraser and Sylvia M. Barnard. Once these contentious issues were settled, better relations ensued all round. Hook's own reward was that in the municipal cemetery of Leeds there was affront neither to Church nor Dissent.[43] Impressed by the vicar's co-operativeness over commutation, the Council reciprocated warmly. Their changed attitude relieved Hook from stress and enabled him to engage more widely in varied projects for social betterment.

Hook's Achievement

According to W. R. W. Stephens, Hook found Leeds in 1837 'a stronghold of Dissent' and left it in 1859 'a stronghold of the Church'. An analysis of the Religious Census of 1851 (detailed in the Endpiece) shows that the ratio of churchgoers in Leeds in 1836 differed little from that of 1815. However, the quality of Church life in the town had improved immeasurably. The incipiently reviving parish of 1836–37 had become, under Hook's guidance and leadership, a confident, united community whose organization, particularly at the Parish Church, was now a model for other English parishes. The services at St Peter's were noted for their ordered beauty and the quality of the organ and choral music. Hook, as vicar, was outstanding as a preacher, and drew many by his warmth and understanding. Within the main township the Anglican churches were now well distributed, especially in the poorer districts, all seats being free in churches from 1845, and used extensively by the poor. By 1859, when Hook was preferred to the Deanery of Chichester, in vitality, activity and renown, if not in members, Leeds had indeed become 'a stronghold of the Church', and remained so for many years after Hook's departure from the town.

[43.] *LI*, 24 Dec. 1836, 7 Jan., 1 Apr. 1837, 11, 25 Apr. 1840; *LM*, 24 Dec. 1836, 2, 9 Mar., 4 May, 30 Nov. 1844, 13 Sept. 1845, 30 Oct. 1847, 15 Dec, 1849; Barnard, pp. 6–8, 10–12; Chadwick, *Victorian Church*, I, 75–95, 142–58; Cornish, I, 158–81; Fraser, 'Churchwardens', pp. 17, 20–21; Gilbert, pp. 162–65; Moorman, pp. 329–36; Ward, pp. 126–34, 191–98; Woodward, pp. 490–91, 509–11.

Leeds and The Religious Census of 1851

Attendance at Sunday worship was recognized in the nineteenth century as a public affirmation of denominational allegiance. The Religious Census of 1851 provided a unique opportunity of comparing the relative numerical strengths of Church and Dissent. The year also represented the high point of Hook's endeavours in Leeds, with the growing network of smaller parishes firmly in place and controversies resolved. For 1851 Nigel Yates extracted attendance figures for Leeds township, which may be compared with Baines's estimates in 1837 of relative denomination strengths. In ratio form of Dissenters to Anglicans the latter represented 2:1. Yates's figures for Census Sunday, 30 March 1851, indicated 1.81:1 for morning services and 1.71:1 for evening. Taken together, a perceptible Anglican improvement may be inferred. In broad terms for every eight practising Dissenters in the township there were around 4.5 Anglicans in 1851, as compared with 4 in 1837. Such a conclusion is supported by the many evidences of Anglican activity in the period.[1]

B. J. Coleman calculated an index of attendance (IA) showing denominational attendances as a percentage of population and also as a percentage share (PS) of the aggregate attendance of all denominations. To later ages the general level of religious observance in 1851 appears extremely high among the North's largest provincial towns. Leeds (IA 47.4) and Liverpool (IA 45.2) registered the highest attendances, Manchester (IA 34.7) and Sheffield (IA 32.1) being markedly lower.

For Anglican percentage shares Liverpool (PS 40.7) registered highest; Leeds (PS 34.5), Manchester (PS 34.4) and Sheffield (PS 34.3) noticeably less so. Coleman's calculations suggest that the West Riding was one of the bleakest parts of England for Anglicanism, with Halifax (PS 56.8) being a notable exception. The Anglican low point, however, was at Bradford (PS 22.9). Throughout the Riding the Methodist denominations together (PS 42.3) provided the stiffest competition against the Church, especially in Leeds (PS 41.9) and Halifax (PS 41.4). For Leeds E. P. Hennock's analysis showed Wesleyanism (PS 25.4) separately, thereby establishing it as the largest Methodist denomination in the town, and the Church consequently as the largest single denomination. Even so, it was indisputable that, in the main

---

[1.] *LM*, 4 Mar. 1837; Coleman, pp. 5–7; Yates, 'Religious Life', p. 261.

township and the wider borough alike, Protestant Dissenters were numerically predominant.[2]

As previously mentioned W. R. W. Stephens claimed, Hook found Leeds in 1837 'a stronghold of Dissent' and left it in 1859 'a stronghold of the Church'. The earlier year represented an informed estimate of a Dissenter to Anglican ratio of 2:1, which was essentially confirmed by the Religious Census of 1851. Dissenters in the 1850s maintained their numerical preponderance. By 1858, when there were thirty-six churches in Leeds, Dissenters possessed ninety chapels, three for Wesleyans in the centre each matching the Parish Church for seating. Decennial rises in population from early in the century meant that, in spite of strenuous efforts since 1836, the ratio of inhabitants to churches in 1855 (5270:1) was little different from 1815 (5236:1).[3] However, under Hook's influence, the quality of Church life in Leeds was improved immeasurably.

[2.] Coleman, pp. 6–7, 20–21, 40–41; Hennock, *Fit Persons*, App. III, p. 357; H. Perkin, *The Origins of Modern English Society, 1780–1880* (1969), pp. 199. n. 2, 201.

[3.] Fenteman, pp. 49–50; Huntington, p. 118; Lang, p. 14; Morgan, p. 48; Rusby, p. 69; Stephens, *Hook,* II, 392; Wood, *Church Extension*, pp. 15, 29–30; Yates, *St Saviour's*, p. 33; see Chapter I and Tables 1.1, 7.1, 7.2, 7.3, 7.4.

List of Sources and Bibliography

A. MANUSCRIPTS AND TRANSCRIPTS

Pusey House, Oxford
Hook Archives
British Library, London
 Gladstone Papers, Letters
Bodleian Library, Oxford
 Wilberforce Papers
 MS Eng. Lett.
Brotherton Library Special Collections
 Society of Friends, Carlton Hill Archives
West Yorkshire Archive Service, Leeds
 Leeds Parish Church, Parish Records of St Saviours, Ripon Diocesan Archive

B. REPORTS ETC.

Bishop of Ripon's Visitation Charges 1844, 1847, 1850 [Bishop T. Longley]
Church Missionary Society [CMS] *Annual Reports*
London Society for Promoting Christianity among the Jews [LSPCJ] *Annual Reports*
Orders in Council Ratifying Schemes of the Ecclesiastical Commissioners for England, with separate *General Index to the end of 1854*
Ripon Diocesan Church Building Society [RDCBS] *Annual Reports*
Society for the Propagation of Christian Knowledge [SPCK] *Annual Reports*
Society for the Propagation of the Gospel [SPG] *Annual Reports*

C. BOOKS AND PAMPHLETS

Addleshaw, G. W. O., and F. Etchells, *The Architectural Setting of Anglican Worship: An Enquiry into the Arrangements for Public Worship in the Church of England from the Reformation to the Present Day* (1948)
Ashwell, A. R., and R. G. Wilberforce, *Life of the Right Reverend Samuel Wilberforce*, 3 vols (1880–82)
Atkinson, M., *Practical Sermons (with a Memoir)* (1812)
Barnard, S., *To Prove I'm Not Forgot: Living and Dying in a Victorian City* (Manchester, 1990)
Beckwith, F. M., 'The First Leeds Baptist Church (the Old Stone Chapel, 1779–1826)', *Baptist Quarterly*, n.s. VI, pp. 72–82, 116–24, 166–71.
Beresford, M., 'The Face of Leeds, 1780–1914', in *Modern Leeds*, pp. 72–112
Beresford, M., *East End, West End: The Face of Leeds during Urbanisation, 1684–1842*, *PTh.S.*, LX and LXI (1988)

Best, G. F. A., *Temporal Pillars: Queen Anne's Bounty, the Ecclesiastical Commissioners and the Church of England* (Cambridge, 1964)

Binfield, C., *So Down to Prayers: Studies in English Nonconformity, 1780–1920* (1977)

Briggs, A., *History of Birmingham, II: Borough and City, 1865–1938* (1952)

Brown, F. K., *Fathers of Victorians: the Age of Wilberforce* (Cambridge, 1961)

Brown, L. M., 'Modern Hull', in *Victoria County History: County of York, East Riding, I, The City of Kingston upon Hull*, ed. by K. J. Allison (1969), pp. 215–77

Bunnett, R. J. A., *Leeds Parish Church of St Peter* (Gloucester, *c.* 1950)

Carpenter, S. C., *Church and People, 1789–1889* (1933)

Chadwick, O., Editor's Introduction, in *The Mind of the Oxford Movement*, ed. by O. Chadwick (1960)

Chadwick, O., *The Victorian Church: Part One, 1829–59* (1987)

Church, R. W., *The Oxford Movement: Twelve Years* (1891)

Clarke, P., *Jubilee 150: Worship, Work and Witness at St George's Church, Leeds, 1838–1988* (Leeds, 1989)

Coleman, B. I., *The Church of England in the Mid-Nineteenth Century: A Social Geography* (1980)

Collier's Encyclopedia, IX (1967)

Connell, E. J., and M. Ward, 'Industrial Development, 1780–1914', in *Modern Leeds*, pp. 142–76

Cornish, F. W., *The English Church in the Nineteenth Century*, 2 vols (1910)

Curnock, N., ed., *The Journal of the Rev. John Wesley A.M.*, 8 vols (1909–16)

Dalton, H. W., 'Walter Farquhar Hook, Vicar of Leeds: His Work for the Church and the Town, 1837–48', *PTh.S.*, LXIII (1990 for 1988), 27–79

Dikes, T., *A Sermon Preached on 17 February 1811 (on the Death of the Rev. M. Atkinson)* (1811)

Elton, A., and B. Harrison, eds, *Leeds in Maps* (Leeds, 1989)

Fellowes, E. H., *English Cathedral Music from Edward VI to Edward VII* (1941)

Fenteman, T., *An Historical Guide to Leeds and its Environs* (Leeds, 1858)

Fraser, D., 'The Leeds Churchwardens, 1828–1850', *PTh.S.*, LIII (1973), 1–22

Fraser, D., 'Poor Law Politics in Leeds, 1833–1855', *PTh.S.*, LIII (1973), 23–49

Fraser, D., *Urban Politics in Victorian Britain* (Leicester, 1976)

Fraser, D., ed., *A History of Modern Leeds* (Manchester, 1980)

Fraser, D., 'Politics and Society in the Nineteenth Century', in *Modern Leeds*, pp. 270–300

Forster, G. C. F., 'The Foundations: From the Earliest Times to *c.* 1700', in *Modern Leeds*, pp. 2–21

Gilbert, A. D., *Religion and Society in Industrial England: Church, Chapel and Social Change, 1740–1914* (1984)

Gill, C., *A History of Birmingham, 1: Manor and Borough to 1865* (1952)

Gladstone, W. E., *Dean Hook: An Address Delivered at Hawarden* (1879)

Grady, K., 'Commercial, Marketing and Retailing Amenities, 1700–1914', in *Modern Leeds*, pp. 177–99

Grady, K., *The Georgian Public Buildings of Leeds and the West Riding, PTh.S.*, LXII (1989)

Grantham, G. P., *A History of St Saviour's* (Leeds, 1872)

Haig, A., *The Victorian Clergy* (1984)

Heeney, B., *A Different Kind of Gentleman: Parish Clergy as Professional Men in Early and Mid-Victorian England* (Hamden, CT, 1976)

Hennock, E. P., *Fit and Proper Persons: Ideal and Reality in Nineteenth-Century Urban Government* (1973)

Hennock, E. P., 'The Anglo-Catholics and Church Extension in Victorian Brighton', *Studies in Sussex Church History*, ed. by M. Kitch (1981), pp. 173–83

Hole, C., *Early History CMS* (1896)

Hook, W. F., *Questions and Answers on Confirmation* (1834)

Hook, W. F., *Scriptural Principles as Applicable to Religious Societies* (1841)

Hook, W. F., *A Letter to the Right Reverend the Lord Bishop of Ripon on the State of Parties in the Church of England* (1841)

Hook, W. F., *Mutual Forbearance Recommended in Things Indifferent* (1843)

Hook, W. F., *Letters to the Parishioners of Leeds* (Leeds, 1844)

Hook, W. F., *The Three Reformations: Lutheran; Roman; Anglican* (1847)

Hook, W. F., *The Duty of English Churchmen and the Progress of the Church in Leeds* (1851)

Hook, W. F., *Pastoral Advice to Young People Preparing for Confirmation* (n.d)

Hook, W. F., *The Church and its Ordinances*, ed. by W. Hook, 2 vols (1876)

Hook, W. F., *Parish Sermons*, ed. by W. Hook (1879)

Huntington, G., *The Church's Work in our Large Towns* (c. 1864)

Hylson-Smith, K., *Evangelicals in the Church of England, 1734–1984* (Edinburgh, 1988)

Jackson, M., *Oxford Tracts Unmasked* (1838)

Jebb, J., *Three Lectures on the Cathedral Service of the Church of England* (Leeds, 1841)

Jowitt, J. A., (Tony), 'The Pattern of Religion in Victorian Bradford', in *Victorian Bradford: Essays in Honour of Jack Reynolds*, ed. by D. G. Wright and J. A. Jowitt (Bradford, 1982)

Kirk, G. E., *Farnley, Leeds: Its Chapelry, Chapels and Present Church, with Lists of Local Clergy* (Leeds, 1951)

Kitson Clark, E., *Leeds Parish Church* (1931)

Kitson Clark, G., *Churchmen and the Condition of England, 1832–1885* (1973)

Lang, C. G., ed., *Church and Town for Fifty Years, 1841–1891* (Leeds, 1891)

Lawn, R. G., 'The City of Leeds and its Methodism', *Methodist Magazine* (July 1930)

Leeds Directories, 1834 and 1839

Leeds Poll Books, 1834, 1835, 1837

Leeds Intelligencer

Leeds Mercury

Le Patourel, 'Medieval Leeds: Kirkstall Abbey; The Parish Church; The Medieval Borough', *PTh.S.*, XLVI (1963), 1–21

Liddon, H. P., *Life of Edward Bouverie Pusey*, 4 vols (1894–98)

Linstrum, D., *West Yorkshire Architects and Architecture* (1978)

Longley, C. T., *A Letter to the Parishioners of St Saviour's, Leeds, by the Right Rev. the Lord Bishop of Ripon: with an Appendix of Documents* (1851)

Lowther Clarke, W. K., 'Confirmation', in *Liturgy and Worship: A Companion to the Prayer Books of the Anglican Communion*, ed. by W. K. Lowther Clarke (1936), pp. 443–57

Lumb, G. D., and J. B. Plaice, eds, *Extracts from the Leeds Intelligencer and the Leeds Mercury*, *PTh.S.*, XL (1955).

Machin, G. I. T., *Politics and the Churches in Great Britain, 1832 to 1868* (Oxford, 1977)

McLachlan, H., 'Diary of a Leeds Layman, Joseph Ryder', in *Essays and Addresses* (Manchester, 1950)

Mayhall, J., *The Annals and History of Leeds, and Other Places in the County of York, from the Earliest Period to the Present Time* (Leeds, 1860)

Middleton, R. D., *Newman and Bloxam: An Oxford Friendship* (1947)

Middleton, R. D., *Newman at Oxford: His Religious Development* (Oxford, 1950)

Moore, R. W., *History of the Parish Church of Leeds* (Leeds, 1877)

Moorman, J. H. R., *A History of the Church in England* (1963)

Morgan, C. J., 'Demographic Change, 1771–1911', in *Modern Leeds*, pp. 46–71

Morris, R. J., *Class, Sect and Party: The Making of the British Middle Class, Leeds 1820–1850* (Manchester, 1990)

Nelson, J., *The Journal of Mr John Nelson, Preacher of the Gospel, Written by Himself* (1826)

The Parochial System of the Church of England opposed to the Present Condition of the Parish of Leeds (Leeds, 1842)

Perkin, H., *The Origins of Modern English Society, 1780–1880* (1969)

Pevsner, N., *The Buildings of England: Yorkshire, the West Riding* (Harmondsworth, 1959)

Pollen, J. H., *Narrative of Five Years at St Saviour's, Leeds* (Oxford, 1851)

Port, M. H., *Six Hundred New Churches: A Study of the Church Building Commission, 1818–1856, and its Church Building Activities* (1961)

Proby, W. H. B., *Annals of the 'Low Church' Party in England down to the Death of Archbishop Tait*, 2 vols (1888)

Prochaska, F. K., 'Philanthropy', in *Cambridge Social History of Britain*, III, ed. by F. M. L. Thompson (Cambridge, 1990)

Read, D., 'North of England Newspapers (c. 1700–c. 1900) and their Value to Historians', *Proceedings of the Leeds Philosophic and Literary Society, Literary and Historical Section*, VIII (1957), 200–15

Read, D., *Press and People, 1790–1850: Opinion in Three English Cities* (1961)

'Report upon the Condition of the Town of Leeds, by a Statistical Committee of the Town Council, October 1839', *Journal of the Statistical Society*, II (1839–40)

Rowell, G., *The Vision Glorious: Themes and Personalities in the Catholic Revival in Anglicanism* (Oxford, 1983)

Rusby, J., *St Peters at Leeds, being an Account Historical and Descriptive of the Parish Church*, ed. by J. G. Simpson (Leeds, 1896)

Savage S., and C. Tyne, *The Labours of Years: The Story of St Saviour's and St Hilda's, Leeds* (Oxford: Cowley, 1976)

Shattock J., and M., Wolff, eds, *The Victorian Periodical Press: Samplings and Soundings* (Leicester, 1982)

Sprittles, J., *Leeds Parish Church: History and Guide* (Gloucester, c. 1954)

Sprittles, J., *Links with Bygone Leeds, PTh.S.*, LII (1969)

The Statement of the Clergy of St Saviour's, Leeds, in reference to the recent Proceedings against them (Leeds, 1851)

Steele, E. D., 'The Leeds Patriciate and the Cultivation of Learning, 1819–1905: A Study of the Leeds Philosophical and Literary Society', *Proceedings of the Leeds Philosophical and Literary Society* (1978), pp. 183–202

Stephens, W. B., 'Elementary Education and Literacy, 1770–1870', in *Modern Leeds*, pp. 223–49

Stephens, W. R. W., *The Life and Letters of Walter Farquhar Hook, DD, FRS*, 2 vols (1878)

Stephens, W. R. W., *A Memoir of the Right Hon. William Page Wood, Baron Hatherley*, 2 vols (1883)

Stock, E., *The History of the Church Missionary Society*, 3 vols (1899–1916)

Stoughton, J., *Religion in England from 1800 to 1850*, 2 vols (1884)

Stranks, C. J., *Dean Hook* (1954)

Sykes, L., and K., eds, *Sketches of the Life of Edward Jackson* (1912)

Taylor, R. V., *The Biographia Leodiensis . . . from the Norman Conquest to the Present Time* (1865)

Teale, W. H., ed., *The Seven Sermons Preached at the Consecration and Reopening of the Parish Church, Leeds, with an Introduction* (Leeds, 1841)

Thomas, W., ed., *The Jubilee of Queen Street Chapel, Leeds, with Memorials of the Church and its Pastors from the Beginning* (Leeds, 1875)

Thompson, H. W., *A Short Account of Holy Trinity Church, Leeds* (Leeds, 1927)

Unwin, R. W., 'Leeds Becomes a Transport Centre', in *Modern Leeds*, pp. 113–41

Varley, E. A., *The Last of the Prince Bishops: William Van Mildert and the High Church Movement of the Early Nineteenth Century* (Cambridge, 1992)

Virgin, P., *The Church in an Age of Negligence: Ecclesiastical Structure and Problems of Church Reform 1700–1840* (Cambridge, 1989)

Wade, W. L., *West Park Congregational Church (Queen Street Memorial) Leeds, 1672–1972: Three Hundred Years of Witness* (1972)

Walton, M., *Sheffield: Its Story and Its Achievements* (Sheffield, 1948)

Ward, W. R., *Religion and Society in England, 1790–1850* (1972)

Webster, C., *R. D. Chantrell, Architect: His Life and Work in Leeds 1818–1847*, P.Th.S., 2nd Series, 2 (1992)

Webster, D., 'Parish' Past and Present: 275 Years of Leeds Parish Church Music* (Leeds, 1988)

Wesley, S. S., *A Few Words on Cathedral Music and the Musical System of the Church, with a Plan of Reform* (1849)

Wilson, R. G., *Gentlemen Merchants: The Merchant Community in Leeds, 1700–1830* (Manchester, 1971)

Wilson, R. G., 'Georgian Leeds', in *Modern Leeds*, pp. 24–43

Wood, F. J., *Four Notable Vicars* (Leeds, 1910)

Wood, R. J., *Church Extension in Leeds* (Leeds, c. 1964)

Wood, R. J., *Holy Trinity, Leeds: A Short History of the Church and its Ministers* (Leeds, 1966)

Woodhouse, T., 'The Working Class', in *Modern Leeds*, pp. 353–88

Woodward, E. L., *The Age of Reform, 1815–1870* (Oxford, 1938)

Yates, N., *The Oxford Movement and Parish Life: St Saviour's, Leeds, 1839–1929*, Borthwick Papers, 48 (York, 1975)

Yates, N., *Leeds and the Oxford Movement: A Study of High Church Activity in the Rural Deaneries of Allerton, Armley, Headingley and Whitkirk in the Diocese of Ripon, 1836–1934*, PTh.S., LV (1975)

Yates, N., 'The Religious Life of Victorian Leeds', in *Modern Leeds*, pp. 250–69

Yates, N., *Buildings, Faith and Worship: The Liturgical Arrangement of Anglican Churches, 1600–1900* (Oxford, 1991)

D.   UNPUBLISHED THESES

Adams, P. A., 'Converts to the Roman Catholic Church in England, *c.* 1830–1870' (BLitt, Oxford, 1977)

Chance., P. F., 'Religion and Politics in Birmingham, 1830–1850' (BPhil, Open University, 1982)

Coombs, P. B., 'A History of the Church Pastoral Aid Society 1836–1861' (MA, Bristol, 1960)

Elliott, C. M., 'Social and Economic History of the Principal Protestant Denominations in Leeds, 1760–1844' (DPhil, Oxford, 1962)

Ford, C. S., 'Pastors and Polemicists: The Character of Popular Anglicanism in South East Lancashire, 1847–1914' (PhD, Leeds, 1991)

Herring, G. W., 'Tractarianism to Ritualism: A Study of Some Aspects of Tractarianism outside Oxford, from the Time of Newman's Conversion in 1845, until the First Ritual Commission in 1867' (DPhil, Oxford, 1984)

Jacques, D. N., 'The Clergy of the Diocese of Ripon 1836–1888, with particular reference to the Influence of the Oxford Movement' (MPhil, Leeds, 1988)

Lowerson, J. R., 'The Political Career of Sir Edward Baines (1800–1890)' (MA, Leeds, 1965)

Nockles, P. B., 'Continuity and Change in Anglican High Churchmanship in Britain, 1792–1850' (DPhil, Oxford, 1982)

Smith, M. A., 'Religion in Industrial Society: The Case of Oldham and Saddleworth, 1780–1865' (DPhil, Oxford, 1988)

Stephenson, A. M. G., 'The Formation of the See of Ripon and the Episcopate of its first Bishop, Charles Thomas Longley' (BLitt, Oxford, 1960)

Walters, J. D. P., 'The Impact of Anglican Evangelism on the Religious Life of Wolverhampton and its Locality in the Period 1830–1870' (MPhil, Council for National Academic Awards, 1984)

Index